British Comedy Cinema

British comedy cinema has been a mainstay of domestic production since the beginning of the last century and arguably the most popular and important genre in British film history.

This edited volume will offer the first comprehensive account of the rich and popular history of British comedy cinema from silent slapstick and satire to contemporary romantic comedy. Using a loosely chronological approach, essays cover successive decades of the 20th and 21st centuries with a combination of case studies on key personalities, production cycles and studio output along with fresh approaches to issues of class and gender representation. It will present new research on familiar comedy cycles such as the Ealing comedies and *Carry On* films as well as the largely undocumented silent period along with the rise of television spin-offs from the 1970s and the development of animated comedy from 1915 to the present.

Films covered include: *Sing As We Go*, *The Ladykillers*, *Trouble in Store*, the *Carry On*s, *Till Death Us Do Part*, *Monty Python's Life of Brian*, *Notting Hill* and *Sex Lives of the Potato Men*.

Contributors: Laraine Porter, Lawrence Napper, C.P. Lee, Tim O'Sullivan, Alan Burton, Sarah Street, James Chapman, Andrew Roberts, Richard Dacre, Peter Waymark, I.Q. Hunter, Justin Smith, James Leggott and Paul Wells.

I.Q. Hunter is Reader in Film Studies at De Montfort University. He is the co-editor of the *British Popular Cinema* series.

Laraine Porter is Senior Lecturer in Film Studies at De Montfort University and the Director of the annual British Silent Film Festival.

British Popular Cinema

Series Editors: Steve Chibnall and I.Q. Hunter
De Montfort University, Leicester

At a time when there is a growing popular and scholarly interest in British film, with new sources of funding and notable successes in world markets, this series explores the largely submerged history of the UK's cinema of entertainment.

The series rediscovers and evaluates not only individual films but whole genres, such as science fiction and the crime film, that have been ignored by a past generation of critics. Dismissed for decades as aberrations in the national cinema and anaemic imitations of American originals, these films are now being celebrated in some quarters as important contributions to our cinematic heritage.

The emergence of cult genre movies from the apparently respectable lineage of British film emphasises the gap between traditional academic criticism and a new alliance between revisionist film theorists and extra-mural (but well-informed) cinema enthusiasts who wish to take the study of British film in unexpected directions. This series offers the opportunity for both established cineastes and new writers to examine long-neglected areas of British film production or to develop new approaches to more familiar territory. The books will enhance our understanding of how ideas and representations in films relate to changing gender and class relations in post-war Britain, and their accessible writing style will make these insights available to a much wider readership.

Books in the Series:

British Crime Cinema
Edited by Steve Chibnall and Robert Murphy

British Science Fiction Cinema
Edited by I.Q. Hunter

British Horror Cinema
Edited by Julian Petley and Steve Chibnall

British Historical Cinema
Edited by Claire Monk and Amy Sargeant

British Queer Cinema
Edited by Robin Griffiths

British Women's Cinema
Edited by Melanie Bell and Melanie Williams

British Comedy Cinema
Edited by I.Q. Hunter and Laraine Porter

British Comedy Cinema

Edited by
I.Q. Hunter and Laraine Porter

Routledge
Taylor & Francis Group

LONDON AND NEW YORK

First published 2012
by Routledge
2 Park Square, Milton Park, Abingdon, Oxon OX14 4RN

Simultaneously published in the USA and Canada
by Routledge
711 Third Avenue, New York, NY 10017

Routledge is an imprint of the Taylor & Francis Group, an informa business

British Library Cataloguing in Publication Data
A catalogue record for this book is available from the British Library

Library of Congress Cataloging in Publication Data
British comedy cinema / edited by I.Q. Hunter and Laraine Porter.
p. cm. – (British popular cinema)
Includes bibliographical references and index.
1. Comedy films – Great Britain – History – 20th century. 2. Comedy films – Great
Britain – History – 21st century. I. Hunter, I.Q., 1964-II. Porter, Laraine.
PN1995.9.C55B75 2012
791.43'61709410904 – dc23
2011040908

ISBN: 978-0-415-66665-7 (hbk)
ISBN: 978-0-415-66667-1 (pbk)
ISBN: 978-0-203-14633-0 (ebk)

Typeset in Perpetua
by Taylor & Francis Books

Printed and bound in Great Britain by the MPG Books Group

Contents

Illustrations

Contributors

Alan Burton is presently Director of Studies for Film Studies at Hull University. He has published widely on British film-making and film-makers, including collections on Basil Dearden and Michael Relph, and the Boulting brothers.

James Chapman is Professor of Film Studies at the University of Leicester and editor of the *Historical Journal of Film, Radio and Television*. He has wide-ranging research interests in the history of British cinema, television and popular culture, and his recent works include *Inside the Tardis: The Worlds of 'Doctor Who' — A Cultural History* (2006), *War and Film* (2008), *Projecting Empire: Imperialism and Popular Cinema* (2009, with Nicholas J. Cull) and *British Comics: A Cultural History* (2011). *Projecting SF: Science Fiction and Popular Cinema*, again with Nicholas J. Cull, will be published in autumn 2012.

Richard Dacre is the author of *Trouble in Store: Norman Wisdom — A Career in Comedy* (1991). After spells with the Other Cinema Collective, managing London's Scala Cinema, and working on the cult children's TV series *Cloppa Castle*, he ran Flashbacks film memorabilia shop, and remains the distributor of Mike Leigh's debut feature *Bleak Moments*. He now divides his time between writing, lecturing and tour guiding. Published work includes contributions to *Time Out*, *Primetime* and *Movie Collector*, plus segments for *The British Cinema Book* (1997, updated 2009), *The Encyclopedia Of British Film* (2003) and *Directors In British And Irish Cinema* (2006).

I.Q. Hunter is Reader in Film Studies at De Montfort University, Leicester. He has published widely on British cult and genre cinema, including *British Science Fiction Cinema* (edited, 1999) and *British Trash Cinema* (forthcoming, 2012).

C.P. Lee is Senior Lecturer in Film Studies at University of Salford and organiser of their annual International Comedy Conferences. He has written and presented a series of documentaries for BBC Radio 4 on topics ranging from regional film-making to Northern soul and has appeared on many documentaries for both the BBC and Channel 4. His published work includes chapters published in historical journals, academic textbooks and books on popular culture. He is the author of five books — *Like The Night: Bob Dylan and Manchester's Free Trade Hall*, *Shake, Rattle & Rain: Popular Music Making in Manchester 1955/1995*, *Like A Bullet Of Light: The Films of Bob Dylan*, a personal memoir *When We Were Thin* and, most recently, in collaboration with Dr. Andrew Willis, *The Lost World of Cliff Twemlow*. He is also the leading expert on North-West film and curates a website that acts as an open-access resource for the history of the Mancunian Film Studio (www.itsahotun.com).

James Leggott lectures in Film and Television Studies at Northumbria University. He is the author of *Contemporary British Cinema: From Heritage to Horror* (2008) and the co-editor of *British Science Fiction Film and Television* (2011). He has published on various aspects of British film and television culture, including social realist cinema, television comedy, reality television and the work of the Amber Collective.

Lawrence Napper is a lecturer in the Department of Film Studies at King's College London. His book *British Cinema and Middlebrow Culture in the Interwar Years* was published by University of Exeter Press in 2009. He has also published on British musicals and is currently working on a study of British war films of the 1920s.

Tim O'Sullivan is Professor of Media and Cultural History in the Faculty of Art, Design and Humanities at De Montfort University. He has written widely on aspects of film and television history, including (with Alan Burton) *The Cinema of Basil Dearden and Michael Relph* (2009) and more recently a study of television and the 1948 Olympics in Britain.

Laraine Porter is Senior Lecturer in Film Studies at De Montfort University's Cinema and Television History Centre. She is also the Director of the British Silent Film Festival which she founded in 1998 in partnership with the British Film Institute. Until 2008, she was the Director of Broadway Media Centre in Nottingham and the majority of her career has been spent at the intersection between higher education and the film industry. She has co-edited several volumes of essays on British cinema before 1930 including *Pimple Pranks and Pratfalls* (2000) on British silent comedy.

Andrew Roberts is a barrister with an MA in Contemporary British History from the University of London who is making (majestic) progress towards a PhD in 'The Middle Classes in Post War British Cinema' at Brunel. He contributes film articles to *Sight and Sound, History Today, The Observer, The Independent* and *The Guardian*.

Justin Smith is Principal Lecturer in Film Studies at the University of Portsmouth. A cultural historian with a specialism in British cinema, his research interests and writing cover film fandom, reception and exhibition cultures, identity and popular memory. He is the author of *Withnail and Us: Cult Films and Film Cults in British Cinema* (2010) and, with Sue Harper, *British Film Culture of the 1970s: The Boundaries of Pleasure* (2011). He is the Principal Investigator on the AHRC-funded project 'Channel 4 Television and British Film Culture', www.c4film.co.uk.

Sarah Street is Professor of Film at the University of Bristol. Her publications include *Cinema and State* (with Margaret Dickinson, 1985), *British National Cinema* (1997 and 2009), *Costume and Cinema* (2001), *Transatlantic Crossings* (2002), *Black Narcissus* (2005) and (with Tim Bergfelder and Sue Harris) *Film Architecture and the Transnational Imagination: Set Design in 1930s European Cinema* (2007). Her latest book is *The*

Negotiation of Innovation: Colour Films in Britain, 1900–55 (forthcoming, 2012). She is a co-editor of *Screen* and of the *Journal of British Cinema and Television*.

Peter Waymark is a journalist who has written extensively about cinema and television for *The Times* and regularly contributes obituaries to the paper on actors, directors and writers. He was awarded a PhD by the Open University for a thesis on 'Television and the Cultural Revolution: The BBC under Hugh Greene'.

Paul Wells is Professor and Director of the Animation Academy at Loughborough University. He has published widely in the field of animation studies including *Understanding Animation* (1998), *Re-Imagining Animation* (2008) and *The Animated Bestiary* (2009). He is also an established writer and director in radio, TV and theatre conducting workshops and consultancies worldwide based on his book *Scriptwriting* (2009). He is Chair of the Association of British Animation Collections (ABAC).

Acknowledgements

The editors would like to thank all the contributors (some of whom kindly stepped in at very short notice), Natalie Foster and Ruth Moody at Routledge, the staff of the BFI library, and colleagues in the Cinema and Television History Research Centre (CATH) at De Montfort University for their support and patience during the editing of this book. Steve Chibnall was especially helpful in supplying images from the Steve Chibnall Collection.

Every effort has been made to obtain permissions to reproduce copyright material and if any proper acknowledgement has not been made we apologise and invite copyright holders to inform us of the oversight.

I.Q. Hunter would like to give special thanks (for everything) to Elaine Street and Laraine Porter would like to thank Martin Halliwell and her dad Ken Porter who loved Frank Randall and taught her all the best catchphrases.

1 British comedy cinema

Sex, class and very naughty boys

Laraine Porter and I.Q. Hunter

Comedy is the most popular of all genres in British cinema, sustaining the film industry in times of economic slump in the 1920s and 1970s, and drawing mass audiences when other genres fail. From adaptations of Oscar Wilde to showcasing Northern comedians, from sex comedies to 'rom-coms', the comedy film has dominated production, created major stars such as Peter Sellers and Hugh Grant, and often reached an international audience with cult hits like *Withnail and I* (1987) as well as slapstick blockbusters like *Bean* (1997). Along with horror, it is the genre that has created the most dissonance between critics and public, particularly in terms of personalities like Gracie Fields and George Formby, series such as the *Carry Ons* and popular TV spin-offs like *On the Buses* (1971), but also *Four Weddings and a Funeral* (1994) and *Love Actually* (2003), which inspired a good deal of critical bile. Distaste for populism and the sheer vulgarity of much British comedy arguably misses the point. The strength of British comedy lies in its continuing appeal to niche markets and tastes. Whether Northern or Southern, intellectual or bawdy, verbal or visual, British comedy has nimbly adapted itself to a diverse range of cultural identities.

Despite this richness, and its continuing ability to thrive in spite of low budgets and fickle audiences, British comedy cinema has never really had its due and this book sets out, in its own modest way, to redress this. Critical focus has mostly been on Ealing, notably Charles Barr's seminal study of the relationship between production practices and the films themselves (Barr 1977); 'quality' satires like the Boulting brothers' *I'm All Right Jack* (1959); enduring personalities like Will Hay and Moore Marriott; and the *Carry Ons*, which finally gained critical approval for embodying 'the standpoint of the common man, offering a proletarian, democratic version of what cinema might provide' (Gerrard 2008: 37). Recent critical attention has also focused on Richard Curtis's internationally acclaimed rom-coms, but there are swathes of British comedy left untouched. Virtually nothing has been written on the silent period for example, which is almost universally assumed to have been eclipsed by Hollywood. This is partly because the production of British comedies has always been patchy and, for the most part, aimed at niche tastes and domestic audiences. Few British comedy films have achieved instantaneous international appeal. Historically, critics have also been responsible for overlooking or denouncing popular or 'low' comedy, which has often taken them out of their comfort zones and away from their main interests in literary adaptations and social realism – in other words, more legitimate British cinema.

Equally, much British comedy cannot be reclaimed in terms of its cult status or transgression, though some critics have re-evaluated it in terms of its ability to connect with or reflect working-class tastes. But there too lies a problem, given comedy's innate ability to transcend boundaries. How can we assume a simple equation between low comedy and working-class tastes or literary comedy and middle-class tastes? Andy Medhurst has done much to bring these issues to critical attention, particularly in understanding the relationship between the bawdy and carnivalesque and what it means to be British in a much wider sense (Medhurst 2007). But much of British comedy cinema has been overlooked, patronised or misunderstood; Launder and Gilliat, the *Doctor* films of the 1950s and 1960s, TV spin-offs of the 1970s and so on. This book, without claiming to be comprehensive, takes another look at what is hiding in plain sight, this absolutely central, but often overlooked genre of British cinema.

Throughout its history, British comedy has also grappled with the unease and confusion about what it is to be British, not least because humour is considered intrinsic to the British 'character'. Rudeness and irony, understatement and farce – each has some claim to define the essence of Britishness. British comedy can variously be characterised as a comedy of class, social and sexual embarrassment, thwarted ambition and a love–hate relationship with convention, conformity and the Establishment in all its forms. In this latter respect, British comedy has often explored the space between consensus and revolt, both in terms of small communities, as in Ealing comedies such as *Passport to Pimlico* (1949) and *Whisky Galore* (1949), or through Norman Wisdom's disruptive little-man-outsider in farces like *Trouble in Store* (1953). The fine lines between conformity and anarchy, normality and chaos, and the genteel middle-class reserve of stereotypical Britishness, have been tested to breaking point throughout its history; from the early Mitchell and Kenyon silent shorts to the present day films of Simon Pegg (*Shaun of the Dead* (2004)) and Chris Morris (*Four Lions* (2010)). As Marcia Landy says, referring specifically to Ealing and Launder and Gilliat, British comedies are frequently 'carnivalesque':

> They focus on dominant social institutions – the public school, the world of commerce and industry, political parties – and turn them on their head. In these narratives, the complacency of the status quo and the rigidity of social structures is [sic] threatened by eruptions of physical and psychic energy.
>
> (Landy 1991: 333)

It would also be wrong to characterise British popular comedy only in terms of 'low comedy', for literate and sophisticated satire – the traditions of university wit and the cruel political cartoons of Cruickshank and Gilray – have always existed alongside pratfalls and bawdy. Important too is that 'eccentric' British strain of whimsy, surreal nonsense and downright silliness that leads from Lewis Carroll and Edward Lear to the anarchic 'madcap comedy' of The Crazy Gang, The Goons (who made two films, *Down Among the Z Men* (1952) and *The Case of the Mukkinese Battlehorn* (1956)), Richard Lester's *The Bed Sitting Room* (1969), Monty Python and Viv Stanshall's *Sir Henry at Rawlinson End* (1980) (Spicer 2007: 106–9).

Many comedy films have also been vehicles for comedians whose reputations were forged on stage and in other media. The influence of radio and television has been absolutely crucial. British comedy films since the 1960s have also had a close relationship to stand-up and the satirical sketch show format of the Cambridge Footlights and *Beyond the Fringe*. The genre's history is understood more easily in terms of its intersection with other media and its comic stars (from Betty Balfour to Rowan Atkinson), than its screenwriters and auteurs, notwithstanding the likes of T.E.B. Clarke and Richard Curtis. As Richard Dacre has suggested, British film comedy 'divides into two traditions: films which rely on the writer and films which rely on a star entertainer' (Dacre 2009:107). However, from the 1940s onwards, significant continuities have been ensured by certain studios (Ealing, Hammer), series (*Old Mother Riley*, the *Doctor* films, *St. Trinian's*, *Carry Ons*) and production teams (the Boultings, Launder and Gilliat, Betty Box, Monty Python and Working Title). These brands forged audience loyalties and gave producers the confidence to invest in recurring formulae.

Lack of large-scale finance is a perennial issue faced by the British film industry, and comedy is no exception. The inadequate returns from the domestic market have either required Hollywood co-productions, often with the inclusion of American stars, or kept production costs low and proportionate to the smaller UK market. Small-scale producers from the 1920s to the 1950s, such as Mancunian Films, aimed product at niche markets, but limited their costs by allowing their comedians simply to 'do their business' in front of the camera, which satisfied audiences' desires to see their favourite local comedians in the same way that the DVD-of-the-comedy-gig does today.

The key strength in British comedy cinema is its ability to draw on all these cultural traditions. Britain's highly demarcated regional cultures, language, accents and class continue to provide fertile ground for comedy based on difference, incongruity and the clash of opposing forces. Although regional differences are crucial (Northern and Scottish comedians, in particular), at the heart of British comedy, as with so many British genres, is class and its abiding theme – the tension between consensus and transgression.

An historical overview of British cinema comedy

The impulse to produce film comedy came with the very first experiments in the new medium at the end of the 19th century. The simple single sight-gag, borrowed or reworked from Music Hall, Circus or Pantomime, lent itself easily to film and was guaranteed to produce a reaction from audiences. Getting a laugh, along with creating surprise or wonder, was all important to early cinema showmen and women, who competed for attention with the ribald attractions of the fairground. The very first exhibition of the Lumière brothers' Cinematograph in the UK at the Polytechnic of London on 20 February 1896 consisted of actuality films and the earliest known film comedy, *L'Arroseur Arrosé* [*The Waterer Watered*] (1895). British producers rapidly got on the bandwagon, copying the film's simple gag format, and again it was a comedy, R.W. Paul's *The Soldier's Courtship* (1896), which is often credited with being the first 'made up' British film (Low 1948: 85). Comedy was therefore the first fictional film genre to be both exhibited and produced in the UK. Paul's film, like many others produced at this time, was essentially a *coitus interruptus* comedy, in which a soldier courting a pretty young nursemaid has his intentions defeated by an 'old maid' who insists on sharing their park bench.

From these early short single-gag films, British film comedy developed alongside the institution of cinema itself. The arrival of comfortable purpose-built cinemas in the 1910s allowed longer narratives which required more complex plotting and character-isation. The development of the intertitle as an agent of comedic delivery later required the skills of writers, who included A.A. Milne; and soon adaptations from Noël Coward, H.G. Wells and Oscar Wilde appeared on the screen. But just as that first R. W. Paul comedy carries the DNA of the sex comedy, so other silent comedies laid down the templates for most of the subsequent sub-genres of British comic cinema. In particular, the early comedies of social or sexual embarrassment, such as *Mr Poorluck's First Tiff* (1910), in which the eponymous 'hero' has to win back his wife from his mother-in-law after he is discovered flirting at a party, or *A Wild Goose Chase* (1908), in which an elderly man is chased off by an enraged goose when he tries to kiss the young woman who owns it. Many early comedies combined sex with the comic chase, a for-mula that Benny Hill would revive in the 1970s, while others in which policemen, vicars and shopkeepers are fair game for comic torment, established a thread of anti-authoritarianism that would run throughout British comedy and find perfect expression in the great Ealing films such as *The Lavender Hill Mob* (1951).

Gender and age are important demarcations of comic difference in these early years: amorous young men attempt to woo nursemaids, children are a perennial nuisance, and old maids are the butts of often cruel physical comedy. Suffragettes and independent 'new women' were popular figures of fun in 'henpecked husband' revenge comedies. These were partly a response to their perceived threat to the social and sexual order, and Suffragettes were sometimes played by men in drag to suggest their denatured femininity, but these comedies were also produced at the time of the Suffragette 'outrages' – acts of arson and suicide, reported in cinema newsreels that would have been screened alongside the comedies.

Class was a defining comic factor by the First World War as cinema strove for cultural legitimacy and started to reflect the wider range of comic modes which it imported from literature and theatre. This period also saw Hollywood secure its domination of the film industry and thereby the market for comedy. British cinema would never compete on equal terms again. This forced British films to adopt their own distinct forms of comedy, paying homage to Hollywood but asserting the difference and uniqueness of British humour. Pimple, the most prolific and popular home-grown comedian who emerged just prior to the First World War, was derided by American impresario Mack Sennett for his lack of subtlety and coarse burlesque humour. But films like the cheekily-titled *Pimple Has One* (1915) in which a drunk Pimple, mistaking a woman's request for help in fastening her boot for a come-on, literally whitewashes the screen to conceal the impropriety, or *Pimple's Battle of Waterloo* (1913), a parody of the serious feature film *The Battle of Waterloo* (1913) with Pimple's Napoleon falling off his (Pantomime) horse, attacked by Suffragettes and surrendering ignominiously to marauding Boy Scouts. These were fast, furious, and cheap, but sometimes ingenious burlesques that knowingly mocked their own lack of production values and parodied British cinema's pretensions to high culture. Although Pimple could never be compared to Chaplin, his popularity was indicated in a 1915 audience poll of Britain's favourite stars where he ranked number six, not far behind Chaplin in third position (Hammond 2000: 58).

Laraine Porter, in her chapter on early and silent British comedy, notes that the enduring reliance on Music Hall gags meant that British comedy often lagged behind other national cinemas until the period after the Great War, when a new wave of creative talent began to explore cinema's potential for satire. Exceptions to this included actress-producer Florence Turner, who successfully hybridised Music Hall and cinema on both sides of the Atlantic, though sadly, unlike many of her successors, her early transatlanticism did little for her film career, though her departure back to the US in 1916 left a noticeable gap in British production (Low 1950: 79)

The early 1920s saw a wave of character and romantic comedy dramas adapted from popular writers of the time, such as the Manning Haynes adaptations of W.W. Jacobs's short stories including *The Head of the Family, The Skipper's Wooing* and *Sam's Boy* (all 1922). These overlooked and forgotten films remain fresh and funny today and in no way justify being eclipsed by Hollywood or ignored by film historians. Sophisticated film satire emerged at the beginning of the 1920s, in the work of Adrian Brunel and Ivor Montagu, who worked largely as independents showing films in the emerging Film Society movement, but who attracted a range of eager creative talents including Elsa Lanchester and Charles Laughton, H.G. Wells and Lord Beaverbrook. Brunel made several burlesques for Gainsborough including *Cut it Out: A Day in the Life of a Censor* (1925) in which a director and his cast are frustrated by Harper Sunbeam, an interfering censor who represents The Society for Detecting Evil in Others. The 1920s

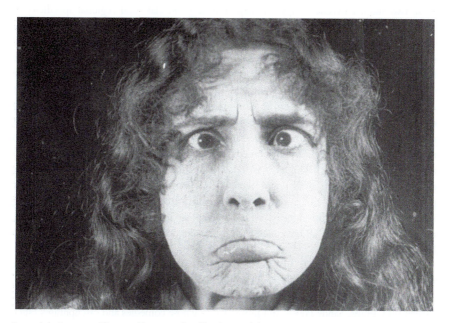

Figure 1.1 American Florence Turner in her 'facial comedy' *Daisy Doodad's Dial* (1914).

ended with the likes of Hitchcock and Asquith both embracing the genre, with films like *Champagne* and *The Farmer's Wife* (both 1928) and *The Runaway Princess* (1929) respectively, though neither director was particularly proud of his silent comedy output.

The arrival of the Talkies in 1928 further isolated non-Anglophone domestic cinemas. Britain's linguistic relationship with the US proved both a blessing and a curse for British cinema, as Hollywood's slicker productions could easily beat British films in audiences' affections. At the same time, language barriers ensured that French and German national cinemas, with which Britain had benefited from close creative ties during the silent period, forged their own comedic identities. To this day French and German comedies remain largely bound to their national cultures and are rarely exported. Silent comedy, which had flourished as an international language, now required verbal gags rather than sight ones, but even Chaplin was reluctant to abandon his silence and waited until 1940 to release his first proper Talkie, *The Great Dictator*.

David Sutton has argued that 1930s British comedy cinema, emerging from a mixed pedigree of silent cinema, Variety and Music Hall alongside newer theatrical forms of revue and farce, fused with new sound technology to create a more interactive 'open' entertainment form that owed more to live entertainment than the traditional 'closed' forms of narrative cinema (Sutton 2000: 23). This resulted in comedies that combined story with song and dance numbers that were largely dominated by popular comedians. In Hollywood, the new sound technology was exploited in the verbal gymnastics of 1930s Screwball comedies whilst in Britain it was used to play on the North–South divide, promoting Northern working-class comedians such as Gracie Fields and George Formby, and largely eschewing Hollywood glamour for the down-to-earth asexuality of these two stars. Lawrence Napper's chapter focuses on class and regional specificity in comedy films of the 1930s, drawing on contemporary criticism to argue that the likes of Fields and Formby, The Crazy Gang and Arthur Lucan are still subject to cultural snobbery. Many critics fail to analyse these films in context or simply do not appreciate the humour. More importantly, their continued critical denigration, often at the expense of the so-called realist films of the decade, is symptomatic of a wider problem. Whilst *Housing Problems* (1935) is seen as a masterwork of authenticity, despite its pitying objectification of its working-class subjects, *Sing As We Go* (1934), with its upbeat message, resists the patronising dismissal of middle-class commentators. Problems in representing the working class in comedy are central to Napper's argument. This was as much an issue in the 1930s as it is today, with social and popular historians, then as now, arguing over the validity and accuracy of comedic representations. As Napper points out, we need to adopt a much more sophisticated framework for understanding the popularity of 1930s comedy, whose appeal to its working-class audiences may require a considerable effort of historical imagination. Perhaps you simply had to be there.

C.P. Lee's study of John E. Blakeley's Mancunian Films complements Napper's chapter in that it focuses on regionally specific Northern humour. Mancunian Films featured comedians such as the inimitable Frank Randle, female impersonator Norman 'over-the-garden-wall' Evans, Sandy Powell and Jimmy James whose comedies and catchphrases (such as Powell's 'Can you hear me, mother?') relate directly back to Music Hall, but still

Figure 1.2 Gracie Fields in *Sally in Our Alley* (1931). Image courtesy of the Steve Chibnall Collection.

provide inspiration for contemporary Northern comedians such as Peter Kay. That these comedies were largely overlooked is testament not to their lack of merit, but to the persistent London-bias of the major studios, stars and critics. This is a comedy of accents, quotable catchphrases and the pitting of an essential 'Northerness' against the South, but it also celebrates Northern regional specificity including the Lancashire/ Yorkshire divide.

Andrew Roberts, writing on the *St. Trinian's* films, points to the dominance of the institution in British comedy, and especially the public school, hospital and factory. His chapter charts the development of *St. Trinian's* and the school film, such as the series' immediate precursor, Launder and Gilliat's *The Happiest Days of Your Life* (1950), as well as *Boys Will Be Boys* (1935) and others featuring Will Hay's seedily disreputable school master, against post-war changes to the British education system – the rise in independent public boarding schools, the inception of the Eleven Plus examination and the democratisation of quality education for the masses. Roberts's rich contextualisation also considers the origins of the school films in popular school stories from the beginning of the 20th century. Authors such as Enid Blyton helped romanticise the boarding school as a chummy, benign institution offering opportunities for midnight feasts, harmless japes at the expense of eccentric French mistresses and a safe haven for girls to explore their pre-adolescence. The erotic component of the films was always present; the sixth formers in even the first *St. Trinian's* romp, *The Belles of St. Trinian's*

(1954), are sexually precocious. But when the later *St. Trinian's* films shed their celebration of grubby-kneed, anarchic girlhood in favour of salacious 1960s sex kittens, whose endless display of stocking-tops rendered them the voyeuristic objects of masculine desire, then the films effectively lost the plot. The recent *St. Trinian's* films (2007, 2009) picked up on the latter tradition, with mixed success, but perhaps the non-sexualised adolescent girl could not survive beyond the 1950s.

The most celebrated cycle of British comedies was produced by Ealing Studios from 1947 to 1957, starting with *Hue and Cry* (1947) and including such classics as *Whisky Galore* (1949), *The Lavender Hill Mob* (1951), *The Ladykillers* (1955) and, often considered the summit of British film comedy, *Kind Hearts and Coronets* (1949). Tim O'Sullivan's chapter analyses the continuities in the films' celebration of anarchy and idiosyncrasy in this tight little island, and especially highlights the differences between 'core' canonical comedies such as *The Ladykillers* and overlooked deviations from the usual 'Ealing style' as *Another Shore* (1948) and *Meet Mr Lucifer* (1953). O'Sullivan emphasises that Ealing's films were, as Landy says, 'distinctively middle class in their outlook, and they probed tradition, loyalty, community, and social responsibility, expressing a distaste for overreaching and crass materialism' (Landy 1991: 370).

As Norman Wisdom's official biographer, Richard Dacre knows his subject better than most and his chapter on one of Britain's greatest comic stars comprehensively covers Wisdom's career as a Super Gump or 'little man' in the Chaplin tradition of pathos and sentimentality. Wisdom is a cosily unthreatening but nevertheless disruptive figure in a stable and regimented nation. Wisdom was often at odds with his studio bosses and fought to keep the integrity of his character as well as for opportunities to display his considerable talents for dancing and musical performance. That he achieved success around the world, especially in Communist Albania where he became a national hero, is testament to the universality of his little-man-against-the-world comedy. Like Chaplin, Benny Hill and Mr Bean, Wisdom transcended linguistic and cultural barriers, though his films' combination of sentimentality and pratfalls often grated with critics.

The 1950s was an especially rich period for comedy. Terry-Thomas, Ian Carmichael, Leslie Phillips, Alastair Sim, Joan Greenwood, Margaret Rutherford, Joyce Grenfell and Peter Sellers all found a constant supply of work in films by the Boulting brothers, Launder and Gilliat, and in the Rank Studio comedies such as the *Doctor* series, beginning with *Doctor in the House* (1954). Before the sexual and social revolutions of the 1960s, Britain could still believe it was a nation of slightly eccentric shopkeepers, school teachers and hapless crooks, and films like *The Green Man* (1956) and *Too Many Crooks* (1959) constructed comic universes where such characters could thrive. In retrospect, the 1950s were a – perhaps *the* – Golden Age of British comedy, benefitting from the confluence of a spirit of post-war change, a wealth of talent – much of it nurtured through ENSA (the Entertainments National Service Association) – and kept afloat by healthy audience numbers, relative financial stability and a British film industry which maintained continuity by the approximation of a studio system.

Meanwhile, radio – always a medium able to take risks – provided significant opportunities for new comedy talent and ideas. Radio comedies like *It's That Man Again, Round the Horne, The Goon Show* and *Hancock's Half Hour* offered training grounds for comedians such as Peter Sellers, Kenneth Williams, Spike Milligan and Tony Hancock.

Having started their career, polished their craft or gained inspiration from their experiences in the Second World War, these men used radio to explore a purely aural comedy of accent and intonation, innuendo and, with *Round the Horne's* Julian and Sandy, the gay language of Polari alongside experimentation with the BBC's sound effects library.

The twin Boulting brothers flourished during this period. Alan Burton tracks the press response to their comedies, which satirised the Establishment and its enemies in *Private's Progress* (1956) and *I'm All Right Jack* (1959). The Boultings' comedies owed much to the theatrical styles honed in the 1920s and 1930s by Noël Coward and W. Somerset Maugham, who interweaved satire and social comment within traditions of literary comedy, but they also used physical comedy and innuendo as a way of reaching out to wide audience. Their films move fluidly between the two main forms of British comedy, slapstick and middle-brow farce. However, the Boultings gravitated towards mild sex comedies, such as *A French Mistress* (1960), by the end of the 1950s. Few producers were able to resist the liberalisation of post-war attitudes and the Boultings found themselves competing for audiences in a very crowded field. British cinema too was changing and the new wave of realist 'kitchen sink' films of the late 1950s and 1960s heralded an era of permissiveness.

Sarah Street analyses one of the most admired scene-stealers of this period, Margaret Rutherford, whose roles as an indomitable and eccentric middle-aged single woman embodied many characteristics often identified with Englishness in films such as *Blithe Spirit* (1945), *Passport to Pimlico* (1949), *The Importance of Being Earnest* (1952) and four turns in the 1960s as Agatha Christie's Miss Marple. Rutherford's comedy was located in her brilliant and precise co-ordination of facial expressions and body language alongside her no-nonsense sartorial style. Throughout her career she moved effortlessly between stage and screen and created her own unique persona, bringing nuance with subtle gradations of strength and vulnerability, lightness and shade, bewilderment and confidence – latitude not afforded younger, sexier actresses of the time. Rather than being the butt of the joke, Rutherford turned eccentricity into a positive characteristic and something to be celebrated, not least for its irreducible Englishness. Her comedic skills were much in demand and she worked with several different directors from the Boulting brothers to Anthony Asquith, though surprisingly perhaps, in only one Ealing comedy (*Passport to Pimlico*).

The most significant British comedy film star of this period was Peter Sellers, a master of character acting through disguise and silly voices from the innovative insanity of The Goons to Inspector Clouseau in *The Pink Panther* (1963) and his multi-character appearances in Stanley Kubrick's mordant *Dr Strangelove, or How I Learned to Stop Worrying and Love the Bomb* (1964). His talent for impersonation and accents contributed to his first job, when he telephoned the BBC pretending to be Kenneth Horne, star of the radio comedy *Much Binding in the Marsh*. As a result, he was offered a role with Ted Ray in *Ray's A Laugh* and subsequently with Harry Secombe, Spike Milligan and Michael Bentine in *The Goon Show*. Sellers was as famous for his troubled personal life as he was for his comic genius and like Tony Hancock came to epitomise the comedian-as-manic-depressive, whose comic genius draws on a fragile and troubled ego. Hancock never became a film star, though *Hancock's Half Hour*, which ran concurrently on radio and television, was a national institution. Hancock's comedy of heroic grumbling and thwarted social pretension is played out in a world of dingy bedsits, urban alienation, dull jobs and bad weather. He made only two films. *The Rebel* (1961), in which he gives up his job as an office clerk to pursue his vocation as an artist, mocks both Parisian and British pseudo-intellectual pretension. Many of his regular cast appear and Irene Handl is unforgettable as his cantankerous and interfering landlady who objects to Hancock using his bedsit as a studio and the idea that he may have entertained nude female models. Hancock's second film role was *The Punch and Judy Man* (1962), in which he plays an unhappily married Punch and Judy man in a sleepy 1950s seaside resort. Based on his own memories of growing up in Bournemouth, the film is less highly regarded than *The Rebel*.

The most durable of all British comedy series began in 1958 with *Carry On Sergeant* and continued till *Carry On Emmannuelle* in 1978. James Chapman argues that the *Carry Ons* managed, on remarkably low budgets and with great consistency and ingenuity, to track the changes from consensus to permissive liberalism. Far from being made obsolete in the 1970s by the sex comedies, they actually reflected the period's cultural changes with surprising accuracy, tackling mass tourism in *Carry On Camping* (1969) (the highest grossing film in the UK that year), labour relations in *Carry On At Your Convenience* (1971), and the novel terrors of feminism in *Carry On Girls* (1973). Far from being critically overlooked they are now regarded as iconic celebrations of queerness and subversive bawdy (Colin MacCabe ranked *Carry On Cleo* (1964) and *Carry On Up the Khyber* (1968) as two of the greatest British films),[1] and Kenneth Williams, through his letters and diaries, has been re-evaluated as a brilliantly acerbic witness to British cultural change since the 1950s. Chapman notes that the early *Carry Ons* shared the world and the aesthetic of realism of the British New Wave or kitchen sink films, before the New Wave went off in more experimental comic directions with *Tom Jones* (1963), *Billy Liar* (1963) and *Morgan: A Suitable Case For Treatment* (1966), and the *Carry Ons* turned to genre and costume parody.

The satire boom of the 1960s pioneered by *Beyond the Fringe* left, in the short term, few traces in the cinema. Peter Cook, the presiding comic genius of the boom, floundered in *The Rise and Rise of Michael Rimmer* (1970) and Paul Morrissey's burlesque of *The Hound of the Baskervilles* (1978), and only *Bedazzled* (1967), an updated Faust story, made much impact with audiences or critics and became a cult film. Dudley Moore went on to Hollywood stardom in *10* (1979) and *Arthur* (1981), while Alan Bennett wrote *A Private Function* (1984) on the way to becoming a national treasure.

Arguably the most brilliant comedy of the 1960s and 1970s was on television. Sitcoms continued the social realist tradition of exploring working-class life, as well as middle-class insecurity, while sketch shows like Spike Milligan's *Q* and *Monty Python's Flying Circus* integrated satire and silliness. Writers such as Ray Galton and Alan Simpson, and programmes such as *Till Death Us Do Part*, *Steptoe and Son*, *The Likely Lads*, *Fawlty Towers*, *Dad's Army*, *The Fall and Rise of Reginald Perrin* and *The Good Life* explored race, nostalgia, social aspiration and, above all, the subtleties of class. The majority transferred equally successfully from TV (mostly ITV) to feature films, such as *Please Sir!* (1971), *On the Buses*, *Bless This House* (1972) and *Love Thy Neighbour* (1973), but almost all were critically disregarded. Critics once again proved out of step with popular taste. Peter Waymark discusses the voracity with which cinema embraced the TV sitcom film – around 30 were made in the 1970s and 1980s – and the challenges of producing 90-minute feature films from 30-minute episodic comedies (a typical solution was having their cast go on holiday, as in *Holiday on the Buses* (1973) and *The Likely Lads* (1976)). This was achieved with only occasional success, as it was often the restrictions of the TV format that gave the sitcom its creative strength. Waymark cites the *Porridge* spin-off (1979) as a failure precisely because, once the film 'opened-up' the series' set-up and abandoned the claustrophobia of the prison cell, the material lost its comedic *raison d'être*. The cinema spin-offs were also able to take advantage of 'A' or 'AA' certification to include more risqué material than their TV versions. *Dad's Army* writers, Croft and Perry, were pressurised by producers Columbia to include more innuendo in the film version, putting their characters at odds with audience expectation and ultimately leaving Arthur Lowe, as Captain Mainwaring, visibly uncomfortable at having to deliver *double entendres* out of character.

The 1970s also saw cinema attendances go into free fall, with many city centre cinemas being converted into bingo halls. If television was keeping audiences at home, then cinema needed to compete with increasingly risqué adult-oriented material, including both horror and sexploitation films. Along with (and similar to) the sitcom films, a key comedy form of the early 1970s was the sex comedy, whose strains of rudeness and appalling bad taste I.Q. Hunter's chapter pursues from *Confessions of a Window Cleaner* (1974) to contemporary gross-out films like *Fat Slags* (2004) and *Sex Lives of the Potato Men* (2004). As well as being overwhelmingly sexist, 1970s sex comedies updated the *Carry On* formula to popularise the values of individualistic permissiveness. As one of the few buoyant genres at the time, they attracted some unexpected veteran directors and producers – Val Guest made *Confessions of a Window Cleaner* and Betty Box produced *Percy* (1971), directed by Ralph Thomas, who was more usually associated with the *Doctor* films. Hunter notes the recent revival of the sex comedy, with films such as *Preaching to the Perverted* (1997) and *Swinging with the Finkels* (2010), but also that these 'low comedies' are largely disconnected from the tradition of working-class bawdy now represented by end-of-the-pier comedians such as Roy 'Chubby' Brown.

Monty Python in a sense dominated British comedy cinema in the late 1970s and 1980s. They produced the two best British comedies of the 1970s and some of the most quotable and quoted lines in the history of film comedy. Justin Smith traces the production history of the Pythons' ventures on screen from the sketch compilation, *And Now for Something Completely Different* (1971), to *Monty Python's The Meaning of Life* (1983). Smith argues for *Monty Python's Life of Brian* (1979) as the Pythons' masterpiece (though *Monty Python and the Holy Grail* (1974) is the more prominent cult film in the US). The Pythons were the common denominator of many, perhaps most, British film comedies till the late 1990s – *Jabberwocky* (1977), *Clockwise* (1986), *The Missionary* (1982), *Erik the Viking* (1989), *A Fish Called Wanda* (1988), *Personal Services* (1987), *Time Bandits* (1981), *A Private Function* (1984), *Consuming Passions* (1988) and *Nuns on the Run* (1990). At the same time Terry Gilliam's cultishly-surreal, dystopian comedy *Brazil* (1985) saw his talents flourish as a director in his own right. However, arguably, it was Cleese's television series *Fawlty Towers* that achieved the most universal success across audience demographics.

In the 1980s, *A Fish Called Wanda* was the major box office hit, combining international stars (Oscar-winning Kevin Kline) with a self-deprecating restatement of old-fashioned English traits such as social embarrassment:

> Wanda, do you have any idea what it's like being English? Being so correct all the time, being so stifled by this dread of, of doing the wrong thing, of saying to someone 'Are you married?' and hearing 'My wife left me this morning,' or saying, uh, 'Do you have children?' and being told they all burned to death on Wednesday. You see, Wanda, we're all terrified of embarrassment. That's why we're so ... dead.

A Fish Called Wanda encouraged a trend for rom-coms, typified also by the gentle comedies of Bill Forsyth (*Gregory's Girl* (1981), *Local Hero* (1983)) and Richard Curtis (*The Tall Guy* (1989)), which made similar contrasts between British reserve and aptitude for embarrassment and American energy and vulgarity. In the 1920s, critics had argued that American stars brought vim and vigour to the screen, whilst British actors could only perform 'reserved' and it appeared that little had changed in six decades since American producer Samuel Goldwyn, searching for something positive to say about British actors in 1924, remarked that ' ... no ... actor ... can enter a drawing room like an Englishman' (Low 1971: 303).

The 1980s were a transitional period in comedy. There were generational and political shifts in stand-up, TV and then film. A new wave of post-Python alternative comedy, nurtured on the live comedy circuits and owing as much to the Edinburgh Fringe Festival as to Oxbridge, emerged on TV in series such as *The Comedy Store*, *The Young Ones*, *Not the Nine O'Clock News* and *The Comic Strip Presents* ... and then spilled over onto film. This marked a change from the comedy of Working Men's Clubs typified by Bernard Manning and his ilk in the ITV series *The Comedians*, and the sitcom movies with their casual sexism and racism. It represented too a rejection of the culture and traditions of working-class comedy, at a time when the working class was being dismantled by the Right and tagged as racist and reactionary by the Left. Comedians such as Manning, Freddie Starr, the exiled but internationally beloved Benny Hill, and Roy 'Chubby' Brown found a new home on video. (Only Brown transferred to film, with *UFO* (1993), a self-consciously politically incorrect retort to the New Wave of comedy.) Demographic and social divides in British comedy were as keen as ever. At the same time, an older generation of comedians, such as Frankie Howerd and Kenneth Williams, enjoyed renaissances with a new generation and became national treasures just before their deaths, though an attempt to update the *Carry On* series with *Carry On Columbus* (1992) was a disaster despite the presence of several contemporary New Wave comedy stars.

Alternative comedy was a combination of Pythonism, satire and politics. Its stars – Rowan Atkinson, Rik Mayall, Ade Edmondson, Lenny Henry, Richard Curtis, Robbie Coltrane, Emma Thompson, Stephen Fry and Hugh Laurie – rapidly progressed to film, and not only comedy (Thompson won an Oscar for her screenplay for *Sense and Sensibility* (1995)). Simon Pegg described the process thus:

[A]lternative comedy did not begin with the *Comic Strip* but rather regenerated through the ages like Doctor Who, the mantle being passed on to the next generation of subversives (often directly): Spike Milligan (*The Goons*) appeared in *Monty Python's Life of Brian*, Terry Jones (*Monty Python*) appeared in *The Young Ones*, Ben Elton (*The Young Ones*) introduced Vic Reeves at *The Secret Policeman's Ball* ... , etc. The connections are many and varied, and although the style of comedy evolves and mutates, the desire to undermine the norms of comedy remains constant and a new incarnation will emerge as the older version is assimilated into the mainstream and disempowered.

(Pegg 2010: 209–10)

The slow-burning triumph of the 1980s, a one-off completely outside the prevailing trends and one of the greatest British cult films, was *Withnail and I* (1987). Set at the fag-end of the 1960s, 'the greatest decade in the history of mankind', it shared characteristics with the tradition of British 'bed-sitcoms' like *Steptoe and Son* or *Hancock's Half Hour* – desperate men stuck in homosocial pairings, dealing with compromise, sell-out, poor domestic hygiene and stunted social ambition. Its cult built slowly – especially in the US – after a lukewarm initial response in cinemas, indicating the extent to which the British cinema industry had lost touch with its audiences. It was simply not able to market this kind of film to an appropriate demographic. Though writer Bruce Robinson's follow-up to *Withnail*, *How to Get Ahead in Advertising* (1989), also starring Richard E. Grant, met with less success and failed to attain cult status, perhaps because it appeared to be self-consciously courting it.

The exigencies of the British film industry and the fine line between achieving cult status and being consigned to cinema's scrapheap are illustrated by Vivian Stanshall's (of the Bonzo Dog Doo-Dah Band) foray into comedy *Sir Henry at Rawlinson End*, a film which undeservedly fell through the cracks. Based on his LP, the film is a daft masterpiece of British eccentricity about Sir Henry (Trevor Howard) and his decadent and decaying aristocratic family attempting to exorcise the ghost of his brother Humbert, who was accidentally killed in a drunken duck-shooting accident. As a portrait of mad and debauched British aristocracy in free-fall, it has no rival.

The most successful product of the *Comic Strip* generation was Richard Curtis, whose rom-coms from *The Tall Guy* to *Notting Hill* (1999) projected an imaginary Britain (or rather London) and relied on American stars to lend the films some international appeal. He wrote one of the key comedy hits of the 1990s, *Four Weddings and a Funeral* (1994), which attracted critical opprobrium as a conservative 'heritage film' as blandly unreal as 1950s comedies and, like *Notting Hill* and the epic *Love Actually*, offering Blairite fairy tales of upward mobility at a time of sharp social divisions. But, as James Leggott elsewhere points out, 'to condemn these stories for their representation of a city free from social and ethnic tensions is to overlook their potency as fantasies of reassurance and unity' (Leggott 2008: 70). Hugh Grant emerged as the most important British comedy star since Cary Grant, and perfected a style of diffident bumbling Englishness, which has been described as 'essentially the Ian Carmichael "silly ass" transmogrified for a more permissive cinema' (Mackillop and Sinyard 2003: 2); but he was equally good as a cad in *Bridget Jones's Diary* (2001). In his chapter Leggott discusses Richard Curtis as a national institution, as famous for his charitable endeavours with Comic Relief as his comedy output, but whose inoffensive, feel-good comedies also achieved true transatlantic success.

Four Weddings inspired numerous rom-coms, such as *Sliding Doors* (1998) and *Wimbledon* (2004), set in a stylised and gentrified Britain cleaned up for international consumption; even Woody Allen got into the act with *Match Point* (2001) and *You Will Meet a Tall Dark Stranger* (2010). Like TV make-over shows and property programmes, the films often struck critics as nostalgic encomiums to middle-class complacency and materialism.

Writer Nick Hornby supplied the material for several romantic comedies, starring the likes of Colin Firth (*Fever Pitch* (1997); Firth is now Britain's biggest star), Hugh Grant (*About a Boy* (2002)) and John Cusack (in the US-UK co-production of *High Fidelity* (2000)). The films explored masculine fragility and insecurity among homosocial groupings (football, single fathers, the record store), but always in the guise of female-friendly romantic comedies. The ever-so-slightly-damaged, but vulnerable, New Man/New Lad protagonists are waiting for the right woman to rescue them from their over-investment in mates and hobbies. But it is in these male groupings that the comedic banter is at its funniest rather than with the 'final couple' at the films' resolution.

In complete contrast was *The Full Monty* (1997), the other key hit of the 1990s, which echoed and inspired a number of comedies that mourn ambivalently for a lost working-class way of life – *Brassed Off* (1996), *Billy Elliott* (2000), *Kinky Boots* (2005) and more recently *Made in Dagenham* (2010). All focused on regionally specific working-class life and work, rooted in disappearing manufacturing industries and blue-collar workforces. These films, striving for authenticity, seek to recreate the communal comedies of the 1950s in a post-industrial age where few of their audiences will have experienced life and work in large factories. The films are both nostalgic for, and critical of, the decline of these masculine communities and offer a counterpoint to Richard Curtis's comedies of individualism and Thatcherite self-improvement.

From the early 1990s, a new generation of British Asian writers and directors such as Meera Syal and Gurinder Chadha used comedy to negotiate inter-generational clashes and the gaps between their ambitions as British citizens and the expectations of their Asian heritage. *Bhaji on the Beach* (1993), *East is East* (1999) and *Anita and Me* (2002) all dissipate the potential for racial, social and familial disharmony into comedy, pitching their second-generation Asian protagonists into a Britain that is bemused rather than hostile. What this new generation of Asian comedic talent brought to the screen was the ability to see Britain's class system and social divide from the perspective of an outsider searching for meritocracy in a society on the verge of change.

Comedy in the 2000s has explored altogether riskier areas of racial and cultural difference, such as Islamic fundamentalism and terrorism. Chris Morris's controversial *Four Lions* (2010) finds unsettling humour in the ineptitude of Muslim would-be bombers, including one who blows himself up. In a Britain after the '7/7' bomb attacks in 2005, *Four Lions* undoubtedly pushes at the limits of comic taste, but manages to negotiate these by humanising its characters and creating some truly funny moments which transcend its potentially unfunny and sensitive subject matter.

Animation has been a staple of British comedy cinema from the lightning cartoon sketches of the early 20th century. Paul Wells discusses the rich tradition of British animated comedy which continues to thrive in the short-film format, supported in the 1980s and 1990s by Channel 4's *Fourmations* series and by the British Animation Awards. Animated comedy, by its very nature, is able to create its own universe from scratch, to overturn the laws of physics and to transmogrify the human body into a multiplicity of forms – from simple stick figures to anthropomorphic blobs. As such, it has proved a useful medium to explore human fragility in all its guises, from dysmorphia to fears about ageing and corporeal decay. Wells's title, borrowed from Alison Snowden and David Fine's Oscar-winning *Bob's Birthday* (1993), a superb comedy of social embarrassment and mid-life marital crisis, is a perfect example. Animated comedy has also proved both a safe haven and a creative space for women animators to explore attitudes to female sexuality and desire. In *Girls Night Out* (1988), Joanna Quinn's quiescent middle-aged Welsh housewives, who turn into a rapacious gang when confronted with a male stripper, are the dark underbelly of the middle-class Women's Institute-types of *Calendar Girls* (2003). Quinn's graphic style and use of shifting perspectives perfectly captures the phallic confidence of her male stripper before the removal of his metaphorical cod-piece (a posing pouch) by the mischievous Beryl. No discussion of British animated comedy can ignore Nick Park's creations, Wallace, the cheese-loving Lancastrian inventor, and his long-suffering dog, Gromit, who, along with Mr Bean, remain among the UK's biggest comedy exports.

Since the 1990s, comedy settled into a number of modes: gentle, character-driven 'Britcoms' with some international appeal; and vehicles for TV stars. Some of the latter were successful, such as *Bean* and *Shaun of the Dead*, but many, especially youth-orientated bad taste low comedies like *Guest House Paradiso* (1999) and *Lesbian Vampire Killers* (2009), were commercial and critical disasters. In fact, it is arguable that, ever since the sitcom film of the 1970s, British comedy has been significantly weakened by its continuing reliance on TV for so much of its material.[2]

Other recent comedies such as *Starter for 10* (2006), *Cemetery Junction* (2010) and *Submarine* (2010) have explored what it is to be young, male, working class and living in 'the sticks'. Here comedy lies in ambition-about-to-be-thwarted, ranging from getting to university to losing one's virginity in the most cringingly embarrassing ways possible. James McAvoy and Benedict Cumberbatch, not known as comedians, are superb in *Starter for10*, essentially a town-and-gown comedy of class and social shortcomings based around that quintessentially British television institution, *University Challenge*. Ricky Gervais and Stephen Merchant's *Cemetery Junction* set in the eponymous 1973 suburb is the story of three working-class lads striving to break from the cul-de-sacs of their expectations and the lassitude of their parents. This is territory more usually explored by Shane Meadows, himself a gifted comedy actor, who started his feature film career with the comedy *Small Time* (1996) about a group of low-budget thieves whose ambition rarely extends beyond stealing dog food. *Submarine*, based on Joe Dunthorne's novel of the same name, is a male confessional echoing an earlier television series, *The Secret Diary of Adrian Mole Aged 13 3/4*, about a 15-year-old fantasist coming of age in an unforgiving Swansea.

If many of British cinema's homosocial comedies addressed young men, then young female audiences had their equivalent in *Bridget Jones*-like comedies of sexual embarrassment, thwarted romance and personal revelation, which aimed to connect with female experiences of self-deprecation and poor body image. Older female audiences found their spokeswomen in Julie Walters in *Educating Rita* (1983) and Pauline Collins in *Shirley Valentine* (1989), the taken-for-granted housewife who finds sex and romance after she runs off to a Greek island. Willy Russell's courageous heroine struck an instant chord with a generation of women who felt that their only function was to feed inattentive and ungrateful husbands. Both films did incredibly good business, but only a few subsequent films exploited this rarely-served but extremely lucrative demographic – *Dancin' Thru The Dark* (1990), for example, also by Willy Russell, and the rom-com musical *Mamma Mia!* (2008), whose success took the British exhibition industry completely by surprise.

The increased popularity of the feature-length cinema documentary has also spawned its satirical sibling the 'mockumentary'. Using hand-held cameras, vox pops and location filming, this tradition of spoofing can be traced back to Christopher Guest's seminal *This is Spinal Tap* (1984) about 'the sights, the sounds, the smells of a British rock band on tour'. Often featuring the director-as-personality, these films parody the kind of techniques pioneered by the likes of Michael Moore, Nick Broomfield and Werner Herzog in their issue-based personality-driven and rhetorical documentaries. British comedian, Sacha Baron Cohen, found international fame and US/UK co-production deals as a wannabe gangster in *Ali G Indahouse* (2002), a spin-off from his Channel 4 TV character, and as a cringingly embarrassing Kazakhstani film maker in *Borat: Cultural Learnings of America for Make Benefit Glorious Nation of Kazakhstan* (2006), a major international hit. By comparison, *Morris: A Life with Bells On* (2009) is a gentle but hilarious satire on Morris Dancing that sees the much-derided English form exported to California, where it is embraced as a gay cult and celebrated for its campness. *Morris*, a low-budget indie production, garnered plaudits on the international film festival circuit, but failed to secure a theatrical release in the UK. Its success has largely been through computer downloads, a DVD release and screenings among the UK's alternative village-hall exhibition circuits.

With the inception of the UK Film Council in 2000, British film comedy was, along with horror and gangster films, one of the three key low-budget genres backed with funds from the National Lottery. A number of independent, niche comedies were the result including *A Cock and Bull Story* (2006), which features some of Britain's top TV comedy talent, including the successful pairing of Steve Coogan and Rob Brydon in the film within a film attempt to film Laurence Sterne's supposedly unfilmable novel, *Tristram Shandy*. The film rewards several viewings for its overlapping dialogue and banter between its protagonists. In terms of political comedy, the Blair years provided ample opportunity for biting satire, particularly based around the figure of the maniacal spin-doctor. Writer Armando Iannucci's *In the Loop* (2009), another Lottery-supported film, was spun off from the television *The Thick of It*, but featuring a strong US sub-plot to assist the film's passage across the Atlantic.

It has often been the infrastructural inadequacies and incapacity, rather than the merits of individual films, which have let the side down – witness *Withnail and I* which suffered from a lack of imagination in the 1980s cinema exhibition sector. British comedy cinema has been characterised by an abundance of talent and inventiveness at all levels of production, but its greatest strength is in screenwriting. Unlike Hollywood comedy, with its team-based writing, British comedy has tended towards the individual (and double acts), the eccentric and occasionally the auteurist. It has pushed at boundaries, despite some run-ins with the BBFC, and produced some truly ground-breaking films like *Monty Python's Life of Brian* and *Four Lions*. It has benefitted from being able to take risks and experiment with new ideas in both radio and television. Public subsidy, through the National Lottery and UK Film Council, has also assisted in getting more niche comedies into production, but ultimately the inadequate size of the domestic market has meant that the majority of films need to achieve international recognition, particularly in the US, to make any return on investment. This is a problem for more Anglocentric comedy, more culturally specific than Britain's other great export, heritage cinema. Lack of investment in marketing and distribution has consigned many merit-worthy British comedies to the straight-to-DVD market, or seen them languishing at the further reaches of independent cinema schedules.

Notes

1 www.carryon.org.uk/articles8.htm
2 This argument is made at www.guardian.co.uk/film/2009/nov/12/british-comedy-movies.

Bibliography

Barr, C. (1977) *Ealing Studios*, London: David & Charles.

Dacre, R. (2009) 'Traditions of British comedy', in R. Murphy (ed.), *The British Cinema Book*, 3rd edn, London: British Film Institute/Palgrave Macmillan.

Gerrard, S. (2008) 'What a Carry On! The decline and fall of a great British institution', in R. Shail (ed.), *Seventies British Cinema*, London: British Film Institute.

Hammond, M. (2000) '"Cultivating Pimple": Performance traditions and the film comedy of Fred and Joe Evans', in A. Burton and L. Porter (eds), *Pimple Pranks and Pratfalls*, Trowbridge: Flicks Books.

Landy, M. (1991) *British Genres: Cinema and Society, 1930–1960*, Princeton: Princeton University Press.

Leggott, J. (2008) *Contemporary British Cinema: From Heritage to Horror*, London and New York: Wallflower.

Low, R. (1948) *The History of the British Film 1896–1906*, London: George Allen and Unwin.

——(1950) *The History of the British Film 1914–1918*, London: George Allen and Unwin.

——(1971) *The History of the British Film 1918–1929*, London: George Allen and Unwin.

Mackillop, I. and N. Sinyard (2003) 'Celebrating British cinema of the 1950s', in I. Mackillop and N. Sinyard (eds), *British Cinema of the 1950s: A Celebration*, Manchester and New York: Manchester University Press.

Medhurst, A. (2007) *A National Joke: Popular Comedy and English Cultural Identities*, London and New York: Routledge.

Pegg, S. (2010) *Nerd Do Well*, London: Century.

Spicer, A. (2007) 'An occasional eccentricity: The strange course of Surrealism in British cinema', in G. Harper and R. Stone (eds), *The Unsilvered Screen: Surrealism on Film*, London and New York: Wallflower Press.

Sutton, D. (2000) *A Chorus of Raspberries*, Exeter: University of Exeter Press.

2 From slapstick to satire

British comedy cinema before 1930

Laraine Porter

It has long been accepted that British comedy took its own pratfall when Variety entrepreneur Fred Karno sailed for the US in 1912 taking with him two of the greatest silent clowns that the world would ever know – Charlie Chaplin and Stan Laurel.[1] From that point onwards, received wisdom tells us that silent comedy was so dominated by Hollywood that there was little space, or need, for other national cinemas to compete. Silent comedy crossed language barriers and was easily exported around the world and Chaplin's international reputation was unassailable.

Cinema historians have largely overlooked or dismissed this period in British film comedy, often in unfair comparisons with Hollywood, and although Britain never produced anyone to rival Chaplin, nor did any other country. It has long been asserted that even minor Hollywood comedians outshone the British. Historian Rachael Low identifies a number of reasons why British silent comedy in the 1910s failed to gain a foothold, including the often parlous financial state of the industry, an over-reliance on stage farces, inappropriate performance styles, a lack of mimetic skills needed for silent cinema and more importantly, a lack of stars:

> The most successful humorous films here, as in America, were those of Chaplin. It is true that the economic conditions of the industry militated against a similar worldwide success on the part of any British comedian, but it is also only too obvious that there was no British comedian deserving of such success ... But lesser American comedians, too, were favourably compared with their British counterparts at the time.
>
> (Low 1950: 168)

Social historians have not always been kind to this period in British comedy either. Thomas Burke writing in 1934, looking back to the 1900s and lamenting the decline of the Music Hall, describes his distaste for the 'crude' film comedies audiences were flocking to see:

> In 1908 the movies were practically unknown to intelligent people. At first the performers were anonymous; nobody thought that the public could possibly care about the lay figures who were going through those banal motions. A little later they were given nick-names of the crude schoolboy sort – 'Fatty,' 'Skinny,' etc. There came a time when a man mentioned to me with surprise that his

children, who were receiving a serious education, were infatuated with this idiotic entertainment ...

(Burke 1934: 141)

But despite critical dismissal, cultural snobbery and resentment that the cinematograph was ousting the Music Hall, comedy was a cornerstone of British cinema from the outset. Popular audiences loved it.

This chapter will examine its development from the short films of the 1900s and 1910s starring performers such as Pimple, Did'ums and the Tilly Girls, in sketches with their roots in Edwardian Music Hall, Pantomime and Variety, to 1920s feature films by directors such as Adrian Brunel, Manning Haynes, Alfred Hitchcock and Anthony Asquith. It will examine key trends in British silent comedy from the beginning of the 20th century, tracing the roots of literary and satirical comedy with the involvement of writers such as A.A. Milne, H.G. Wells, Noël Coward, Elizabeth von Arnim and P.G. Wodehouse. Silent comedy also spans some of the most momentous events of the 20th century from the Edwardian summer leading up to the Great War, the rise of the Suffragette and 1920s modernity, industrial uncertainty and unrest, to the Stock Market collapse of 1929. It starts with the first film screenings in 1895, covers the development of cinema as an institution around 1910, the arrival of the feature film in 1913, the near collapse of the British film industry in the mid-1920s, and the shift towards sound cinema by 1928.

This chapter is divided into five schematic sections: the frenetic period of the early pioneers and short film comedies made before the First World War; the transformative period during the war with the arrival of feature comedies and the dominance of Hollywood; the early 1920s and the development of sophisticated satire; the subsequent literary adaptations; and finally, the mid to late 1920s and the consolidation of the silent comedy aesthetic before the arrival of sound. Much of this history must be written in relation to Hollywood which consolidated its international stranglehold by 1914, perfecting slapstick and knockabout comedy within its emergent and highly efficient studio and star systems, whilst British cinema refined and reworked traditions based in the Music Hall, alongside theatrical and literary traditions of farce, irony, satire and drollery. Witty intertitles would later purvey subtle irony, but most early comedies relied on exaggeration rather than the virtuoso performance or skilful comic pathos. But by the mid-1920s Britain had a range of comedic star performers like Betty Balfour and comedian-director Walter Forde, alongside character actors like Gordon Harker, and even serious actor-director Guy Newall who played the 'Silly Ass' character in Géza von Bolváry's film adaption of Arnold Ridley's stage play *Ghost Train* (1927) with considerable comedic talent.

The beginnings of British film comedy: Pioneers and early trends

The early period in British cinema (1895–1902) is populated with comedies that delight in the technical possibilities of film, combined with popular slapstick sketches and pratfalls borrowed from Pantomime or Music Hall. Many films exploit the effects of speed, mechanization and modernity on late Victorian and Edwardian life, whilst early Suffragette and 'henpeck' comedies can be seen as a backlash against changing social and sexual relations and the status of women. Trick films such as *The Greasy Pole* (1899) and *The Bathers* (1900) which simply reverse the motion of attempts to take down a flag and men diving into a lake respectively were a sub-genre in their own right as were films of lady cyclists, still a novelty at this time.[2] 'Facials' showing comic faces in extreme close-up, such as *The Big Swallow* (1901), revel in the novelty of the close-up and were screened as fairground attractions, competing with the hurly-burly of showmen and women hawking their sideshows. The 'facial' sub-genre enjoyed relative longevity and full expression in the 1914 Florence Turner vehicle, *Daisy Doodad's Dial* (of which more later), which displayed the Music Hall star's talent for facial gymnastics in a way which would have been impossible on the stage. Parodies and spoofs of serious films began early. *The Cheese Mites* (1903) in The Unseen World series sensationally used microscopic cinematography and was quickly parodied in *The Unclean World* (1903) in which a professor spits out his lunch to examine it under a microscope, revealing insects which turn out to be clockwork. This kind of self-referential satire would later be developed in the 1920s by directors such as Adrian Brunel and marks the beginning of a key form in British cinema comedy.

Inevitably, Britain's Edwardian class system was ripe for being undermined by comedic displays of social anarchy and the early comedies of Blackburn-based Mitchell and Kenyon (M&K) often display unprovoked scenes of comedy violence and *reductio ad absurdum* plots.[3] In *The Interrupted Picnic* (1906) a bucolic lunch is suddenly disrupted by a mob, including a child riding a donkey, that simply chases off the picnickers, steal their food and trash the site. M&K's early comedies can be read as the comedic underbelly of their Factory Gate films in which hoards of workers file peaceably past the camera on their way to the massive Edwardian factories. In M&K's comedies, the crowd turns angry, and their sheer numbers must have caused unease among the factory owners and middle classes in a society which relied on mass working-class compliance and consensus with long hours in monotonous jobs. These anarchic comedies often end up in unmotivated violence or aggression directed at authority figures such as police-men, teachers and vicars, with children as young as two or three years old literally dragged into the action. M&K's northern comedies are distinct from those produced by their southern counterparts (largely in London and Brighton) in their use of Blackburn locations but also in the pacing of their plots, which move at lightning speed from calm, quotidian scenes to complete routs in a matter of seconds. Surreal humour is also evident in their films such as *Diving Lucy* (1903) in which a pair of legs in striped stockings, stick feet-first out of a village pond. Assuming a drowned woman, onlookers, including the ubiquitous Copper, deploy a park bench and plank to effect a rescue only to pull out a pair of fake legs attached to a placard saying 'Rats'. Inevitably, the hapless Copper falls into the pond. It is unclear what external references audiences might have brought to this self-contained comedy lasting less than two minutes, which opens with the animated intertitle: ' ... £100 Reward ... Lost!!! ... Her Husband Thinks She Might Have Stuck at the Bottom ... But Somebody Said "Rats"!!!'? Did it echo a Variety sketch or did it emerge as a cinematic gag in its own right? Was it a Suffragette gag? It is still funny, but the full contextual meaning, as with many of these early sketch-comedies, is lost to us now.

Children were the source of several comic trends with characters such as Did'ums, the truly awful eponymous curly-haired boy-child who starred in several Clarendon shorts from 1910 to 1912 and whose plots include baby-stealing, tormenting police-men, swapping hotel room numbers and so on. Did'ums and his ilk flout the Edwardian idea of childhood innocence as does *Our New Errand Boy* (1905), featuring producer James Williamson's son Tom as the delivery boy who plays cruel, unmotivated tricks on customers. Hepworth's Tilly girl comedies of the 1910s pre-empt the St. Trinian's mob by more than 40 years. Largely directed by Lewin Fitzhamon, they feature teen actresses Alma Taylor and Chrissie White, who as out-of-control young women, unfettered by Edwardian ideals of ladylike behaviour, reflect burgeoning female eman-cipation in their youthful physicality, freedom from restrictive corsetry, defiance and rebelliousness. They delight in unprovoked cruelty in films that see them tormenting sick people in their bed in *Tilly the Tomboy Visits the Poor* (1910), attacking passers-by with a fire hose in *Tilly and the Fire Engines* (1911), and knocking down the guests at an afternoon tea party in *Tilly's Party* (1911). These comedies proved that women could perform slapstick as well as their American counterparts and opened a window of opportunity for British comediennes, never fully exploited. For despite the success of these early comedies, both White and Taylor would go on to perform serious 'drawing room' roles in the 1920s, leaving their bad-girl alter-egos behind.[4]

Whilst the Edwardian Tillys wreaked havoc in the middle-class streets and parlours of leafy Walton-on-Thames and the nightmare-child Did'ums had clearly been over-indulged, then the M&K children and Williamson's *Errand Boy* represent the invisible hordes of working children who helped fuel the Edwardian economy. That children were often left to fend for themselves and each other in the Edwardian home is a source for concern, translated into comedy. *When Daddy Comes Home* (1902) and *When Mama's Out* (1909) both feature 'home alone' children whose parents return from work to domestic comedy mayhem.

These child and teen comedians are essentially amoral and single-minded in their pursuit of gratuitous mischief, gleefully punishing anyone who crosses their path. The elderly and the sick staid Edwardian ladies, teachers or vicars are all ripe for a comedic bashing. The fun lies in the contrast between the children's lowly social status and their ability to create unbridled havoc among unsuspecting adults. Their youthful speed and agility are exploited in the comic chase, but it is their complete lack of sentiment for their victim that undermines notions of childhood innocence. They are a comedic outlet for anarchy, violence and frustration in a tightly class-bound and hierarchical society in which children of working-class parents were at the bottom of the social and economic heap. As performers, they also provided a pool of cheap and available labour for films that relied on kiddie-comic slapstick rather than character development.

If anarchy fuelled the plots of M&K comedies, then we can see the origins of sex comedy in films by George Albert Smith such as *Hanging out the Clothes: Master, Mistress and Maid* (1897) or *The Kiss in the Tunnel* (1899), where saucy (one might say, sala-cious) men steal illicit kisses from women. The eroticized figures of the maid resisting the attentions of the master of the house and the young woman travelling alone who attracts amorous young men are the focus of common plotlines. *Percy's Persistent Pursuit* (1912) sees the eponymous protagonist trying to woo a young woman and losing his

Figure 2.1 The Tilly girls: Chrissie White and Alma Taylor (author's own image).

trousers when chased off by a gang of 'maids' and *A Race for a Kiss* (1904) sees a jockey and motorist race for a woman's favours. In the pre-First World War comic universe, unchaperoned young women were fair game for male attention, whilst older women, no longer sexually attractive, become figures of fun. G.A. Smith's grotesque *The Old Maid's Valentine* (1900) has a bespectacled, fussily dressed, middle-aged woman mistaking a joke card for a Valentine. The comedy lies in her thwarted expectations and the very idea that an older woman should consider romance.

Gendered comic stereotypes predated cinema by several centuries, but cinema adopts them with enthusiasm and rapidly capitalizes upon its ability to show close-ups, particularly of women's legs and ankles. Early cinema starts to fragment the body, paving the way for the sexualized use of close-ups (of legs, faces, breasts) that will come to dominate the representation of women in classic cinema. Early comedy was also responsible for developing cinematic language in many other ways including positioning the spectator as voyeur. G.A. Smith's *As Seen through a Telescope* (1900) is shot from the perspective of a man spying on a bicycling couple and delivers a close-up on the woman's ankle being petted by her partner.

As social and sexual relations shifted with the rise of the 'new woman' and women's suffrage, then so too did British comedy exploit the figure of the Suffragette and her male victim the 'henpeck'. As early as 1899, the Bamforth Company produced *Women's Rights* in which two women 'gossiping' behind a fence have their skirts nailed down by eavesdropping workmen. *Milling the Militants: A Comical Absurdity* (1913) features a husband who dreams of becoming Prime Minister and re-introducing ducking stools as female punishment, when he is left to look after the children whilst his wife attends a Suffragette demonstration. *The Suffragette's Downfall; or Who Said 'Rats'* (1911) is another Suffragette punishment film in which the husband plots to prevent his wife joining the suffrage movement and gets her to sign an agreement promising to stay home and do the housework.[5] *Mr. Henpeck's Revolt* (1909) features a 'henpeck', ridiculed for doing his wife's shopping, who gets drunk in revenge. *Wife The Weaker Vessel* (1915), starring ex-Tilly Chrissie White, is another revenge comedy in which a henpecked husband, jealous of his bachelor friend, tricks him into marrying a physical education instructress who quickly asserts her dominance in an early fantasy of male masochism.

The newly assertive Suffragette was a gift to comedy. She materialized as the harridan, the gossip, the errant wife and mother and, most importantly, an emasculating force on Edwardian masculinity. These films exploit the comic combination of the dominating wife and ineffectual husband, recognizable from Music Hall, which Donald McGill would later develop in his seaside postcards. These films also offer comic expression for unease in the shift in post-Victorian gender relations in which women threatened to neglect the home and husband – a threat which is dissipated by turning her into a figure of ridicule. In their characterization and stereotyping, these early gender comedies contain the seeds of multiple later representations, like the spinsterish Suffragette, Thirza Tapper, in Hitchcock's *The Farmer's Wife* (1928), discussed later.

During a period which saw the growth of the late Victorian cities and the mass migration from the countryside to newly expanded cities, the comically exaggerated bumpkin at odds with modernity is exploited in films such as *The Countryman and the Cinematograph* (1901) where the 'yokel' in the cinema is unable to differentiate between screen and reality, *Farmer Giles in London* (1909) in which the naïve farmer is robbed of his clothes, and *Farmer Jenkins' Visit to the White City* (1910). These films establish the distinction between the 'uneducated' rural classes and the sophisticated and urbane metropolitan, allowing audiences a laugh at what they had left behind and where they themselves had come from.

Corporeal punishment, disembodiment and death are common outcomes of many early comedies which pitch the human body against symbols of modernity such as electricity, the bicycle and the motor car. As the pace of life increased then so too did the potential for human catastrophe and the fast pacing of silent comedies is a product of the machine age. Films like *How it Feels to be Run Over* (1900) and *How to Stop a Motor Car* (1902) used trickery to satisfy curiosity about being knocked down by a car – road deaths being a relatively common experience despite the lack of vehicles – or to play with fantasies of mortality in reconstructing the human body after catastrophes. However, in *Mary Jane's Mishap or Don't Fool with the Paraffin* (1903) and *Explosion of a Motor Car* (1900), death is the final gag. *A Lesson in Electricity* (1909) and *Overcharged* (1912) both play with the body exposed to electrical currents. Comedies of physical transformation that pitched humanity against machines can be understood as expressing insecurity at the pace of change and mechanization. In *An Over-Incubated Baby* (1901), Professor Bakem's incubator promises to speed up baby's growth by 12 months in one hour, but the inevitable mishap sees baby emerging as an old man.

During the pre-war period, comedies based on racial difference are largely confined to Jewish and Oriental protagonists. The racist stereotype of the spendthrift Jew crops up in comedies like *The Robbers and the Jew* (1908) where the joke is on a Jewish man who is robbed after coveting his money. Later in the 1920s, racist expressions relating to black people crop up more frequently in comedies, though no more so than in other genres. Where it did occur, racism in comedy reflected the changing idea of threat from migrant communities shifting from Chinese, Jewish and black to German by 1914.

World War I and the transformation of cinema

The long Edwardian summer that ended in 1914 saw the development of a series of independent producers scattered around London, Blackburn, Holmfirth, Brighton, Sheffield and Walton-on-Thames, whilst bespoke cinemas screening repeat programmes of shorts, newsreels and features sprang up in all major cities. The longer film required plotting, character development and narrative motivation; the single-gag film was losing its attraction, but remained the staple of many smaller production companies until 'the decline of the open market [during the War] made more important feature comedies essential' (Low 1950: 161). But British producers were loath to invest in comedy and by 1914, British comedies remained half the length of their American and European counterparts. While Chaplin, Arbuckle, Linder, Normand and Sennett were already known around the world, Britain entered the war with Pimple. This period also sees the demarcation between low comedy and high culture in British cinema. Rachael Low comments:

> [T]he less well-known exponents of Music Hall slapstick still constituted the bulk of Britain's film humour and the more important companies rarely exerted any

great efforts in this direction ... it was into drama that British producers flung all
their resources after 1911, and the significance of stage plays and stage players was
so great that their absence in the sphere of humour is the more striking.

(Low 1949: 182)

The war, as it unfolded, was not a subject for comedy, though comedy was used to
undermine the reviled Hun or the Objector in propaganda films such as *Conscription*
(1915), in which a group of men attempting to avoid conscription are ridiculed. Cinemas
were widely used as recruiting stations and film put to efficient use as propaganda, but
it is only in the post-war period, and at a safe emotional distance, that feature comedies such as *Old Bill 'Through the Ages'* (1924), based on Bruce Bairnsfather's 'Old Bill'
comic strip, were produced. Low identifies three distinct trends in comedy films during
the war: first, the short, often violent, potboilers that climaxed in 'unpleasant surprises'
featuring the likes of Winky, Tubby, Weary Willie and Tired Tim; second, comedies
that developed story and character around recognisable Music Hall acts and personalities;
and third, comedies that progressed the art form by fusing plot and personality. As film
length increased, then so did the need to invest in production values and personalities.
Music Hall stars such as George Robey, Lupino Lane and Billy Merson all produced
films, but cinema's inability to translate the verbal banter of the Music Hall often left
the punchline to the intertitle with varying degrees of success.

Pimple, played by Music Hall star Fred Evans, emerged with a vengeance just prior
to World War I, churning out burlesques of popular events and developing his earlier
Smiler character. That Evans was able to parody the war with impunity in *Pimple Enlists*
(1914) testifies to both his popularity and his refusal to accept sacred cows (Hammond
2000: 58). Despite his popularity in Britain, Evans' roughly-hewn burlesque style did
not endear him to future historians or international audiences and he was massively
overshadowed by his American counterparts, particularly Chaplin who was consolidating
his popularity during 1914–15. Evans' comedy is broad, fast and unsubtle. His face,
bizarrely painted to accentuate his nasal-labial lines with darkened cheeks and paler
circle around his mouth, now appears more appropriate to circus than cinema. Michael
Hammond has pointed out that Evans' lack of appeal to American producers like Sennett
was due to his heavy use of 'limey make-up' (Hammond 2000: 60), which linked him
back to familiar British pantomimic traditions but was at odds with contemporary
Hollywood tastes. Whilst Karno, Chaplin and Laurel had crossed the pond, Evans and
his ilk would endure with British audiences only.

Someone who did cross the Atlantic, both ways, was actress and producer-director
Florence Turner. In 1914 she produced the extended facial comedy *Daisy Doodad's Dial*,
in which she competes with her husband (Tom Powers) to win a gurning competition,
unselfconsciously practising in public and eventually being arrested for breach-of-
the peace. The narrative motivation for her facial acrobatics diminishes at the end of the
film when she falls asleep only to dream of her distorted faces and ends with her reprising her 'facials' directly to camera. Here the film harks back to earlier facial comedies
and the 'cinema of attractions' where narrative was progression relinquished in favour
of pure spectacle.[6] Turner's prodigious talent for impersonation was evident in her skit on
Sarah Bernhardt in *Film Favourites* (1914) in which she sits in full Elizabethan costume and

curly wig, eyes rolled and hands clasped in exaggerated pose, spoofing Bernhardt's celebrated portrayal of Elizabeth I in the 1912 film *Les Amours de la Reine Élisabeth*. There is a clear interplay between high and low culture here as the celebrated Bernhardt was largely unassailable in her middle-class theatrical appeal. As a popular film and Music Hall star, Turner was able to mimic the great actress and parody the serious theatricality of Bernhardt's roles. She also impersonated Chaplin in the same series (see Figure 2.2).

Figure 2.2 Florence Turner imitating Charlie Chaplin in *Film Favourites* (1914). Image courtesy of the BFI.

East is East (1916, released 1917), produced by and starring Turner and co-producer Henry Edwards, is a rare example of a British feature comedy from this period which successfully combines subtle cinematic performance with broader Music Hall gesture. The film is a comedy of class and romance in which Turner and Edwards, as Victoria and Bert, enjoy an easygoing platonic friendship as hop-pickers who, along with a motley group of itinerant workers, follow the Kentish harvest (see Figure 2.3). The film is a celebration of kinship amid a picturesque English countryside populated by chirpy East Enders. The bucolic equilibrium is overturned when Turner hears of a legacy from a rich relative and relocates to the wealthy West End, leaving Bert to seek his fortune alone. His success comes from an entrepreneurial fish and chip venture exploiting a glut of dogfish, whilst she languishes, ill at ease among her 'social betters'. The two are eventually reunited when Victoria, on a nostalgic trip to Kent, stops to look at the idyllic cottage they both dreamed of owning, only to find that Bert had already purchased it. That East will always be East in terms of class and aspiration and the West End will always be populated by superficial snobs is the clear message of this film, which anticipates several later representations of loveable Cockneys in Balfour's Squibs series.[7] But the American Turner successfully performed an East Ender, without indulging in the kind of stereotyping that would characterize later attempts (witness Dick Van Dyke in *Mary Poppins* (1964)) and successfully hybridized British Music Hall

Figure 2.3 Henry Edwards and Florence Turner as East End hop-pickers in *East is East* (1916). Image courtesy of the BFI.

tradition with American film talent satisfying popular audiences and film critics alike. The deleterious effects of World War I on the British film industry took their toll on Turner and Trimble's production company and the two returned to the US in 1916. Turner's career declined in the US, prompting her return to the UK in 1920 where she made several successful films before ending her career as an all-but-forgotten Hollywood extra in the 1930s.

Post-World War I: Adrian Brunel and the development of satire

If the majority of British comedy up until the Great War had its origins in Music Hall and Variety, another strand of literate, satirical comedy developed in the 1920s pioneered by independent film-maker Adrian Brunel. Brunel satirized existing film forms: the Topical Budget newsreel in *A Typical Budget; the Only Unreliable Film Review* (1925), G.E. Studdy's animated cartoon character Bonzo in *The Topical Bonzette* (1925), the stage musical *Chu Chin Chow* in *Two-Chinned Chow* (1923) and the annoyingly popular song 'Yes We Have No Bananas' in *Yes, We Have No-!* (1923). *So This is Jollygood* (1925) is a sophisticated satire on the inadequacies of the British film industry in relation to Hollywood and produced as part of the Gainsborough Burlesque Series. Directed by the fictional Tex Ringworm (a pun on director Rex Ingram), it deploys Brunel's trademark combination of non-fiction footage and stock-shots with ironic intertitles and performed satirical sequences. It starts with a declamation that Jollygood's stars live in grand houses, cutting to a stock-shot of Buckingham Palace, whilst a Victorian slum is described as the 'dwelling of the typical British star'. The Rapid Film Corporation – (where '11 stories are rejected every 29 1/3 seconds') – shows script editors throwing rejects over their shoulders at lightning speed into a waste-paper basket wielded by a studio lackey. April Showers who 'guarantees to make any story unrecognizable' goes through scripts with titles like 'Sheik Stuff' by Ethel M. Dull (a play on Edith M. Hull, the author of *The Sheik*, the vehicle that launched Valentino) with a spoof of 'Rubarb Vaselino' who 'makes every film-fan's flappers' feelings flutter'. Inevitably, the British version of Valentino is an effete poseur. The announcement that 'Villains are easy' is accompanied by Tom Mex, in the style of actor-director Erich Von Stroheim as 'the man you hate to love' (as opposed to 'the man you love to hate'). The burlesque of a stage melodrama 'The Wise Child or Where Are My Parents?' shows a grandmother in a bare kitchen ostentatiously ordering a small boy 'go little Bertrude, get your money box', cutting to a close-up of her sobbing face as a hand moves into frame to deliver fake tears through a dropper. Enter the child's mother and the villain who would take her honour with the intertitle 'shall she sell herself to provide sustenance for her Old Fashioned Mother? Never. Better let the Old Girl die', hilariously undermining traditional melodramatic sentiment. *Crossing the Great Sagrada* (1924) elegantly spoofs Captain Angus Buchanan's serious (and popular) autobiographical travelogue *Crossing the Great Sahara* from the same year. Here Brunel satirizes the heroic tone and imperialist pomposity which characterized many travelogues from this period. Holmes, Sweet and Holmes, his explorers, are, with the aid of found ethnographical footage, taken across the desert to the African jungle but somehow end up at the YMCA in Wapping. Comedy is derived from the mismatch between image and intertitle, juxtapositions of found footage and amateur performance and the feigned 'incompetence' of film technique. His films made much of their lack of finance when compared to the originals they spoofed and we can trace a direct link between Brunel in the 1920s to the Pythons in the 1970s.

Brunel was part of a group of literati who dabbled in satirical 'amateur productions', including Elsa Lanchester, Charles Laughton, H.G. Wells, A.A. Milne (who wrote the intertitles for Brunel's films), Evelyn Waugh, Lord Beaverbrook and Ivor Montagu along with cinematographer Freddie Francis. H.G. Wells wrote three surreal comedies for Montagu (though Lanchester claims he wrote them for her), including *Blue Bottles*, *Daydreams* and *The Tonic* (all 1928), clearly influenced by Continental surrealist films of Luis Buñuel and Salvador Dalí.[8] Cinema was starting to appeal to the intelligentsia and despite widespread opprobrium from many quarters (in 1923 the poet John Drinkwater claimed that the cinema 'has no existence as an art',[9] and Augustus John, George Bernard Shaw, General William Booth among many others all joined in the condemnation), Oxbridge-educated young people were finding employment in the industry and other creative intellectuals were starting to explore cinema's potential as art.

The early 1920s: Adaptations of comic novels and stories

H.G. Wells became interested in the cinema through his son Frank, who worked in the film industry, and although he could not be persuaded to write feature film scripts, he did sanction the production of two successful romantic comedies adapted from his humorous novels. Wells' involvement was significant in that he was at the forefront of respected authors working in cinema. *The Wheels of Chance: A Bicycling Idyll* (novel 1896, film 1922) and *Kipps: The Story of a Simple Soul* (novel 1905, film 1921) both starred comedian George K. Arthur and were directed by American Harold M. Shaw. *The Wheels of Chance* follows the adventures of Mr. Hoopdriver (Arthur), a dreamy draper's apprentice who sets out on a lone cycle touring holiday around the Kentish lanes where he encounters the attractive Jessie, who is trying to escape her lothario suitor and stifling middle-class life. Jessie's presence negates Hoopdriver's already precarious bicycle skills in a series of gently comedic interludes that offer a fascinating glimpse of both turn-of-the-century cycling and the standards that British silent comedy could attain with the combination of story, script, location, director and star. This winning combination was not to be repeated beyond these two films as Shaw returned to the US only to die in a car accident in 1926, whilst Arthur, probably the closest British cinema produced to an actor capable of Chaplinesque pathos, moved to Hollywood and a long and successful film career. The lure of Hollywood proved very strong in the mid-1920s when the British film industry lurched from crisis to crisis and was easily outbid for the best of its homegrown screen talent.

The director/writer husband-and-wife team of Manning Haynes and Lydia Hayward and their company Artistic Films did prevail in the British industry, however, producing several sophisticated comedy-romances adapted from W.W. Jacobs' short stories including *The Head of the Family* (1922), *A Will and a Way* (1922), *Sam's Boy* (1922), *The Skipper's Wooing* (1922) and *The Boatswain's Mate* (1924). Set among rural communities and around the Medway and Thames during the twilight days of the small cargo ships that operated there, the films balance character humour with comedic plots and evocative location shooting. *Sam's Boy* begins with the newly orphaned, eponymous boy (played by Bobbie Rudd, a superb child actor, now all but forgotten) desperate to latch onto a new father figure to save him from the dreaded workhouse. The crew of the ketch 'Nancy Bell' take pity on him, but this being a comedy, they see an opportunity to torment their captain by convincing him that the boy is his long-lost love-child and their ageing boss now needs to face up to his responsibilities and the wrath of his wife. The boy sticks like glue to the captain as a means of survival and in a near perfect balance of pathos and comedy, the story is a portrait of a dying way of life and the vulnerability of orphaned children. *The Skipper's Wooing* uses the same ensemble cast in a tale about a lovesick captain in a race against time to woo a young woman engaged to a sleazy travelling salesman.

Haynes' production of these Lydia Haywood adaptations garnered excellent contemporary reviews. *Kinematograph Weekly* praised the acting, photography and production in keeping with the spirit of Jacobs' stories:

> the seascapes are an artistic triumph in themselves, and there are some excellent shots of the London Docks. … In this film too, he has made another find in Bobbie Rudd, who is quite one of the most natural and clever child artistes now acting for the films.
>
> (*Kinematograph Weekly*, 2 March 1922)

It goes on to advise exhibitors to 'BOOM IT WITH EMPHASIS ON W.W. JACOBS', suggests a link-up with booksellers, and stresses that it is an 'all-English' production in which 'Bobbie Rudd's name is worth publicity for he is assured of future success'.

The Boatswain's Mate again stars Haynes and Haywood regular Johnny Butt as an ageing ne'er-do-well pub regular who sees his opportunity to 'marry a pub' by wooing Mrs. Walters, the feisty widowed landlady of the Beehive Inn, played by Florence Turner. 'You always propose after the third pint' is her resigned response to his attentions and the film's intertitles feature witty stick-cartoons offering wry proto-feminist comments on the action. When Butt claims, 'Mrs. Walters, you need a man to look after you', the accompanying cartoon shows a woman cleaning the house, whilst her man sits reading in an armchair. Meanwhile, the enigmatic Victor McLagen plays a very eligible bachelor returning from the war, out of work and on the road, whom Butt engages in a plot to stage an armed robbery on the pub, from which he can 'rescue' and impress his intended. Naturally, it all goes wrong and it is McLagen who gets the girl (and the pub). The film was based on Suffragette composer Ethel Smyth's one-act opera of the same name, about a woman's attempts to outwit her suitor, which was first performed in 1916 with Mrs. Walters loosely modelled on Emmeline Pankhurst.

The *Motion Picture Studio* magazine described these films as 'healthy and wholesome British humour' which capture the essence of Jacobs' 'delightful stories'. It then goes on to express hope for the future:

> The sincerity and simplicity of these pictures makes me hope that the clever producer will one day be accorded greater resources in something rather different.

Meanwhile, these comedies eclipse all other British efforts along similar lines. They are, incidentally, well edited, and the sub titles are not only crisp and clever, but actually punctuated correctly!

(*The Motion Picture Studio*, 26 January 1924)

It is a poignant but telling footnote to the fortunes of British silent film comedy that W.W. Jacobs is now a rarely-read author, Bobbie Rudd disappeared without trace, little is known about the talented screenwriter Lydia Hayward, and the films are largely forgotten. Perhaps their gentle bucolic subjects became unfashionable once audiences began to prefer the urban subjects and sex and flapper comedies produced later. Perhaps they were too small, unassuming and domestic to have ever been exported. But these Haynes and Hayward productions hint at what British comedy could achieve with their quintessentially homegrown subjects and source material, their superb evocation of place and casts of mildly eccentric comic characters. They also represented a bridge between the character and slapstick comedies of the 1910s and the longer feature comedies of the later 1920s. Meanwhile, we can only question why these films have been overlooked by film historians and critics over the past 90 years.

Another mode of British comedy in development during this period were the P.G. Wodehouse farces, including *The Clicking of Cuthbert: The Long Hole* (1924) from the author's golfing stories, in which two posh 'twerps' compete for the same woman by playing a ten-mile linear game of golf over open country. En route, they encounter the mud of an English summer, thieving dogs, a lot of water and the need to extricate balls accidentally pitched into motor cars. Their caddies provide the pratfalls, whilst the two golfers, obsessed with fair pay, argue over, but play fast and loose with, the rules. Needless to say, neither of them considers whether their contested love-object was available. Here there is a distinction between the burlesque physical comedy and roughly-hewn characterization of the 'lower orders' (the caddies) contrasted with the largely verbal comedy of their better-off and better-looking golfing masters.

The mid to late 1920s: Feature film comedy and British comedy stars

In 1925, Lydia Hayward wrote the screenplay for an urbane comedy, *We Women*, directed by W.P. Kellino, which follows the adventures of Billie and Dollie (Beatrice Ford and Pauline Cartwright) as they grapple with poverty, miserable landlords, a variety of jobs as hostesses and dancers, the advances of amorous bosses and the search for romance. This rare, female-centred caper comedy is a British response to the Hollywood flapper comedies which starred the likes of Colleen Moore and Clara Bow. Female audiences across Europe flocked to see these glamorous American stars whose style they emulated like mad. But, as with Chaplin and slapstick comedies earlier, Hollywood also excelled at this particular genre. The fact that *We Women* has all but disappeared owes more to its failure to compete with Hollywood for the audience's affection than to the quality of the film itself.

One female star who did successfully compete for audience affection with Hollywood was Betty Balfour, 'the Queen of Happiness'. Balfour, with her trademark cocky

Figure 2.4 Cinema programme for Betty Balfour in *Squibs MP* (1923). Image courtesy of the Steve Chibnall Collection.

attitude, broad dimpled smile and vivacious mimicry, was Britain's biggest star during the 1920s and her career is worthy of some consideration here. Her roles see her move from chirpy Cockney flower seller in her early *Squibs* films to exotic dancer and flapper in later films such as *A Little Bit of Fluff* (1928). Balfour's career also indicates the battle for narrative control and agency of the 1920s comic actress, who was pitted against the increasingly circumscribed roles for women in the late silent feature comedies.

Born almost a generation after Florence Turner, Balfour's career exists entirely in the age of cinema, but she too started in the theatre as a child entertainer, working with Karno and hosting her own revue. She was already well-established and popular by the time she made her feature film debut, aged 17, in George Pearson's *Nothing Else Matters* (1920). Here she plays a hapless serving girl with a performance style derived from her stage act: all funny walks, ungainly postures and a repertory of facial expressions ranging from mischief to pathos. Pearson films her in full-body shots, allowing her to dominate the screen and display her comedy talents to the full. As such, her performance is neither fragmented, to emphasise her face or part of her body, nor sexualised. The four *Squibs* films that develop her ingénue Cockney flower seller from 1922 to 1923 represent the highlight of a film career that spanned 25 silent features, a period working in Europe and eight sound films made between 1930 and 1945.[10] Producer/director Pearson had himself offered to divorce his wife and marry Balfour on the set of *Blinkeyes* in 1926; effectively ending their working partnership when Balfour rejected him.

Despite being Britain's only truly international star, and the nearest the British industry produced to Hollywood's flapper comediennes, Balfour's career diminished rapidly from 1930 and she eventually attempted suicide in 1952 after a failed return to stage acting. Her film career follows an interesting trajectory and starts to decline as she grows out of her gamine *Squibs* roles in the mid 1920s. By 1928, in Wheeler Dryden's, Syd Chaplin vehicle *A Little Bit of Fluff*, she's become Mamie Scott, an exotic dancer described in an intertitle as 'the actress whose head has been turned by press agents and peroxide' and who is 'celebrating the tenth anniversary of her twenty fifth birthday'. Already, at age 25, jokes are being made at her character's expense in terms of looks and age. In other words, she is becoming the butt of the joke, the comic object rather than the comic subject. She is no longer allowed to create and perform in her own autonomous comedic space, as she had in her earlier films. Her co-star, the 43-year-old Syd Chaplin, is, by contrast, given considerable screen space to play out clichéd and repetitive comedy routines which impede narrative progress. The fact that the film was directed by Wheeler Dryden, Chaplin's half-brother, possibly explains this indulgence.

It is not Balfour's skills as a comedienne that diminished by the late 1920s, but the changing narrative opportunities for women in British film comedy. In Hitchcock's 1928 film, *Champagne*, she plays a vivacious aviatrix and society girl who defies her father and flies out to join her lover on his cruise, ditching her aeroplane in the Atlantic. Balfour would have offered significant identification pleasures to female viewers for her combination of glamour, fun and social status. However, despite an energetic and spirited comedic performance, her comic objectification is evident from the start of the film when Hitchcock establishes a series of lascivious looks from a menacing and predatory male who starts to stalk Balfour's character as soon as she arrives.

In these later roles there is a tension between the narrative containment of Balfour's performance and her own attempts to transcend her comic objectification. By 1928, the conditions for the ways in which men and women are represented in mainstream cinema are firmly in place. For 1920s comediennes, the shift to feature-length narratives and solidifying generic conventions also limited the kind of roles available and prescribed a particular set of looks, physical features and performance styles, considerably more so than it did for their male counterparts. The dominance of melodramas, literary adaptations and middle-class romantic comedies tended to position women as dramatic and comedic objects, as noble victims, quietly suffering wives and mothers, daughters and sisters; roles which demanded a demure, restrained acting style that entailed a considerable amount of 'body draping'[11] to facilitate the more static, *tableau vivant* performance where the female character remains stable within the mise-en-scène in order to display costume, styling and passive sexuality to the best advantage. In contrast, Balfour was described by the *Newcastle Chronicle* as 'the only British film actress who really lets herself go'.[12]

Britain's other key star during this period, Walter Forde, was the son of Music Hall comedian Tom Seymour. Forde directed more than 60 comedies for his company Nettlefold Productions, in a film career that spanned four decades between the 1910s and 1940s and included a succession of *Walter* movies. Forde was able to combine slapstick, sight gags, comic personality and plot in films such as his night-in-the-museum caper *What Next?* (1928). Here he plays a bric-à-brac salesman who unwittingly purchases a truly ugly, but valuable, candlestick coveted by a mad archaeologist and pursued by a useless detective and his haughty assistant (see Figure 2.5). The plot culminates in a series of frenetic and brilliantly-timed set pieces involving revolving doors, suits of armour and crashing weaponry worthy of any modern-day caper film. As producer,

Figure 2.5 A vexed Walter Forde in *What Next?* (1928). Image courtesy of the BFI.

director and actor, Forde was able to fashion his own projects around his comic persona and rework and refine his repertory of gags.

Aside from *Champagne*, which he described as the 'lowest ebb' in his output,[13] Britain's other key auteur Alfred Hitchcock, made another foray into silent comedy with *The Farmer's Wife* (1928), also a collaboration with writer Eliot Stannard. *The Farmer's Wife*, made just before *Champagne*, was based on a successful Eden Philpotts stage play about a middle-aged widower-farmer, Samuel Sweetland (Jameson Thomas), searching for a new wife. Aided by his farmhand, played by the wonderfully phlegmatic Gordon Harker, and his housekeeper Araminta (Lilian Hall-Davis), he conspires to appoint the second Mrs Sweetland. The comedy plays out across a series of set-pieces with the farmer's desperate attempts to woo unsuitable candidates including the twitchy Suffragette Thirza Tapper and the over-ebullient postmistress Mary Hearn, before realising that the perfect candidate is right under his nose. Araminta, hopelessly in love with the farmer, merges into the shadows, unable to express her own feelings until the denouement. Of all the characters in the film, she is the most physically attractive, but also the most passive, having no narrative or comedic agency; her role is simply to watch and wait with a demeanour more appropriate to 19th-century melodrama than late 1920s comedy. It would be hard for Betty Balfour to occupy the role of passive female onlooker and Hitchcock's Araminta looks decidedly old-fashioned in a world of energetic, comedic flappers.

Another young British auteur cutting his teeth in romantic comedy was Anthony Asquith with the Ruritanian romantic pursuit *The Runaway Princess* (1929) based on Elizabeth von Arnim's 1905 comedy novel *The Princess Priscilla's Fortnight*. The film, barely mentioned in Asquith's biographies, tells the story of a princess (Madie Christians) who escapes her stultifying existence and arranged engagement to an effete and effeminate Count, by fleeing to London. The film is a curious riches-to-rags romantic comedy pursuit with a proto-feminist heroine determined to make her own way and experience life as a commoner. In London, she takes a series of jobs in milliners and fashion houses whilst being pursued by a handsome and mysterious detective from her homeland. The escapee princess was a potent identification figure for young women in the inter-war period; beautiful, independent and feisty, yet belonging to a Hapsburgian royal dynasty. The fictional 'Ruritania' crops up in a number of films in the late 1920s as a fantasised, Mittel-European patrician principality where princesses are courted by Hussars in chocolate-box palaces. It is both part of, but distinct from, modern Europe with its encroaching depression and alienating modernity, and offered a fantasy narrative space for romantic comedy. Harry Lachman's *Weekend Wives* (1928) is an altogether racier, modernist romantic comedy set in a sexy and stylish Deauville, where two couples (played by Monty Banks, Jameson Thomas, Annette Benson and Estelle Brody) conduct a French-style bedroom farce with marital deceptions, mistaken identities and lots of nudge and wink humour. The fact that Prince George saw the film three times suggests that the Establishment were no longer ashamed to be associated with British comedy cinema.

Conclusion

This chapter cannot do justice to the largely forgotten and overlooked comedies and comedians of the British silent period. That British silent comedy was overshadowed by

Hollywood is a truism, but so was the silent film comedy of every other nation, and although British cinema never produced a body of work to rival Chaplin's, there is much to celebrate in the wealth of extant material. For example, Walter Forde, a comedian who was able to produce sophisticated feature comedies, whilst still operating in a gag-based comic universe, was the nearest Britain came to a Harold Lloyd.

Cinema embraced comedy from the very beginning, in the knowledge that popular audiences would recognise the gags and personalities from Pantomime and Music Hall; a legacy from which British silent comedy was reluctant to depart. The Great War helped shift British silent comedy into the modern age by acknowledging changes in class and social structure, gender relations, the mobilisation of women and the expectations of returning soldiers for a more equitable society. At this time too, cinema was itself embraced by a new generation of literati and intellectuals who saw its potential as an art form in its own right and propelled British comedy into a new dimension. This influx also helped break down class and cultural barriers and legitimised film comedy for the middle classes.

The emergence of romantic comedy feature films in the early 1920s reflects a shift in emphasis from the earlier slapstick pursuits, but starts to position men and women in particular roles to the detriment of female comic performers, as we have seen with Balfour and the films of Hitchcock. Women needed to look good rather than be virtuoso comic performers. Class, status, age and gender will always be potent issues for comedy and we can witness these being played out in these early films in ways which are completely recognisable to audiences today. Balfour's working-class Cockney alter-ego, Squibs, struck a chord with audiences, as her Lancashire successor Gracie Fields would do in the 1930s: both characters intimately reflected the lives and aspirations of their audiences.

British comedy did benefit from the writing talents of people like Eliot Stannard, Noël Coward, H.G. Wells, A.A. Milne and the creative genius of people like Adrian Brunel. The early 1920s was a time in which a maturing cinema attracted a range of creative talent from other art forms, eager to experiment with its comedic potential. Even establishment figures such as Lord Beaverbrook produced comedies alongside Brunel. During this period too, British cinema lurched from financial crisis to crisis, with the double-whammy of competition from Hollywood and the ravages left by the Great War, but it was largely comedy that sustained the industry in the 1920s with the domestic successes of the Balfour and Forde films. The coming of sound around 1928 ended the careers of around 4,000 cinema musicians in the UK and all those actors who did not respond well to the microphone, but sound had always been *de facto* to film comedy, and some of the earliest sound experiments were in recording variety artistes whose voice was intrinsic to their comedy. Adrian Brunel spoofed the fears around the new technology in a short home movie, *Brunel and Montagu* (1928), in which the two characters play themselves as film producers contemplating suicide. But Brunel embraced sound technology with his early sound film *Elstree Calling* (1930), a revue of the British Variety artistes, many of whom had appeared in silent films and would go on to continue their career in the sound period.

By the end of the 1920s, British comedy had achieved some not insignificant triumphs and of cinema itself in 1932, a report entitled *The Film In National Life* was able to admit that 'A fellow of an Oxford College no longer feels an embarrassed explanation to be necessary when he is recognized leaving a cinema'.[14] Proof, if proof were needed, that the art form had truly come of age.

Notes

1 Chaplin made two trips to the US with Karno, in 1910 and 1912. It was on the later trip that he was spotted by Keystone boss Mack Sennett.
2 Low (1948: 53) states that several companies made 'greasy pole films' as it was common practice to plagiarise gag films at this time.
3 Mitchell and Kenyon were better known for their actuality films and Boer War re-enactments, but also produced a considerable body of short comedies.
4 A description borrowed from Kenton Bamford (1999: 43).
5 There is no apparent link to the use of the word 'rats' in the earlier film *Diving Lucy* (1903), but the use of the word in two Suffragette comedies is an interesting coincidence and it may have had a colloquial association with the suffrage movement.
6 See T. Gunning (2000) 'The cinema of attraction: Early film, its spectator, and the avant-garde', in R. Stam and T. Miller (eds), *Film and Theory: An Anthology*, New York: Blackwell.
7 This lack of social mobility and meritocracy placed *East is East* at odds with the American *Variety Magazine*, a point made by Cook (2000).
8 See Lanchester (1983: 84).
9 *The Bioscope*, 3 April 1923, quoted in Low (1971: 18).
10 *Squibs* (1921), *Squibs Wins the Calcutta Sweep* (1922), *Squibs' Honeymoon* (1923) and *Squibs MP* (1923). In 1935, Balfour reprised the role in a musical remake of her 1921 *Squibs*, this time directed by Henry Edwards.
11 For a fuller and very insightful discussion around acting styles in British cinema, see Christine Gledhill (2003), particularly Chapter 3: Performing British Cinema.
12 The Betty Balfour Collection held at the BFI Library Special Collections
13 Truffaut (1978: 63).
14 *The Film in National Life* (1932) quoted in Low (1971: 17).

Bibliography

Bamford, K. (1999) *Distorted Images: British National Identity and Film in the 1920s*, London: I.B. Taurus.

Burke, T. (1934) *London in My Time*, London: Rich and Cowan.

Cameron, A.C. (1932) *The Film in National Life*, London: Allen and Unwin.

Cook, A.M. (2000) 'The adventures of the Vitagraph Girl in England', in A. Burton and L. Porter (eds), *Pimple, Pranks and Pratfalls*, Trowbridge: Flicks Books

Gledhill, C (2003) *Reframing British Cinema 1918–1928: Between Restraint and Passion*, London: British Film Institute.

Hammond, M. (2000) '"Cultivating Pimple": Performance tradition and the comedy of Fred and Joe Evans', in A. Burton and L. Porter (eds), *Pimple, Pranks and Pratfalls*, Trowbridge: Flicks Books.

Lanchester, E. (1983) *Elsa Lanchester Herself*, New York: St Martin's Press.

Low, R. (1948) *The History of the British Film (1896–1906)*, London: George Allen and Unwin Ltd.

——(1949) *The History of the British Film (1906–1914)*, London: George Allen and Unwin Ltd.

——(1950) The *History of the British Film (1914–1918)*, London: George Allen and Unwin Ltd.

——(1971) *The History of the British Film (1918–1929)*, London: George Allen and Unwin Ltd.

Truffaut, F. (1978) *Hitchcock: Updated Edition*, St Albans: Granada Publishing.

3 'No limit'

British class and comedy of the 1930s

Lawrence Napper

'Fairytale or not, this is probably the worst film I have ever seen'
Andrew Marr on *Sing As We Go*

Andrew Marr's majestic dismissal of one of the most popular British films of the 1930s seems as good a place to start as any. It comes in the midst of his acclaimed BBC television series tracing *The Making of Modern Britain* (BBC, first aired 25 November 2009). Episode 5, which deals with the Depression of the 1930s and the run-up to the Second World War, is entitled 'Little Britain', and the verdict on *Sing As We Go* (1934) is strategically positioned to confirm the logic of this title. Most of the episode is concerned with 'serious' history, albeit anecdotally told. The Depression, the rise of Oswald Mosley, the political machinations of the National Government, the erosion of Empire and the rise of European dictatorships, these are its points of focus. Almost halfway through the episode, though, there is a cut from footage of mass uniformed rallies in Hitler's Germany and Mussolini's Italy, to the Kazoo band sequence from Humphrey Jennings' *Spare Time* (1939). The narration makes clear the visual dissonance of this juxtaposition. 'In Britain,' declares Marr:

> we had a different sense of national destiny. 'Let's look the other way, vote for dull politicians and keep our fingers crossed.' And after all, there were other distractions. None bigger, none louder than Britain's very own superstar of the Talkies – Gracie Fields.

In this account, Fields and the extraordinary success of her films are rendered emblematic not only of popular cinema, but also more generally of working-class leisure activity, and of a 'little Britain' mindset, which apparently seeks to turn away from the great issues of the age and concentrate instead on foolish trivialities. The programme goes on to offer a somewhat skewed account of *Sing As We Go* itself, editing it in such a way that the film is stripped of its satiric qualities, which are co-opted instead by Marr himself. Gracie's stint selling 'Krunchy Wunchy Toffee' on Blackpool's pleasure beach is shown, but instead of her delightful guying of this ridiculous brand name, Marr (imitating her comic delivery without acknowledgement) offers the critique which he implies the film has missed. Inevitably the title number is shown. Gracie, having just been made redundant, refuses to be downhearted but instead is seen 'warbling her way out of the

Figure 3.1 'Our Gracie' in *Sally in Our Alley* (1931). Image courtesy of the Steve Chibnall Collection.

factory gate and into an uncertain future'. The TV producers introduce a cut here away from the clip and back to Marr himself, framed by the dank underside of Blackpool pier. At the same time an echo effect is introduced to the song still playing on the soundtrack, rendering it suddenly sinister in its supposed naivety about what that future might bring. Having delivered his verdict on 'probably the worst film I have ever seen', Marr ends the segment by quoting a contemporary journalist praising Fields' films for their adherence to the '"right spirit of England [...] clean living, and a total absence of anything un-natural"'. 'Except,' adds Marr with ponderous irony, 'the un-natural appeal of Gracie Fields herself. *In history, not everything can be explained.*'

To place this heavy editorialising in context, it is instructive to compare the treatment of *Sing As We Go* with the use of another fiction film earlier in the episode. This comes during the programme's account of the economic depression of the early 1930s, and the grinding poverty suffered in the industrial north. Familiar images from *Housing Problems* (1935) introduce a milieu of ragged children, and back-to-back housing with washing strung across the street. Speaking to camera in a modern mock-up of this setting, Marr tells us of 'a young Lancashire man, Walter Greenwood, living just this kind of life in a slum called Hanky Park'. He emphasises Greenwood's authentic experiences of poverty as directly informing the political anger, which led him to write *Love on the Dole* (1933). An account of the plot of the novel is then accompanied by key images from the 1941 film adaptation directed by John Baxter, notably the montage of Harry searching for work, and Sally's final speech rejecting the respectable values of her parents. Although the film is acknowledged as an adaptation, it is offered as authentic evidence and not mediated in any of the ways that I've noted with regard to *Sing As We Go*. Its presence introduces no discussion of cinema-going as a leisure activity, and no critical judgement is given on the film's success or otherwise, either as a work of art, or as an adaptation of the novel. After the clip of Sally's speech, Marr's commentary confusingly continues to discuss the book ('the gritty dialogue and the realism were totally new to most of its readers'), suggesting that both book and film are interchangeable objects, and furthermore, that (perhaps as a result of their gritty dialogue and realism) both are able to speak directly to modern audiences as testimonies of their period.

I've chosen to start with Andrew Marr not simply to avenge the outrage he perpetrates against 'Our Gracie', but also because his programme neatly exemplifies a popularly held conception of the difference between 'comedy' and 'realism' in 1930s British cinema, which none of the more recent nuanced accounts of that cinema have been able to shift. Films about the working classes, it seems, can be split into two categories. Firstly, there are the serious dramas; committed, realist, transparent, *authentic* representations of working-class life as struggle and poverty. These films can be trusted to carry the weight of history, are used in teaching, and evoked in TV documentaries with (as we have seen) minimal interpretation. Their rarity in the production schedules of the 1930s is itself an indictment of British film-makers in that period, and the few examples – *The Citadel* (1938), *The Stars Look Down* (1940) and *Love on the Dole* (1941) – are cited over and over again as shining islands in the dismal sea of another kind of film. That other film is of course the comedy. Despite its extraordinary popularity with working-class audiences of the period, and its remarkable commitment to representing their culture, it remains somehow inadequate; trivial, irrelevant, apolitical and anarchic, speaking of pleasure and entertainment where we expect to see want and hardship. The comedy film seems so recalcitrant, so alien and unreadable that even the project of history itself must be abandoned in the face of it – '*In history not everything can be explained.*'

Of course, one can't entirely blame Marr for expressing these prejudices, for to a large extent he is reproducing a model which itself originates in the serious critical culture of the 1930s. Faced with the popular films of the time, film writers whose dominant influences had been the rigorous intellectualism of the Film Society and the dour realism of the documentary movement, regularly expressed dismay at the lack of such qualities in the entertainment cinema on offer. This complaint was two-pronged. On the one hand there was a feeling that British films were too narrow in the classes they represented, favouring the West End theatre in their model of reality, and rooted in a poor imitation of the glamour of Hollywood, filtered through the British class system. 'They seem to be taking place in a kind of vacuum or in a world peopled sparsely by a few character actors,' complained J.B. Priestley in 1939. 'When they show us England, it seems to have been taken from a few issues of the *Sketch* and *Tatler* and a collection of Xmas cards. Only the faintest dribble of real English life is allowed to trickle into most of our films … ' (quoted in Stead 1989: 111). On the other hand, when ordinary working-class life *was* represented, it was often criticised for insufficient realism. Priestley himself had produced the script for *Sing As We Go*, presumably as a riposte to the society settings he describes above. Nevertheless, he was astute enough to understand that a purely documentary treatment wouldn't necessarily make for good entertainment. Warning in *World Film News* that the fabric of British working-class life was slower and less cinematic than its American equivalent, he argued against 'miles of celluloid showing us factories and engineering shops, folks sitting down to endless meat teas and a dreary round of housework, machine-minding, football matches and whist drives'. While such material might be suitable for a novel, he suggested, film 'needs a bit of glamour, an increased tempo, a touch of the fantastic, people who are more vivid than the ordinary run of folk: in short, it demands a bonus somewhere' (Priestley 1936: 3). The 'bonus' of Gracie Fields' vivid performance failed to impress C.A. Lejeune, however, who cited *Sing As We Go* as a film which had precisely missed the opportunity to engage seriously with its setting:

> I fancy that there are other problems worthy of being tackled at some expense by our native film industry. At the cost of being repetitious, I suggest that there is still unemployment, there is still shipbuilding, and there is still farming. We have an industrial north that is bigger than Gracie Fields running round a Blackpool funfair.

> (quoted in Richards 1984: 246)

For Lejeune, as for Marr, the problem was not so much that British films failed to represent the working classes, but that they failed to represent them *in the right way*. Lejeune seems to be calling for the seriousness and commitment of documentary modes as an antidote to the frivolity of Gracie Fields, and this rejection of comedy was part and parcel of the intellectual film debates of the 1930s. Making a similar complaint in 1936, a *World Film News* editorial observed that 'working people, when presented at all, are presented only as figures of fun by kind permission of Mr. Gordon Harker or Mr. Sidney Howard' (quoted in Richards 1984: 245).

This comment seems to me to be curiously expressive of the gulf of taste and outlook that lay between middle-class critics and working-class film-goers. While for *World Film News*, the comic mode marked the peripheral nature of the working-class characters represented, for most audiences comedy was central to their understanding of cinema itself. Indeed these working-class 'figures of fun' constituted some of the most popular and best loved entertainers, working in what was unquestionably the most important genre of the decade. Denis Gifford (1973) suggests that 38 per cent of all films made in Britain during the 1930s were comedies, an eloquent demonstration of their industrial importance and continuing appeal to popular audiences. It was to comedy that Walter Greenwood turned when (fresh from the literary success of *Love on the Dole*) he moved into film, scripting George Formby's first major film for ATP, *No Limit* (1935). Formby and Fields may be considered the king and queen of the genre, commanding the highest salaries of any stars of the decade, but they were not alone. Alongside them, as well as Harker and Howard, were stars such as Leslie Fuller, Ernie Lotinga, Max Miller, Arthur Lucan and The Crazy Gang. With the exception of Harker, these stars were never peripheral comic characters in films of otherwise serious intent, but rather they were the central attraction in cycles of films entirely built around their comic personas. Their characters were resolutely working class, but their films shared an obsession about the boundaries of class with those of a range of other comics identified as slightly higher up on the social scale – figures such as Stanley Lupino, Leslie Henson, Jack Hulbert, Will Hay and Jessie Matthews. Contradicting *World Film News* then, we must note that there were numerous films depicting and directed at 'ordinary working people', and that the fact that they are comedies marks them out to that audience as *more* rather than less central to the cinematic culture of the time. Furthermore, as I shall demonstrate later, class and class-consciousness was written into the very fabric of these comedy films, both in terms of the familiarity of the milieu that they presented, and in terms of the various obstacles and challenges which formed the basis of the comic situations they constructed.

The disjunction between the critics' rejection of comedy as a mode of representing 'real' English life and its central importance for producers and audiences is not hard to explain. For the critics, representation – 'putting England on the screen' – was a serious political and ideological project for British cinema. For the audiences on the other hand, cinema's business was primarily to entertain. That is not to suggest that the entertainment wasn't informed by ideology of course, but rather to note that, even in later accounts of popular 1930s cinema, questions of pleasure, entertainment and resistance are downplayed in favour of a dour emphasis on their apparently monolithic ideological operations. From the 1970s onwards, critics offered a re-appraisal of 1930s comedy precisely as an ideological form, and one which operated along resolutely conservative lines. Jeffrey Richards in 1984 reads the films of Formby and Fields as absolutely upholding the status quo – encouraging audiences to identify themselves with the consensus politics of Baldwin's National Government. Roy Armes in 1978 had suggested that the films 'consistently gave their audiences a deeper reassurance through a facsimile world where existing values were invariably validated by events in the film and where all discord could be turned into harmony by an acceptance of the status quo' (Armes 1978: 114). Peter Stead in 1989 argued that 'for years [British] cinema had ignored contemporary problems' and that the comedies of Formby and Fields in particular 'never really amounted to a serious statement ... the challenge to authority tended to come in the attitudes shown to and remarks made about the rich, and perhaps above all from the sheer natural cheekiness of the star' (Stead 1989: 108). Anthony Aldgate in a 1983 article ominously entitled 'Comedy, class and containment' suggested that through comedy films, British cinema 'reflected and reinforced the dominant consensus'. Even Sue Harper in 1997 concluded that 'the [Will] Hay and the Crazy Gang films provided a sense of cultural security for their audiences; the materials of the culture – its myths, its certainties – were laid out in front of them, as it were, and audiences were not expected to get it wrong' (Harper 1997: 95).

'Reassurance', 'consensus', 'containment'; it's a depressing litany, and one that more recent scholars have attempted to counter with an emphasis on performance and film style. Andrew Higson (1995), for instance, concentrates on the formal qualities of *Sing As We Go*, arguing that its weak narrative motivation, its emphasis on the twin attractions of Fields' performance and the pleasurable spectacles of Blackpool's entertainment culture are the result of an active policy of product differentiation from Hollywood

Figure 3.2 The Crazy Gang – Flanagan and Allen, Nervo and Knox, Naughton and Gold in *O-Kay for Sound* (1940). Image courtesy of the Steve Chibnall Collection.

alternatives – an acknowledgement that this film is rooted in, and addresses, a popular culture which is closer to 'home'. Andy Medhurst (1986) and David Sutton (2000) also argue for the cultural specificity of these films, pointing out that they are built around performers and performance styles familiar from the extra cinematic culture of Music Hall and the end-of-the-pier show. Medhurst emphasises the way that comedy and identity are bound together, often along national and regional as well as class lines. 'Above all else,' he says, 'comedy is an invitation to belong', and while that invitation may refer to a fictional communal identity which is constructed by the comedy itself, one which is 'temporary, contingent, fluid and contested', this does not diminish its power as a pleasurable lived experience. Importantly, Medhurst warns that the sense of belonging which comedy fosters does not necessarily go in any particular ideological direction – 'the direction of comedic politics is contingent on time, place, practitioner and audience' (Medhurst 2007: 19). Most recently, Steven W. Allen has used an analysis of Will Hay's comic persona to suggest that 'the interpretation of British cinema of the Thirties as one purely of consensus is too emphatic'. Allen reads Hay's portrayal of a series of blustering, incompetent and fake official figures as an active critique of the nation as 'governed by the regulations of etiquette, language, conformity and deference'. Hay's emphasis on the misuse of 'official' language articulated a 'specific dissent from the cinema of consensus' which Allen (following Richards) sees in the films of Formby and Fields. 'Hay's films,' he concludes, 'do not depict the conventional harmonious community but instead correspond to a society in transition and full of insecurities which the consensus policies of the Thirties attempted to mask' (Allen 2006: 263).

Allen's model chimes with my own understanding of the 1930s as a 'society in transition' (Napper 2009: 9). However I would argue that his focus on a single comic figure leads him to overlook the ways in which *all* of the comedy films of the period (including those of Formby and Fields) used language (verbal, behavioural and cinematic) to highlight the tensions experienced by audiences living through that transitional process. These comedies in fact were structured around the very tension between a communal sense of belonging, and the acknowledgement that such belonging was temporary, contingent and marked by the boundaries of class. The remainder of this chapter will sketch a few examples of how this might have worked in practice across a selection of films. My approach here is influenced by Robert Darnton's warning that in reconstructing the mentalities of the past through analysis of popular narratives we should not necessarily 'expect to find direct social comment or metaphysical allegories so much as a tone of discourse or a cultural style which communicates a particular ethos and world view' (Darnton 2001:15). Darnton is actually talking about the peasant folk narratives of 18th-century France, but in the light of the common conception of comedy as 'wish fulfilment' or 'fantasy', it might also be worth recalling his observation that whenever the protagonist of a folk tale is granted three wishes, his first request is always for a good meal – 'in most of the tales' Darnton comments, 'wish fulfilment turns into a program for survival, not a fantasy of escape' (Darnton 2001: 34). In trying to move away from the rather reductive insistence on consensus ideology, the idea of comedy as offering a 'program for survival' seems to me a rather useful corrective.

As I have already noted, the key theme of all of these comedies is class. Class isn't codified here politically (as it is for instance in *Love on the Dole*), rather it is understood as the dominant logic of a series of restrictions operating on the characters. These restrictions can't be overturned, but they must be negotiated in a variety of ways for the characters to survive. One might argue that almost all of the comedies of the 1930s are structured around the restrictions of class, strikingly codified in terms of space. Typically they involve a comic protagonist who is embedded within their classed space, but who through a series of mishaps is catapulted out of that space into an unfamiliar one, generally higher up the social scale and with more rule-bound or more 'serious' codes of conduct. Comedy is built out of the dissonance between the protagonists' mode of being and the expectations and social codes of those around them. Either they must adapt to these new codes of behaviour in order to succeed (as in the more middle-class comedies of Jessie Matthews and Jack Hulbert), or retreat to their own space. Most commonly of course, they stay, hovering between acceptance and rejection, and creating comedic chaos out of their disavowal of the rules of behaviour, often securing success in spite of the incongruence of their presence. Thus Gracie Fields, finding herself singing at an upper-class party in *Look Up and Laugh* (1935), in *Love, Life and Laughter* (1934) and in *Sally in Our Alley* (1931), is unable to maintain the grace and poise expected of an aristocratic entertainer, reverts to her more natural comedic style (sending up her audience and their 'mannered' behaviour) and as a result is ejected from the soirée. George Formby is similarly transported to spaces where he doesn't belong – the TT Races in *No Limit* (1935) and the RAF in *It's In the Air* (1938). While less obviously 'classed', these spaces are nevertheless identified with more privileged rivals who are privy to codes of professional and social conduct to which Formby is not. Formby of course prevails in most of his films, despite his inability to modify his behaviour, and his constant anxiety about that inability. Arthur Lucan's Old Mother Riley (who appeared in a series of films from 1937 onwards) similarly refuses to modify behaviour, although she displays no anxiety about the fact, revelling in the chaos she creates (for instance in Parliament in *Old Mother Riley, MP* (1939)). The Crazy Gang films also operate broadly along this model – typically opening with the Gang either busking or on the run (both in *Alf's Button Afloat* (1938)), they are catapulted into a more mannered space (a film studio in *O-Kay for Sound* (1940), the Navy in *Alf's Button Afloat*), where comedy continually arises from their disregard for the rules of behaviour. These are broad generalisations of course, but they serve to underline my point that these comedy films absolutely emphasise the *differences* between classes, and the restrictions operating on working-class characters, rather than the continuities and similarities suggested by the consensus model.

I'd like to turn now to a more detailed consideration of a specific film to draw out some of the more nuanced ways in which issues of class might still operate in comedy films that do not stage the bald encounters to be found in the likes of Fields and Formby, but which nevertheless might still offer their audiences a 'programme for survival' in a society marked by transition. For Leslie Fuller as Bill in *One Good Turn* (1936), class equates to a financial uncertainty which must always be countered by Bill's wit and enterprise. Bill runs a mobile snack bar from a horse-drawn van. His sidekick Georgie points out that if he continues to offer credit to his customers he will be unable to pay his back-rent and will be thrown onto the street. Faced with a clearly starving regular, he feels unable to uphold the rule, but a drunken toff is fair game for his enterprise and in an extended gag he fools this customer into thinking an empty bun is a sausage sandwich. Later on he has a run-in with a rival operating a motorised coffee stall – a marked contrast to Bill's old-fashioned horse-drawn van. Although initially foiled, the rival returns when Bill and Georgie are absent and gives away Bill's stock for free, rendering him penniless. He's already lent the money he saved for the rent to his landlady's feckless son, so he's forced to try and smuggle himself, Georgie and the stall's horse, back into the house without the landlady noticing. For Bill then, class operates as a network of nuanced relationships which conditions his reaction to each particular dilemma, as well as to the over-riding fact that every dilemma arises out of his lack of funds. But it also operates on him in other ways. Importantly, space is imbued with class restrictions throughout the film – Bill is associated with the street, and every incident of his moving indoors is marked (as in the sequence sneaking past the landlady) by the need to 'blag' his way into a space from which the owners wish to exclude him, in which he doesn't rightly belong and in which he constantly runs the risk of being 'found out'. Class is also nuanced by modernity. The motorised stall offers an obvious symbol of the threat of modernity, but modernity also colours the class relations of the characters in this period of transition. The landlady's feckless son Jack belongs to a more modern, transitional class – he works in an office, away from the community, and wears a suit. Nevertheless he is happy to mobilise Bill's older class anxieties and loyalties in his threat that unless he can borrow Bill's saved rent money to

Figure 3.3 Arthur Lucan as Old Mother Riley fighting with Garry Marsh in *Old Mother Riley Joins Up* (1940). Image courtesy of the Steve Chibnall Collection.

get himself out of a jam, the shame of his exposure will reflect on the whole family, including his sister Dolly, on whom Bill is 'sweet'. Dolly, too, is associated with modernity, a hopeful chorus girl in the local theatre run by a villainous American producer. A sequence where Bill helps Dolly and her chums get to the theatre by hitching his horse to the front of their broken-down car nicely encapsulates the film's ambivalent attitude to modernity, and rhymes with the earlier sequence involving the rival coffee stall. The real threat of modernity, however, comes from the villainous American producer, who cons Bill's landlady into investing her savings in the show on the promise of a starring role for Dolly, and then plans to abscond with the money, knowing the show will be a flop. The day is saved when Bill retrieves the cash, and then accidentally appears onstage with his horse during the finale of the show, creating an unexpectedly chaotic comic climax, which ensures that the show is a hit and the landlady's investment is safe.

One Good Turn is very satisfying in that it encapsulates a series of very nuanced understandings of the pressures of Bill's class position vis-à-vis money, space and modernity into an entertainment lasting little more than 60 minutes. One might argue that the resolution at the end of the narrative arc dissolves these tensions in line with a 'consensus' reading, but I'd suggest that to do so fails to take account of the way in which the comic pleasures of the film, and of Leslie Fuller's performance, all revolve around the recognition of his frustration at the restrictions he is subject to, and his ingenuity in overcoming them. Fuller's comedy is heavily invested in the spectacle of his enormous face, bursting with exasperation at some points and beaming with knowing deviousness at others. Two deliciously extended sequences might serve as contrasting illustrations of this performance style – the gag around the sausage sandwich mentioned earlier, and a later sequence involving Bill smoking his pipe. Both sequences exemplify the ways in which these comedy films are, as Higson (1995) and others note, aberrant stylistically – happy to dispense with the narrative economy and forward movement of the classical Hollywood style, in favour of the attraction of an extended gag. This of course isn't unique to British comedy, and is to be found in Hollywood's own comedy films; however, it is often accounted for in a British context with reference to the films' low budget status, and reliance on extra-cinematic comic traditions. Fuller's films, made at Elstree under the quota producer Joe Rock, were indeed low budget productions, and Fuller himself was well known as the resident comic at the end-of-the-pier show in Margate, where his comic persona and style were undoubtedly developed and perfected. Nevertheless, despite the fact that these two sequences undoubtedly stop the narrative dead, and are based on 'business' indebted to the Margate show, they are strikingly cinematic in their reliance on editing and close-ups to produce their comic effects. In the first sequence, the drunken customer (identified as upper class by his dinner jacket and accent) insists on a sausage sandwich, despite the fact Bill has just sold all his sausages. Bill satisfies the customer by spreading mustard on his own finger and placing it in a bun – a detail shown us in close up, which then cuts to a carefully constructed shot showing Bill's face head-on in the background, framed by the customer's profile in the foreground. This shot serves to keep the focus on Bill's face as he carefully extracts his finger from the bun just as the customer takes it, conveying both the trickiness of the operation and his satisfaction at its achievement. The customer discovering there is no sausage, of course, the whole sequence including the two-shot is repeated, the focus on Bill's face this time emphasising how close he gets to having his finger bitten off as he extracts it a little too late. The customer still not satisfied, Bill repeats the procedure again, but this time spreads mustard on the customer's own finger and places that in the bun. He wanders off drunkenly with his 'sandwich', to the satisfaction of Bill and the others at the stall at having 'got one over' on the toff.

If that sequence represents Bill's satisfaction at overcoming one of the many restrictions that he faces, I'd suggest its mirror – the pipe sequence – as operating in the opposite direction. Like the sausage gag, it serves no narrative purpose in itself but it comes at a part of the narrative where Bill is at his most frustrated. All his plans have gone awry, he has been ejected not only from the house, but also from the theatre and, penniless himself, he is also now privy to the impending ruin of the others. He and Georgie sit against a wall to rest. Throughout the film, comedy has been made of the physical difference between Bill's bulk and Georgie's compactness. Here it is expressed in a single shot. Bill sits on the left smoking his pipe, Georgie nestles beside him on the right, reading a paper and blissfully unaware of what ensues. The camera tracks upwards to reveal a woman leaning out of an upstairs window, sponging stains off some clothes with a rag soaked in petrol. As she squeezes the excess petrol from the rag, it falls into the bowl of Bill's pipe below, creating a series of little explosions. A series of cuts alternate between the woman and the two-shot of Bill and Georgie, Bill increasingly un-nerved and frustrated by what is going on with his pipe, and eyeing the still oblivious Georgie in suspicion that he is somehow the cause. Eventually he takes his tobacco pouch out and places it beside him while he knocks the pipe out, ready for a refill. A close-up shows us a particularly large load of petrol raining down onto the tobacco in the pouch, which Bill then uses to re-fill the pipe. The pay-off is a massive explosion, which whites-out the screen, before subsiding to show Bill's incredulous face, still holding the now destroyed pipe in his mouth. Georgie, of course, suffers the recriminations. The sequence has no narrative importance, simply functioning as the apotheosis of Bill's frustrations, all of which arise out of the difficulty of negotiating a way through the specific restrictions of class and space. I've emphasised the way in which both of these sequences are highly cinematic in their construction. While they may be based on gags developed in Margate, it is difficult to see how they would work on stage without the assistance of the close-ups and the shot alternations. They also rely on quite a detailed level of banal familiarity in the specific rendering of the milieu offered by the film. Sausage sandwiches from a street snack bar, and sponging fat stains out of old clothes with petrol – the textured richness of these details of working-class life is surely a long way from J.B. Priestley's complaint about the representation of an England taken from 'a few issues of the *Sketch* or *Tatler* and a collection of Xmas cards'.

The richness of this sort of detail surely relates back to Andy Medhurst's point that 'above all else, comedy is an invitation to belong'. Throughout the 1930s, British film audiences struggling with the restrictions of class, and with the anxiety of change, were invited to recognise and understand these struggles and anxieties in the comic protagonists of the films they saw. Sometimes these films fostered that sense of recognition in quite general ways, and sometimes in rather insanely specific ways. Two examples will suffice. In *O-Kay for Sound*, when The Crazy Gang, mistaken for character actors, have been let loose in the props department of a film studio they hear that there is money to be made making up film titles. 'Hear that boys?' says Chesney Allen, 'there are picture titles all around us.' The gang set to work with gusto, making film titles out of the props lying around. Jimmy Gold gives Teddy Knox a motor hooter in exchange for two bob: '*Trader Horn*'. Bud bites the head off a flower: '*Tudor Rose*', and so forth. The success of the sequence relies on the audience's ability to recognise the punning gags as the titles of actual films, creating a sense of belonging across the barrier of the screen in the general sense of a community of film fans. My second example is a lot more specific in terms of class and regionality, and has to do with Gracie Fields' character name in *Sing As We Go* – Grace Platt. Numerous writers have noted the way in which Gracie's character operates as a symbol of her community and its welfare throughout the film. She is even employed as the cotton mill's welfare officer at the end, a fact made much of by consensus readings keen to see her as a mediating figure between employers and workers, but there is a sense in which her very name prepares us for this role from the start. Platt Brothers & Co was one of the largest manufacturers of cotton machinery in Lancashire, and one of the biggest employers in Oldham. I don't wish to revive an emphasis on the consensus theme here, but rather to point out that Grace's name, Platt, can be interpreted as an acknowledgement by the film of a particular belonging for a certain section of its audience – an in-joke if you like. Stamped in cast iron relief on every piece of machinery in all of the mills of Lancashire, 'Platt' might have acted as a nod across the screen to the audiences watching the film who worked that machinery day in and day out – an acknowledgement (like the sashes on the Blackpool Bathing Beauty contestants proclaiming 'Miss Wigan' and 'Miss Halifax') of the connection between holiday atmosphere of the comedy and the more mundane, habitual, specific but unremarked fabric of their everyday lives. On a wider level, I'd argue that the 1930s comedy films as a whole also made this sort of acknowledgement to their audiences, both literally in terms of rendering familiar spaces, comic forms, ways of speaking, relationships and dilemmas on the screen, but also more abstractly in acknowledging the restrictions, negotiations, tricks, anxieties, frustrations, *strategies of survival* necessary for those bound by their class in a class-bound society.

Andrew Marr's despair when faced with the popularity of *Sing As We Go* ('some things in history simply can't be explained'), reminds me of another piece of advice from Robert Darnton in his *histoire de mentalités*. 'When you realize that you are not getting something – a joke, a proverb, a ceremony – that is particularly meaningful to the natives, you can see where to grasp a foreign system of meaning in order to unravel it.' Seeking images of working-class lives in 1930s British cinema, Marr found only frivolity and dubious gags. Maybe he should have looked a little harder.

Bibliography

Aldgate, A. (1983) 'Comedy, class and containment: The British domestic cinema of the 1930s', in J. Curran and V. Porter (eds), *British Cinema History*, London: Weidenfeld.

Allen, S.W. (2006) 'Will Hay and the comedy of consensus', *Journal of British Cinema and Television* 3. 2 (November): 244–65.

Armes, R. (1978) *A Critical History of British Cinema*, Oxford and New York: Oxford University Press.

Dacre, R. (2009) 'Traditions of comedy', in R. Murphy (ed.), *The British Cinema Book*, 3rd edn, London: Palgrave Macmillan.

Darnton, R. (2001) *The Great English Cat Massacre*, London: Penguin.

Gifford, D. (1973) *The British Film Catalogue 1897–1970*, London: David & Charles.

Harper, S. (1997) '"Nothing to beat the Hay Diet": Comedy at Gaumont and Gainsborough', in P. Cook (ed.), *Gainsborough Pictures,* London: Cassell.

Higson, A. (1995) *Waving the Flag: Constructing a National Cinema in Britain*, Oxford: Clarendon Press.

Jenkins, H. and K. Karnick (1995) 'Introduction: Golden eras and blind spots – genre, history and comedy', in H. Jenkins and K. Karnick (eds), *Classical Hollywood Comedy*, London: Routledge.

Landy, M. (2001) 'The extraordinary ordinariness of Gracie Fields: The anatomy of a British star', in B. Babington (ed.), *British Stars and Stardom*, Manchester: Manchester University Press.

Medhurst, A. (1986) 'Music hall and British cinema', in C. Barr (ed.), *All Our Yesterdays: 90 Years of British Cinema*, London: BFI.

——(2007) *A National Joke: Popular Comedy and English Cultural Identities*, London: Routledge.

Napper, L. (2009) *British Cinema and Middlebrow Culture in the Interwar Years*, Exeter: University of Exeter Press.

Priestley, J.B. (1936) 'English films and English people', in *World Film News.* Vol. 1, No. 8, November 1936.

Richards, J. (1984) *The Age of the Dream Palace*, London: Routledge.

Stead, P. (1989) *Film and the Working Class*, London: Routledge.

Sutton, D. (2000) *A Chorus of Raspberries*, Exeter: Exeter University Press.

4 'Northern films for Northern people'

The story of the Mancunian Film Company

C.P. Lee

'Northern comedy' is arguably a genre of its own within British film and has its roots in the Mancunian Film Company. The decline in cinemagoing in the 1950s led to the eventual demise of Mancunian as film-makers but, ironically, TV's insatiable appetite for cheap films saw a brief revival for Mancunian products in the early 1960s. Recently cultural historians have begun to study the company's content in terms of regional comedy, but it has often been overlooked in terms of its place in British film history. This chapter sets out to provide key information on Mancunian's origins, its output and its principal players, to create an understanding of why this studio is worthy of recognition beyond the dusty footnotes of the past and to justify the importance in creating a genre of regional film comedy that paved the way for successive generations of comedy performers many of whom became household names.

Between 1926 and 1967, John E. Blakeley's Mancunian Film Company produced around 60 movies, more than half of them feature length and many made in the company's own studio in Manchester. The majority of the films showcased local performers from Music Hall and Variety and, in displaying their own particular traits of regionalism to wide audiences, 'John E.', as he was known, created for the studio's output the term 'Northern films for Northern people'. Rough and ready or cheap and cheerful depending on how you look at them, the Mancunian Film Company's musical-comedies had only the barest of narratives and seemingly only existed to put across the stage antics of their star performers. Shown at cinemas throughout the North of England, the films were extremely successful in their time and regularly outdrew Hollywood movies at the box office, but through a variety of factors the movies were less well known in the South. When they did break through the 'celluloid curtain', however, they were contenders at Southern box offices. Chibnall and McFarlane state that: 'For example, *Over the Garden Wall* (1950), starring Norman Evans, played the Granada circuit with additional dates on the Odeon and ABC circuits including prestigious seaside resort venues. Total bookings were around 1,500' (Chibnall and McFarlane 2009: 41).

The story of the Mancunian Film Company began in 1908. Market trader James Blakeley entered the world of entertainment when he decided to buy a cinema. Cinema was still considered by many to be too primitive for a sophisticated audience, yet James managed to pack in the crowds. Seeing how lucrative the film business was James sold the cinema and set up a film rental company with his two sons, James Jnr and John E.

Blakeley's Central Film Agency demonstrated a positive flair for cinema business dealings when, in 1915, John E. persuaded his father that a movie called *Tillie's Punctured Romance* would be a big hit. *Tillie* starred Charlie Chaplin in his first full-length comedy and, whilst other rental firms deemed it too long to hold an audience's attention, Blakeley's obtained exclusive rights for the North West of England and in very little time had a financial success on their hands. This is the first example we have of John E.'s ability to intuitively provide cinema experiences that his audiences would flock to for all the years before, during and after the two world wars as the family business continued to operate. In November 1918, he set up his own business as John E. Blakeley Ltd. This wasn't in opposition to the family, rather it was more likely to cover as many bases as possible and maximise potential markets. John E. also got himself more involved in the actual physical processes of film-making being taught the basics of camera and editing by Gerald Summers at The Lancashire Film Studios in All Saints, Manchester. In Lancashire's building at Banba Hall, footage was developed in the basement, two studios and an office shared the ground floor and titles were shot and footage edited on the second floor.

Completely incentivised by his experiences in Lancashire, by 1926 John E. had talked the family into taking the plunge to make their own films and in February 1927 they formed Song Films Ltd. With his canny gift of accurately projecting successful products, John E. produced a series of what we now call 'silent musicals' or 'sing-along silents'. Termed Cameo Operas, he distributed the films along with a quartet of singers who lip-synched by facing the audience and watching the film in a mirror facing the screen. Once again his business acumen proved correct and the 13 two-reelers were financially rewarding and led to John E. trying his luck at making a feature film. The result was *Two Little Drummer Boys* (1928) starring Scottish comic Wee Georgie Wood, which recouped its costs in no time. The coming of sound put paid to this first foray into film-making and John E. went back to distribution and rental. There were no studios in the North equipped with the new sound recording facilities and the game was no longer worth the candle. For the time being John E.'s movie-making was on hold and the company survived through its profits from distribution.

This was all to change though in 1933 with a visit to Manchester by Hollywood stars Laurel and Hardy. Stan Laurel was a contemporary of Chaplin and an acquaintance of John E.'s through his friendship with Bert Tracey, another Music Hall veteran and fellow Mancunian. He had gone to America along with Laurel and Chaplin in the Fred Karno troupe and he too had fetched up in Los Angeles as early as 1913, working as an actor in shorts for the Kalem Company. By 1915, he was working regularly with Oliver Hardy in a string of slapstick comedies, but appears to have come back to England sometime in 1927. Back in Manchester he brought the Blakeleys and Laurel and Hardy together when the Hollywood pair were undertaking a triumphant tour of the British Isles. According to family legend, it was at a meeting in the city's Midland Hotel (see Figure 4.1) when Stan Laurel asked John E. why he wasn't making films any more. The film renter explained that there weren't any suitable studios in Manchester and Stan Laurel provided the perfect answer when he enquired, 'Why don't you rent a studio in London then?' With Bert Tracey to lend him some technical support, John E. thought that it was worth a go. First he had to find a star and he didn't have to look far.

Figure 4.1 James Blakeley and Bert Tracey with Laurel and Hardy at Manchester's Midland Hotel in 1933. Copyright www.itsahotun.com.

John E. was a huge fan of Music Hall and routinely went out several nights a week to catch the latest acts. He would no doubt have heard via word of mouth about an up-and-coming young singer/comic called George Formby. Son of the late, legendary George Formby Snr, George had got off to a shaky start on the Halls, but somewhere along the line had been shown a small string instrument called a ukulele. George learnt the rudiments of ukulele playing and encouraged by his wife Beryl had started to gain a name for his happy-go-lucky manner and daft little songs. Another colleague of Blakeley's, Arthur Mertz, wrote scripts for the young George and took John E. along to meet him one night. A deal was struck that George would star in three films for Blakeley and receive a fee of £100 a week while filming and 10 per cent of the profits.

Calling his new company Blakeley's Productions, John E. invited Bert Tracey to direct, he hired the Albany Studios on London's Regent Street and in May 1933 announced to the trade press that he would make this movie in London but that he was 'actively seeking studios in Manchester' (Williams and Williams 2001: 28). It would be 15 more years before he was able to realise that particular dream. In the meantime, cast and crew gathered together in October 1933 and filming began. Blakeley had raised £3,000 to cover all aspects of the production and Bert Tracey brought it in at £2,750. So it was that *Boots! Boots!* became the first of Blakeley's sound movies and it proceeded to recoup three times its costs within weeks of its release in July 1934 (see Figure 4.2).

Figure 4.2 George Formby and Toni Forde in *Boots! Boots!* (1934), the first of Mancunian's sound films. Copyright www.itsahotun.com.

For people familiar with George Formby's on-screen gormless, harmless persona of his later films, the character he plays in John E's two movies comes as a surprise as he takes on his father's stage character John Willie, a harder edged, occasionally spiteful and definitely trickier persona. George with his 'face like a race-horse, teeth like a graveyard' was present but not very correct and he develops the sly and conniving traits through to the second film *Off The Dole* (1935), made for John E's brand new Mancunian Film Company, as Formby's character is forced into work when threatened with being cut 'off the dole' of the title.

A much larger investment was incurred in the making of *Off The Dole*. Formby had complained that the first film was 'so dark in places you had to strike matches to see it!' (Williams and Williams 2001: 32) and John E. increased the budget. The film's £8,000 outlay would also pay for John E. bringing in a greater number of Music Hall performers, including Stan Little and Stan Pell, whose advertising bills described their act as 'The Schoolboy and the Priest', Dan Young, 'The Dapper Dude Comic', The 12 London Babes, The Twilight Blondes – the list goes on. Within three months, *Off The Dole* had grossed more than £30,000 and had generated the interest of Basil Dean, Head of Associated Talking Pictures. John E. and Basil Dean were both pragmatists and businessmen so a transfer deal was made between them whereby George was bought out of his contract. From his beginnings with Mancunian, George Formby subsequently went on to become 'the highest-earning comedian in British cinema from the mid-30s to the mid-40s, and just before the war, the biggest British star in any genre' (Bradshaw 2011).

John E's Formby movies were distributed nationally through a deal struck with Butcher's Film Service, though for Blakeley his loyalty and interest continued to lie in the success of his films in the North. Here was a ready-made audience for the relatively unsophisticated fare that Mancunian Films were offering. John E. appreciated how the simple, uncomplicated, feel-good quality of his movies was as down to earth as their viewers. It is instructive to remember that he had an intimate knowledge of rental and distribution in this area and would have had a fairly shrewd idea of what his punters wanted to see.

Together with Arthur Mertz, John E. began to write and produce a modest series of entertainments that continued to pay their way and make it worthwhile producing more. What each success did was to consolidate the formula that had come before and create, in essence, those ideas of 'Northern comedy' that exist to this day. He continued to visit theatres scouting out new talent. He had a box at the Palladium Theatre in London, not so much to watch the acts but to watch the audience's reactions to those acts (Cave 1950). John E. and Mertz put together five feature films between 1935 and 1939. In his quest to find a replacement for Formby, Blakeley tried out acts such as Fred Walmsley and Roy Barbour in a movie featuring singer Jenny 'The Generator of Electronic Radiance' Howard and dancer Bertha 'Dainty and Demure' Ricardo, entitled *Dodging The Dole* (1936). Obviously he felt that 'dole' themes would appeal to his working-class audience.

John E. picked up on another theme with 'common' appeal when, on a train journey back from London, he met school teacher and playwright Ronald Gow who presumably talked about the popularity of football pools. Certainly by the end of the journey as the train came into Manchester's Piccadilly Station a new script outline had been written on the back of an envelope and several days later, Ronald Gow was rather surprised to find a cheque for £20 in the post for his scenario! By the time John E. and Arthur had worked their magic on it the script was renamed *The Penny Pool* (1937) and the movie's main star was to be Gracie Fields' brother-in-law, Duggie Wakefield, appearing for the first time in a Mancunian Film.

Duggie Wakefield was another returnee from America where he and his 'Gang', a motley crew of fellow comics, had a moderately successful career starring in short comedies for Hal Roach during the early 1930s. The Gang comprised fellow comedians Billy Nelson, Jack Butler and Chuck O'Neil; they were also sometimes billed as 'Four Boys From Manchester'. The act was quite well known and had performed at a Royal Variety Show in 1931, predating The Crazy Gang's debut there by two years. Duggie had been coaxed back to Britain by his brother-in-law, Tommy Fields, Gracie's brother, and had already appeared in two of her films, but this was the big chance for the Gang to star in a movie. John E. wasted no opportunity in flooding the film with Variety acts of the day. Duggie and his gang slapsticked their way through the usual flimsy Mancunian plot providing plenty of musical interludes from speciality acts like Lou Macari and his Dutch Serenaders, Mascot and Morice 'Those Tap Dancing Fools', Jack Lewis's Singing Scholars and various others. The film climaxes with a gigantic, Busby Berkeley-style ensemble number called 'Keep Fit', all synchronized pumping and strutting and swinging from ropes.

Calling All Crooks (1938) was Mancunian's follow up to *Penny Pool*. This time Duggie and his Gang played members of a detective agency hot on the trail of a con man. Quite how John E. was able to insert what he billed as a 'merry musical burlesque' into this is anybody's guess because sadly the film is lost, but it did contain the usual quota of Music Hall acts including a ventriloquist, several acrobatic dancers and a wild tiger act! *Kine Weekly* commented: 'Laughter was seldom absent from the screen; and was good fun for those who did not take their pleasures too seriously … [it is] a cast iron two-feature programme booking for the masses; particularly those in northern areas' (Williams and Williams 2001: 53).

The film was released in October 1938 and was followed by one of John E.'s very own speciality acts, that of recycling previous film material, as he put out a series of shorts to capitalise on George Formby's new national success. These shorts, also still 'lost', were entitled *Music Hall Personalities 1 to 6* (1938) and *Music Hall Personalities 7 to 12* (1939).

Jeffrey Richards has shrewdly observed:

> Historically, the great value of Mancunian films is that they are almost totally uncinematic. Although John E. was billed as director, the films were not so much directed as staged. The acts do their 'turns' in front of the camera. The films in reality are photographed variety shows, a series of sketches by music hall stars who knew their trade, with musical interludes.
>
> (Richards 1994: 25)

This statement describes more or less perfectly the template that John E. drew up for his movies. However, it can create a problem inasmuch as people have come to regard Mancunian movies as 'primitive'. This is not so. On occasion, John E. demonstrates that he is as capable a director as anyone; see for instance in *What a Carry On!* (1949), a tracking shot across a crowded room moving towards a piano where Josef Locke is waiting to sing. Also evident throughout all his movies is his competent editing from long shot to close-up as well as a knowledgeable use of establishing shot when necessary. However, when it comes to 'the turns', as Richards observes, John E. is content to lock off the camera and let his cast get on with it, a practice put to certain use in the films he made with Frank Randle, his 'star of stage, screen and magistrate's court'.

Frank Randle was described as 'the greatest character comedian that ever lived' by Gracie Fields (Fisher 1973: 177). Born Arthur Hughes in 1901 in Aspull, Wigan he took his stepfather's name of McEvoy and it wasn't until years later the two names Frank and Randle came to him. The young McEvoy would walk to Blackpool and entertain holidaymakers by doing Chaplin impressions. Sent to work in a mill at the age of 13, young Arthur was found asleep at his post by the foreman. Legend has it that the foreman woke him saying, 'Na'then, tha'rt tired out lad. Tha'd better get home and get some sleep,' to which the departing lad replied: 'Aye. And it'll be a long sleep too 'Cos I'm not comin' back!' (Hilton 2001: 8).

Shortly afterwards he went to live in Blackpool taking any job he could. He joined a gymnasium and there he began exercising to extreme. For Randle, keeping fit was a lifelong obsession despite the staggering quantities of alcohol that he drank throughout his career. He believed he'd be immune from illness and live well into his nineties as long as he practised on his Indian clubs every day (a set always stood in his dressing room right up to the very end) and all his life Randle continued to be a most agile tumbler and trampolinist. This led to his first break in show business when he joined an acrobatic troupe, The Three Ernestos. Over the next few years he worked with Astley's Trapeze Troupe, became Arthur Twist when he was in The Bouncing Randles Trampoline Act, and Arthur Heath when the mood took him. In 1929, he finally settled on Frank Randle and became a 'front-cloth' comic, performing his character sketch routines. He also had all his teeth taken out as he believed it to be advantageous for a comic because he could pull more faces. He always kept seven different pairs of false teeth in jam jars in his dressing room, mainly made from papier mâché and needing constant restocking as these he would throw at hecklers.

His slow climb from front-cloth comic to top of the bill lasted until the mid-1930s, by which time Randle had become a firm favourite with audiences, particularly in the North, though he did travel and play everywhere successfully. It was to Blackpool always, however, that Frank owed his allegiance, first topping the bill there in 1938 and appearing there without fail every season throughout his life. In 1939, he was sufficiently successful to form his own company 'Randle's Scandals' which he erratically ran until his death in 1957. By 1940, when John E. first approached him regarding his films, Randle was known as 'King Fun of Blackpool', owned a yacht which he was allowed to have moored on the North Pier, and had established a comic career that was not only brilliant, but one that involved an ongoing battle with the local authorities over the content of his stage act and a popular reputation of being a loose cannon that was never-ending.

John E. was typically astute in picking up this rising star and placing him in his films, though he hedges his bets with the notoriously mercurial Randle at the outset when making the credits for his first film (also his first wartime one), *Somewhere In England* (1940). John E. gives first billing to Harry Korris, a solid comic of Northern lugubriousness who was riding high at the time with a BBC Radio show called *Happidrome*, third billing goes to his radio stooge Robbie Vincent and he places Randle in the middle. But John E. needn't have worried. By the time the film had its premiere on Blackpool's Golden Mile; Frank was, by some accounts, the highest paid comic in the country, earning £1,000 per week (see Figure 4.3).

Somewhere In England was a resounding success and marks the beginning of Frank's film career, which we can divide into two parts. First, the wartime oeuvre of five films, four of which were made for Mancunian. The second part dates from 1947 to 1953 with the four films Randle made at the Mancunian-owned Film Studios Manchester on Dickenson Road, Manchester.

The *Somewhere* trilogy, *In England* (1940), *In Camp* (1942), and *On Leave* (1943), are Army comedies. A Blakeley family anecdote, told to the writer by John E's grandson Mike Blakeley, reveals the prefix entitlement '*Somewhere*' was jokingly used by John E. in order, he said, 'to confuse the enemy'. The titles certainly didn't confuse the audience because these broad, working-class farces were perfectly in tune with wartime cinemagoers. Richards cites the attendance figures for the Majestic, Macclesfield, as a barometer of the films' box-office successes. In 1940, *Somewhere In England* was the fifth

Figure 4.3 Harry Korris and Frank Randle in *Somewhere In England* (1940). Copyright www.itsahotun.
com.

most popular movie shown at the cinema with two George Formby movies ahead of it, *Come On George!* (1939) and *Let George Do It!* (1940). By 1942, its successor *Somewhere In Camp* outdrew all other films, British or American, with the exception of Greer Garson's Oscar-winning *Mrs. Miniver.* In 1943, Randle had vanquished Formby and was the top British attraction at the cinema, second only to Bing Crosby's *Holiday Inn* (1942) (Richards 1994: 29).

These findings are both informative and significant. Not only were Mancunian movies striking the right notes with audiences, Randle himself was seemingly growing more popular than Formby who had reigned supreme at the box office for nearly a decade. Both performers came from Wigan and actually knew each other as boys, both got their first break into films through John E. Blakeley and both personified 'Northernness', though such similarities end there. Randle was the 'yin' to Formby's 'yang', the 'evil twin', the other side of the coin. Whilst each was beloved of audiences their personas, both on-stage and off, couldn't have been more different. After gradually ditching the 'John Willie' character that he'd used in his first two Mancunian films, Formby had taken on a more intimate 'Gosh! What am I doing up here?' approach, appearing simultaneously at once shy and yet cheeky, with a nudge and a wink.

Randle, on the other hand, could easily be classed as 'mad, bad and dangerous to know'. Theatregoers could also be easily classed as those who either loved him or loathed him. The latter camp felt Randle was obscene, a blue comedian. He described himself thusly, 'I'm vulgar, but not filthy' (Williams and Williams 2001: 57). The former found in Randle a man of the people, a man who connected with them in a down-to-earth manner and who related to them by talking to them in their own language about things that others saw as taboo. By today's standards his screen and stage acts are fairly innocuous, but back then they were edgy and often resulted in court appearances.

While other films of the wartime era are propagandistic, or kitted out with a phalanx of stiff upper lips, the *Somewhere* trilogy led by Private Randle are anti-authoritarian, disrespectful and brimming over with contempt for authority. Randle's priapic, toothless, inebriated character rampaged across cinema screens and stages throughout the war, making him one of the most successful entertainers of his generation.

In 1944, John E., anticipating the war's end by a year, brought out *Demobbed*, starring Norman Evans, Betty Jumel and Nat Jackley. A year later he followed that up by putting Randle into civilian life in *Home Sweet Home* (1945), an egalitarian romp that cuts across class barriers, hailing the impending Socialist utopia of the Welfare State. In the obligatory concert sequence, the compere introduces the show by shouting 'Comrades!' At another point Tony Pendrell as Eric says to leading lady Nicolette Roeg (sister of director Nic Roeg), ' ... that's how it must be now that all this is over. Class distinction didn't count in war and it mustn't count now.' It's most unusual to find any kind of political comment, no matter how oblique, in a Mancunian film, but here is John E. presumably mirroring the hopes and aspirations of his predominantly working-class audience

In 1946, John E. put Norman Evans back in front of the camera in a hotel-themed comedy *Under New Management*. Once again John E. was showing his acumen, Norman Evans was a highly popular radio and stage performer who would go on to become one of the first stars of TV with his show *Evan's Above* (1956–8). He'd already showcased one of his most popular characters Fanny Fairbottom, a gossipy, middle-aged housewife whose sketches took place over a garden wall. It was a character that would reappear on screen in 1950 in the Mancunian movie *Over the Garden Wall*, a film notable for co-starring the comic's comic Jimmy James in the first of his only two big-screen outings, both for Mancunian. Evans's housewife character had a large impact on comedy, being the template for Les Dawson's female character Cissie Braithwaite, whose conspiratorial mouthings mimicked the lip reading of Lancashire mill girls and has spilled over today into parts of Peter Kay's stage and screen acts.

Under New Management is significant in that it was the last film Mancunian would make in a London studio. According to family legend, after completing shooting and on the way back to Manchester, John E. and his sons Tom and John decided to seek out investors and open a studio in Manchester. They would also no doubt have been aware of the impending launch of the National Film Finance Corporation (NFFC) which had been set up to ensure that a quota of British films were made each year through the funding of independent productions. It didn't take the family long to set up 'Film Studios Manchester Ltd' in a disused Methodist chapel in South Manchester. There were six members of the board of directors including Frank Randle and John E. Blakeley; the other four were businessmen with interests in cinema ownership. The chapel was converted at a cost of £80,000 into a two-sound stage studio complete with wardrobe department, workshops and a canteen. The sound stages were kitted out with state-of-the-art equipment. Opening its doors for business in 1947, it quickly earned the

Figure 4.4 The chapel in 1955 when the BBC took over the building from the Mancunian Film Studios. Copyright www.itsahotun.com.

nickname in Manchester of 'Jollywood'. Other, unkind souls referred to it as 'the corn exchange' because of the quality of films it produced (see Figure 4.4).

The first movie to emerge from Dickenson Road was *Cup-Tie Honeymoon* (1948) starring Music Hall and radio veteran Sandy Powell, famous for his catchphrase 'Can you hear me, mother?' John E. cast as his wife a young ingénue called Pat Pilkington who, as Pat Phoenix, would later find fame playing Elsie Tanner in Granada TV's *Coronation Street* (1960–73 and 1976–84). The plot of *Cup-Tie Honeymoon* was pretty basic; a rich man's son gives up the chance to play football for England when his local team became a man down. Delighted with his son's soccer skills, his father gives permission for him to marry his girlfriend. While this is going on, Sandy and company run amok in a variety of sub-plots. The end.

There followed in fairly rapid succession a string of Frank Randle comedies, *Holidays With Pay* (1948), *Somewhere In Politics* (1948) (see Figures 4.5 and 4.6) and *School For Randle* (1949). Jewel and Warriss starred in *What A Carry On!* (1949) and the company made good use of Belle Vue Leisure Centre in 1948 producing two mini-features, *International Circus Review* and *Showground Of The North*.

Blakeley allowed his comics a free rein in what they did on screen and, as long as the performers followed the flimsy plots, they were free to perform as they pleased. When filming *Over The Garden Wall*, Jimmy James, Dan Young and Alec Pleon enquired about a half-finished set consisting of a staircase going nowhere and in response John E. simply said, 'Go on lads, be funny' and switched the camera on. Mary Waller worked in John E.'s production office and was mystified at first typing up a

Figure 4.5 Frank Randle in *Somewhere in Politics* (1948). Copyright www.itsahotun.com.

Figure 4.6 Frank Randle in *Somewhere in Politics* (1948). Copyright www.itsahotun.com.

script to see blank pages with one word 'bus' on them and when she asked why, was told it was 'business', indicating the performers were to do their ad-libbed, improvised funny business.

In 1950, as the studio was riding high with the success of *Over The Garden Wall* and with all their films turning a profit, John E. and his team were going into pre-production on their next film, *Let's Have a Murder* (1950) (see Figure 4.7). Mancunian Studios were shocked when the NFFC dropped a bombshell with their announcement that they were withdrawing funding from the studio and demanded the repayment of their loan of £50,000. The likeliest reason is that the Chairman Lord Reith, along with J. Arthur Rank, was known to dislike Mancunian Films and their products. For example, Reith said of *Over The Garden Wall* that he considered it not to be 'of as high a quality as the Corporation would have wished' (Harper and Porter 2003: 11) and by 1951, 'the NFFC was clearly acting as a pre-production censor. More than half the projects that it rejected were refused because it considered their scripts or subjects to be artistically or ethically unacceptable' (Harper and Porter 2003: 12–13).

Undeterred by the funding crisis and the threat of having the receivers sent in, John E. fought on and paid back every penny by May 1951, the time set by the NFFC. He achieved this by using his profits from the films and hiring out the studios to other companies such as Hammer and the CWS Film Unit. Then, after that tumultuous year, Tom Blakeley persuaded his father that the future lay in light comedy and accordingly optioned two plays. The resulting films, *Love's A Luxury* (1952) and *Those People Next Door* (1952), did not follow the traditional Mancunian productions of John E. and they

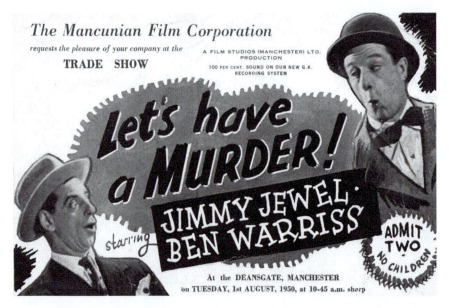

Figure 4.7 Trade show invitation to Mancunian's *Let's Have a Murder* (1950) with Jimmy Jewel and Ben

were neither Northern nor particularly comedy. With the exception of a cameo appearance by Jimmy James in the latter, they didn't even feature Music Hall stars or their acts. Despite the presence of stars such as Jack Warner and the film gaining North American distribution, it would be some years before Tom recouped the investment made.

Reverting to Northern comedy type, John E. set to work on his next project *Shoulder Arms* and made Tom the Production Manager. This movie would be another Army caper starring Frank Randle though by the time shooting began in 1953, they had changed the title to *It's A Grand Life* and John E. had brought in H.F. Maltby to deliver the screenplay. Maltby was a respected actor and writer who had appeared for Gainsborough both in Hitchcock movies and Will Hay comedies. He had worked with Randle in *Somewhere In Civvies* and *Home Sweet Home* and, even though Randle would no doubt veer away from any script whenever he wanted, at least Maltby was used to the man and his ways. The female interest in this film was achieved as Randle's phrase 'Bah gum, she's a hot'un' was brought to personification, by the inclusion of glamorous British star Diana Dors, who said of the filming: 'Randle was mad – and usually drunk in to the bargain. But, as he owned the film company, we had to put up with him shooting guns at the dressing-room wall or dragging his girlfriends by the hair along the corridors' (Dors 1981: 133).

During filming, Randle was sleeping in his caravan in the car park of Rusholme Conservative Club next to the studios, until rain coming through the bullet holes in the roof forced him to move into the dressing room at nights. Randle's alcoholism was legendary. BBC producer Mike Craig interviewed Randle's son Arthur Delaney who said Randle habitually slept with a bottle opener on a piece of string round his neck and the first thing he did when he woke up was reach down for a bottle of Guinness from under his bed and then light up his first Woodbine of the 60 a day he smoked. Certainly, by this time, Randle was careening out of control, frequently walking off set and demanding that various crewmembers be sacked. John E., a devout Catholic, who would make the sign of the cross before every take, was the only one who could control Randle's drunken rages, even having to disarm him on occasion.

Despite his condition, Randle still managed to deliver classic comedy. Whether scripted by Maltby or made up by Randle, it really doesn't matter as it still works as a classic bit of 'business'. In the following scene from *It's A Grand Life*, his Commanding Officer is questioning Randle about an escaped prisoner that he was in charge of.

OFFICER: Now then, Private Randle, what have you to say about this deserter Barnes getting away and stealing the army jeep of which you were in charge?
RANDLE: Oh yes sir. I, er, er … eh?
OFFICER: [Repeats question]
RANDLE: Oh yes, yes … very bad, er, show, sir. Y'see, it's very, very difficult because, er, the chap who told me to look after him must have been daft or somethin'.
SERGEANT: Quiet please! Stand to attention!
RANDLE: Yes, I am …

OFFICER: What are you talking about?

RANDLE: I am at attention. It's me uniform that's at ease. I beg yer pardon sir?

OFFICER: I said what are you talking about?

RANDLE: I don't know sir. He keeps interruptin' me sir. [To sergeant] Be quiet! Be'ave yerself! [To officer, as he reaches for a cigarette] Will yer 'ave a Woodbine sir?

OFFICER: Is this man mad?

SERGEANT: Put that away!

RANDLE: Er, yes ... er ... mind yer own business. Er ... I'm talkin' to the ... corporal, not you. Now, sir [salutes] er ... sorry, cobber. This er ...

OFFICER: What about Barnes?

RANDLE: Ah! That's what we all want to know, isn't it? Yes. 'E's 'opped it. I don't blame 'im. I mean to say, 'e's gone. Y'see, sir, this dog came out of number three trap, and ...

OFFICER: What about Barnes?

RANDLE: Ah! Ah! Barnes! You see, yes, well ... what about it? [To sergeant] Er ... d'you know? No. Well, never mind, doesn't matter. Well, 'is wife, y'see, er, terrible. 'E 'ad four children, er, sir, four, er, all four of 'em, one, either a boy or a child, I'm not quite sure ... and 'is wife ... er ... very, very unfortunate. Er, nasty operation sir, she's 'ad, er, for rubbin' stones, stop stones, I think it's called ... gallstones. 'Ave you seen a gallstone? 'Scuse me sir [grabs paper and pencil]. Look 'ere. Er ... now then. I'll draw yer a chicken. ... Yes ... er ... [officer knocks paper from his hand] Don't yer want a chicken, sir?

OFFICER: What about Barnes?

RANDLE: Yes, er, well, er ...

Randle's comedic presence and the appearance of Dors, described in the credits as 'Britain's Most Beautiful and Glamorous', combined to make *It's A Grand Life* a sustained box office hit (see Figure 4.8). After completing the film, John E. chose to retire and the film's success was a fitting swansong for John E., especially when, in due course, its Army setting was picked up by Granada TV for their highly popular, long-running series *The Army Game* (1957–61). John E. accepted an offer for his Studios from the BBC who established their regional studio there and upon his retirement John E. left Mancunian to continue film production under the supervision of Tom Blakeley who, with the exception of *The Trouble With Eve* (1960), steered clear of comedy film and worked on thrillers, horror and science fiction 'B' features.

Happily for our heritage, fans and comedians alike are able to see a good deal of the works of John E. Blakeley and his Mancunian Film Company with its wealth of comic performances by Variety and Music Hall acts preserved on film. The list is impressive and includes Donovan and Byl's act 'Tumbling Tomfoolery', Betty Jumel's repertoire of funny walks, slapstick and nonsense chat for example in 'The Coalman and the Housekeeper' with Bernard Youens, Dan Young's character of the dapper dude comic, Jimmy James and our Eli's routine as in 'Are you putting it about that I'm barmy?', George Formby's singing for the very first time on screen in *Boots! Boots!* and of course the one, the only Frank Randle in all his comedic roles including his trampolining comedy routine as featured in *Somewhere In Camp*.

Figure 4.8 Frank Randle in *It's a Grand Life* (1953). Copyright www.itsahotun.com.

Bibliography

Bradshaw, P. (2011) 'Will the nation gurn again for George Formby?', *The Guardian Online*, 2 June. Available online: www.guardian.co.uk/film/filmblog/2011/jun/02/george-formby-ukulele (accessed 12 August 2011).

Cave, P. (1950) 'This man makes money out of films', *John Bull Magazine*, 11 March. Available online: www.itsahotun.com/Blakeley/Blakeley_Family.html (accessed 12 August 2011)

Chibnall, S. and McFarlane, B. (2009) *The British 'B' Film*, London: Palgrave Macmillan.

Dors, D. (1981) *Dors by Diana*, London: Macdonald Futura.

Fisher, J. (1973) *Funny Way To Be A Hero*, London: Frederick Muller.

Harper, S. and Porter, V. (2003) *British Cinema in the 1950s: The Decline of Deference*, Oxford: Oxford University Press.

Hilton, J.A. (2001) *A Monkey Up A Stick – Remembering Frank Randle*, Wigan: Aspull and Haigh Historical Society.

Richards, J. (1994) *Stars In Our Eyes: Lancashire Stars of Stage, Screen and Radio*, Preston: Lancashire County Books.

Williams, P.M. and Williams, D.L. (2001) *Hooray For Jollywood*, Ashton-under-Lyne: History On Your Doorstop.

5   Ealing comedies 1947–57

'The bizarre British, faced with another perfectly extraordinary situation'

Tim O'Sullivan

Introduction: Ealing past and Ealing present

> Despite the variety of films we made over the years I suppose it is the comedies with which Ealing will be always identified.
>
> (Balcon 1969: 158)

The year 2011 marks the 80th anniversary of the establishment of Ealing Studios. 'The studio in suburbia – suburban in spirit as well as site,' as Kenneth Tynan was to characterise it wryly in the mid-1950s, noting that even by then the name of 'Ealing' had assumed a certain 'talismanic significance': 'Ealing has become the regimental mascot of the British cinema, devoted to interpreting a national way of life, and taking as its general theme the extraordinary and resilient British, coping with a series of perfectly alarming situations' (Tynan 1955: 4).

Partly in celebration of this anniversary and the coincidence that many of the films have also reached their 60th birthday, restored and digitally re-mastered versions of six of the 'greatest' Ealing comedies are being re-released (yet again) in British cinemas and offers of celebratory, boxed DVD 'classic collector's editions' proliferate on film websites.[1] Quite what contemporary cinema audiences might make of *Passport to Pimlico* (1949), *Whisky Galore* (1949), *Kind Hearts and Coronets* (1949), *The Lavender Hill Mob* (1951), *The Man in the White Suit* (1951), *The Ladykillers* (1955) and their respective 'imagined communities' remains to be seen, but one commentator however has recently noted:

> Whenever the Ealing comedies of the late 1940s and early 1950s re-emerge, a mood of nostalgia invariably overcomes commentators and critics. Despite the subversive edge existing in so many of the films, their celebration of community, consensus and mild but loveable eccentricity is applauded. They are seen as representing an idealised Britain where small-timers invariably thwart big, bad bureaucrats and where tolerance, humour and benevolence rule.
>
> (Macnab 2011: 1)

It is in such terms that these 'core', if not 'canonical', Ealing comedies and their conventionalised projections of 'Britishness' have become key critical touchstones – or millstones, depending on your point of view – for subsequent British comedy film production. As Macnab goes on to suggest, Ealing has acted as an enduring if stubborn 'prism' through which many subsequent British comedy films have been assessed and usually found wanting. For instance, he cites the work of Bill Forsyth in the 1980s – *Gregory's Girl* (1981) and *Local Hero* (1983) – which were routinely ascribed 'Ealing style' status and praised for their reproduction of the 'Ealing tradition'. *A Private Function* (1984) was similarly acclaimed as recapturing the spirit of Ealing. When Charles Crichton reprised his career in British comedy direction with *A Fish Called Wanda* (1988), the film was seen as a 'savage tribute to another Ealing comedy'.[2] Likewise in the 1990s, *Brassed Off* (1996) and *The Full Monty* (1997) were also often seen as having overtones of Ealing. Indeed any relatively small budget British comedy film produced after the demise of Ealing in the mid-1950s has attracted comparison. From Dearden and Relph's *The Smallest Show on Earth* (1957), produced for British Lion in the immediate aftermath of Ealing, but regarded by many as a 'classic' Ealing ensemble comedy, but made paradoxically *after* Ealing,[3] to more recently the closing finale of Ken Loach's *Looking for Eric* (2009), with its perceived and perhaps unexpected element of 'Ealingesque' whimsy and resolution. Similarly, Nigel Cole's *Made in Dagenham* (2010) was lauded as 'the type of film that could have been made by Ealing Studios' (Cole's earlier *Calendar Girls* (2003) had also been compared favourably with the Ealing style). Contemporary reviews of Joel and Ethan Coen's remake and American transposition of *The Ladykillers* (2004) indicated a particularly mixed critical reception which revealed variable degrees of reverence for the Ealing original.[4] More recently, the science fiction film *Attack the Block* (2011) was seen as harking back to the heyday of Ealing comedy. In similar terms, the recent announcement of the adaptation of *The Ladykillers* for the British stage in 2011 attracted critical attention and sparked not a little controversy, much of which rather predictably hinged on the degree to which the script for the forthcoming stage play might 'deviate' from that of the original film. Graham Linehan, the established comedy writer commissioned for the adaptation and committed to more than a simple transcription, found that he was 'ambushed' on the BBC *Today* radio programme. Expected to perform his 'Punch-and-Judy' part in an artificial, gladiatorial, 'ding-dong' confrontation with the theatre critic Michael Billington, he felt that the contrived agenda took him to task about the wisdom of even considering adapting *The Ladykillers* at all.[5]

In these and other examples it is clear that the Ealing comedies represent a significant, sensitive and at the same time jealously guarded part of popular British film heritage; a key component in the nostalgic, *generational*, 'rear-view mirror' of how post-war British society and history is recognised and (mis-) remembered. Understandably, for some writers, even and especially in these times of the avowedly revisionist and non-canonical 'New Film History' (Chapman et al. 2007), perhaps sufficient has already been written about not only Ealing, but also Ealing comedies. Who would want now to walk into this established critical minefield? For instance, a recent and important historical study of popular English comedy adopts this view, seeking to avoid 're-treading well-covered ground – the post-war Ealing comedies', arguing that Barr's celebrated (1977/93) study has already provided not only the comprehensive, but the definitive, astute and final word (Medhurst 2007: 7). On the other hand, Ealing continues to fascinate and provides a magnet for various forms and 'angles' of contemporary film scholarship.

Dissecting Ealing comedies: Jewels in the crown and all that glisters?

> Possibly, when one starts looking for a pattern, one can see it in everything.
>
> (Barr 1977: 134)

Of the 95 feature films made at Ealing under the aegis of Michael Balcon's influential term as Chief Executive (1938–58), about one third can be regarded as comedies. Conventionally, critics have classified those produced up to the mid-1940s primarily as *performance*-led films, vehicles that in the main capitalised on the broad farce or slap-stick of established stage comedy stars and their acts, most obviously in the form of George Formby, Gracie Fields, Will Hay and Tommy Trinder.[6] These account for some 15 films, beginning with *Trouble Brewing* (1939) and ending with the historical extra-vagance of Cavalcanti's *Champagne Charlie* (1944).[7] The comedies made at Ealing after this point (18 films) are distinguished more by script- or story-driven narratives and, although they feature important performances (notably for instance by Alec Guinness and recurrent ensemble casts), it is the scripts (T.E.B. 'Tibby' Clarke [seven scripts], William Rose [three] and others[8]), the directors (Mackendrick [four films], Crichton [five], Hamer [one], Frend [three]) as well as the thematic selection and reiteration of what Kenneth Tynan in 1951 was to characterise as 'the bizarre British', and their 'perfectly extraordinary situations', which was to make the core of these films 'Ealing Comedies' and not just 'comedies made at Ealing' (Tynan 1951).[9]

This 'core' consists of eight films, starting with the studio's first post-war comedy *Hue and Cry* (1947). Full of juvenile energy, the film combines tellingly a fantasy (akin to an anglicised *Emil and the Detectives* (1931)) with the documentary realism of the settings and locations of the raw London bomb-sites, the territory of groups of young schoolboys who join forces to outwit a gang of crooks. The next three films were produced and released in the crucible of 1949; the '*annus mirabilis*' of post-war Ealing, as Barr (1977: 96) has it. *Passport to Pimlico*, a comedy which plays with the contra-dictions between the heady freedoms of local secession at the heart of the capital meeting the ultimate obligations of national, post-war unity, came first. The mischief shifts slightly in *Whisky Galore*, when the community of an isolated Scottish island outpost undermines the bureaucratic state and subverts its attempts to cancel out the storm-sent carnivalesque spirits of its title. *Kind Hearts and Coronets*, however, pursues a very different, darker and superficially much less collective trajectory, as the dis-possessed and vengeful Louis 'comically' murders and philanders his way to his birthright (at the expense of the aristocratic class) – almost. Two years later *The Lavender Hill Mob* features another tale of 'a worm that turns', as a downtrodden, long-serving bank clerk revolts against the chains that bind him and plans, then pulls off, a bullion robbery, to great comic effect and with apparent success until the giddy spree reveals the handcuffs in its finale. The year 1951 also saw *The Man in the White Suit* adven-turously extend the Ealing satirical and ironic comedy agenda as its hero, an eccentric

Candide-like maverick scientist, whose seemingly magical invention of an indestructible clothing fibre that repels dirt, falls foul of the machinations of capital and labour, before romance and rain provide the resolution. In 1953 appeared *The Titfield Thunderbolt*, a mild but intensely nostalgic epitome of one of the principal tropes of Ealing – a rural community challenged by the alienating forces and associated mind-set of modernity. This, the first comedy filmed in (wonderful) colour, is a steam-driven, creaking, leaking and variable tale, and as a result it has understandably not been recognised in the first division of Ealing comedies. Finally, *The Ladykillers* (1955), the last film Mackendrick contributed to the studio, is a significant final milestone (or tombstone?) in the Ealing comedy oeuvre. An unnervingly dark and original comedy, it continues to retain its considerable power in the juxtaposition of a weird and sinister gang of bank-robbers with the sweet innocence of their landlady (Katie Johnson) and all that she represents. The tour de force casting and Technicolor cinematography (by Otto Heller) is complemented by the script's inexorable drive towards the grisly, hysterical and absurd conclusion. Although shot on location in the environs of St Pancras and King's Cross, this film is many, many miles away and in a very different territory to Pimlico – only six years earlier.

If these eight films can be understood as the classic core or the 'first division' of the Ealing comedy, there are an additional four films which are usually regarded as having a more liminal status. They are generally regarded as somehow flawed, predictable, anti-climactic or as rather lame ('below par' and not very funny) attempts to emulate earlier successes. Barr notes that three of them were directed by Charles Frend and

Figure 5.1 The Lavender Hill Mob (1951). Image courtesy of Canal + Image UK.

were indicative of his 'unease with comedy' (1977: 190). They begin with the fourth comedy film produced in 1949, *A Run for Your Money*, a tale of innocents abroad, as two Welsh miners win a trip to London to watch a rugby international and have to run the gauntlet of the metropolis, its feminine wiles, sponging drunks and the inept management of their prize trip. This is potentially promising Ealing material, but ultimately it fails to deliver the 'Ealing feeling' and was understandably overshadowed by its more illustrious precursors of that year. In a similar vein, *The Magnet* (1950) also falls short. In its attempt to recapture the childhood culture and the effervescent energy successfully featured in *Hue and Cry*, the film founders on a thin, convoluted and improbable plot.[10] *The Maggie* (1954) likewise fell awkwardly between several stools. This was Mackendrick's penultimate and least successful film at Ealing (he also intervened in the scripting with William Rose).[11] It is an oddly flat, distorted and charmless twin of *Titfield*, with elements of *Whisky Galore* and associated dollops of Kailyardry thrown in, as a venerable old 'puffer', this time a cantankerous steam-driven cargo boat and its 'lovable' Scottish crew, engage mischievously with an American tycoon, and his money and his/their mission.[12] This rather sorry quartet of films is completed by *Barnacle Bill* (1957), based on Clarke's last screenplay for Ealing. It concerns a seasick naval Captain (Guinness, with multiple flashbacks of his distinguished scion, redolent of *Kind Hearts*), whose obstinate command of a land-connected seaside pier ultimately leads to a re-awakening of a separatist state, rather as in *Pimlico*. 'Like the last twitching of the nervous system after death,' as Barr (1977: 165) was later to pronounce, without irony.

These Ealing comedies have provided a sustained and recurrent focus for British and international film scholarship and criticism since they were produced and released in what was a relatively short period, and operated as a home-grown, cinematic fulcrum and pivot between the late 1940s and the mid-1950s.[13] This was a crucial moment for British film and British society and culture and understandably the films have been interrogated and flayed inside-out to render up what they might reveal about their changing times. This is most often understood in terms of their representation and ideological management or 'reflection' of a shift from an inward, 'safe' and backward (war-ward)-looking state of 'austerity', to an outward, but more threatening, divisive and forward-looking experience of 'affluence' and 'consumerism'.[14] Barr's rightly acknowledged study continues to provide a, if not *the*, key critical touchstone; informed as it is by an in-depth knowledge and sense of the studio arrangements and the shifting politics under Balcon, and an admirably nuanced feel for how the respective textures of the films do, or do not, 'mesh' and work as comedies within the broader cultural and political contexts of their times. Much less celebratory than Perry's (1981) study, Barr's reading of the films tends towards a stern, rather austere pessimism as he charts and laments the shift from the 'mild anarchy' (Balcon 1969: 159) of the immediate post-war years to rapid stagnation and the accelerating, downhill onset of a kind of impotent senility and loss of vigour expressed in an inability to even recognise and keep pace with the actual, changing realities of the time. Significantly, he remains a much quoted but difficult to summarise source – as does Durgnat (1970). What remains instructive and important about Barr's study, however, is its refusal to entirely separate or isolate the study of Ealing comedies from the more general analysis of the Ealing oeuvre as a whole. The comedies were inextricably (and sometimes oddly[15]) linked to other currents and conditions in the studios as they sought profitability across the range of developing post-war film genres – crime thrillers, historical dramas, war films, 'social problem' films, melodramas and so on.[16]

Undoubtedly united by key aspects of their conditions of production and performance, the Ealing comedies have also been divided along a spectrum which recognises major differences in terms of the tilt in the dynamics of their allegorical dimensions and hence their ideological and comical powers. Conventionally, films such as *Hue and Cry* and *Passport to Pimlico* have been grouped as conservative *daydreams*: fantasies allied strongly with Clarke's scripts and their narratives of relatively gentle, comic disruption and disorder which are resolved by the seemingly inevitable restoration of established conformity and order. These disarmingly whimsical and moral 'what if?' fables utilise realistic settings and configure recognisable characters leading mundane and humdrum lives.[17] The films represent a sustained engagement with and examination of communities, testing the 'glue' (a metaphor for Englishness or Britishness) that binds and holds them together, and the characteristic modes of response to times of crisis, usually induced by external threat, challenge or change.[18] The comedy emanates usually from the clash and struggle between the 'insiders' and the 'outsiders' and the reassuring, final triumph of reconciliation, as contending private or sectional interests are compromised or reconciled in order to preserve the original organic integrity of the wider community and its public values. In this process, the extent to which any lasting transformation takes place is a key issue for consideration, as the pebble lands in the pond, causes its comic ripples, but then leaves ultimately an undisturbed, mirror-like surface.

At the other, far darker pole of this spectrum, way beyond cosiness and whimsicality but nonetheless with a twist of quintessential 'Englishness', are the films which are based less on daydreams, but much more on strange and transgressive *nightmares*.[19] Far from celebrating the resilience of national or any kind of imagined consensus or solidarity embodied in the English or British way of life, these films, epitomised in *Kind Hearts and Coronets* and *The Ladykillers*, unleash stories of maverick and dangerous eccentricity, resulting in suspended moral fables based on 'black' (or at least dark grey), understated English comedy, which recount and play with stories of criminal, violent, murderous – and even sexual – desire and their consequences. These films, dealing with themes of repressed and released revenge, resistance and strangely authorised greed, created very different ripples in the cultural pond and are the hallmarks of the work and influence of Robert Hamer and Alexander Mackendrick within the Ealing team ethos and times. Almost imperceptibly, they managed to add a distinctive touch of subversion and, in spite of their recuperative endings, to destabilise a little the established values of Ealing, and its self-conscious projection of Britishness, from the inside.

The filmic devices of voice-over commentary and flashback as well as highly charged, symbolic representations of the 'crowd' and the 'chase' are worthy of further attention in these films, as are, more broadly, their representations of gender and gender relations. These are comic tales of men and women who are not only strangely asexual but almost wholly forced into an unforgiving one-dimensional, patriarchal mould – not a pattern that was repeated uniformly across all of the Ealing output of the time.[20]

This spectrum of much celebrated moments in the heritage of British cinema were of course formed in the gigantic shadow of the recent experience of 'total war' and by the subsequent attempts by British politicians and political parties to forge a way forward from 1945. Barr (1977) and subsequently Richards (1997) extend and buttress their synchronic analysis of this series of particular Ealing comedy films within a firm diachronic appreciation of the shifting targets of the comedies and their political environments and contradictions. In Barr's 'admittedly fanciful' reading of *The Ladykillers*, for instance:

> The gang are the post-war Labour government. Taking over 'the House', they gratify the conservative incumbent by their civilised behaviour (that nice music), and decide to use at least the façade of respectability for their radical programme of redistributing wealth (humouring Mrs W and using her as a front). Their success is undermined by two factors, interacting: their own internecine quarrels and the startling, paralysing charisma of the 'natural' governing class, which effortlessly takes over from them again in time to exploit their gains (like the Conservatives taking over power in 1951, just as the austerity years come to an end).
>
> (Barr 1977: 171–2)

The correspondence is both compelling and entertaining and it is important to read on, as Barr indicates that 'this is not a dimension which needs actually to have been in the mind of anyone involved' (172). For Jeffrey Richards, given the studio's declared political sympathies, it is arguable that the early period of Ealing comedies (1947–51) 'constitute a programmatic attack on the evils that Labour wished to eradicate: entrenched aristocratic privilege (*Kind Hearts and Coronets*), the power of money (*The Lavender Hill Mob*), monopoly capitalism (*The Man in the White Suit*) and colonialism (*Whisky Galore*)' (Richards 1997: 135). The later phase of films, coincident with the Conservative Party's rule (1951–8), he goes on to suggest, are characterised by a retreat from the earlier Labour post-war mission, a reversal which results in revisionist, homological remakes of the earlier films, so, in perfect symmetry, *Whisky Galore* is transformed into *The Maggie*, *Passport to Pimlico* into *The Titfield Thunderbolt*, and *Kind Hearts and Coronets* into *The Ladykillers*.

These are patterns which may be more or less obvious for film historians writing with the undoubted benefit of measured and scholarly hindsight. However, there is a way in which the films also appear to refuse or evacuate any (party) political dimensions, presenting themselves by contrast as a reiteration of timeless comic struggles between the old and the new and of deferential conformity pitted against resistance. Most important here are the ways in which the comedies deal or play with the balance between the good and the bad.[21] Quite how these interpretative frameworks informed or otherwise stimulated audiences' actual laughter (or its refusal) in the cinemas of the 1950s and subsequent generations' in front of TVs, videos and DVDs, remain a relatively unresearched and unanswered question. How do contemporary viewers relate to and make sense of Ealing comedies?

Coda: Beyond the pale: Post-war comedies 'made at Ealing'

For emerging scholars of British film and cinema looking for a challenge, ripe for reclamation, reassessment and possible revision are the six remaining comedy films 'made at Ealing', which deviate from the mainstream 'norm' of Ealing comedy. As early as 1948, Ealing released *Another Shore*, directed by Charles Crichton and starring Robert Beatty and Moira Lister. This is a strange and quirky comic fable, which projects Dublin daydreams of escapism, fuelled by motor insurance scams, and ultimately reined in by romance and a realistic reappraisal of what the world might actually offer. An odd and maverick attempt at a comic experiment, it preceded the establishment of the Ealing pattern. *Meet Mr. Lucifer* (1953) is a landmark film, examining as it does the entry of television into the British home from a cinematic point of view. Predictably it presents television as the agent of Satan, a destructive device capable of wrecking and ruining domestic life as the fortunes of a particular TV set are traced through a number of households (see Stokes 1999: 94–6). *The Love Lottery* (1954) is an interesting attempt at a satire on stardom and celebrity which, untypically for Ealing, features David Niven as a Hollywood film idol who is raffled as a prize in an extraordinary tale of daydreams of love, chance and romance, which finally reconciles the ordinary with the spectacular. In *Touch and Go* (1955) Jack Hawkins plays a successful furniture designer, who, as a result of the British 'hide-bound' rejection of his 'contemporary' style, decides unilaterally to uproot his family and emigrate to Australia and the pro-mise of 'new horizons'. In the end, however, he is unable to carry this through as the domestic ties of his known world hold him back and a suitable reversal and compro-mise results. *Who Done It?* (1956) and *Davy* (1957) are both kinds of throwback to the earlier, pre-war age of Ealing 'performer' comedies, but transported from the era of stage variety into the age of radio and television stardom.[22] In their first leading film roles before television beckoned, Benny Hill, as an amateur sleuth, and Harry Secombe, as an opera singer who-might-have-been, were the respective leads in these two rather sorry 'fag-ends' of Ealing comedy. It was not an especially funny ending:

> Ealing has little enough in common with Oscar Wilde, or with the most famous of his characters. But looking back we can see the story of post-war Ealing as the story of Dorian Gray. Ealing itself determines to remain the same, holding out against the processes of age and change. But time goes by regardless, and the Ealing *picture* inexorably acquires the marks of age.
>
> (Barr 1977: 177)

Notes

1 See recent commentaries on *The Lavender Hill Mob* by Matthew Sweet (2011) and Andrew Gilligan (2011) and on *Kind Hearts and Coronets* by Matthew Dennison (2009).

2 www.rottentomatoes.com/m/fish_called_wanda/

3 See Burton and O'Sullivan (2009: 23–6) and Chapman (1997: 194–202) for relevant discussion of *The Smallest Show on Earth*. *Genevieve* (1953) is often misrecognised as an 'Ealing comedy'. Barr (1977: 165) has noted that 'both of them are as near to Ealing films as they could be without actually being made there'.

4 'The Coen brothers should have left *The Ladykillers* alone' was how one critic headlined it (Patterson 2004).

5 See Brown (2011) and Linehan (2011).

6 See for instance Green (1983: 294), Armes (1978: 180–97) or Pulleine (1997: 115).

7 At least two early and telling films in this period, however, do not conform to type. *Let's Be Famous* (1939) is a comedy which juxtaposes the snobbish and patrician ethos of the BBC (radio) service with the twin 'upstart' incursions of regional broadcasting and commercial advertising culture. Four months later, *Cheer Boys Cheer* (1939) was an early precursor, if not prototype, for one of the kinds of 'Ealing Comedy' to come, when the small, traditional and harmonious family brewing company 'Greenleaf' and its community is threatened by and fights a take-over bid from a modern corporate, industrial giant 'Ironside'. See Barr (1977: 5–6).

8 Clarke's contribution and influence is a notable thread of continuity not only in the comedies but in the output of Ealing as a whole – he scripted 14 films there 1944–57 (see his enjoyable and informative biography (1974) where he notes that his script for *The Lavender Hill Mob* won him an Oscar, but little more than the £1,500 he was paid at the time he wrote it). The other seven comedy scripts drew on members of the Ealing 'in-house' (Red Lion) team of regulars, including input from the respective directors, and Monja Danischewsky, John Dighton, Roger MacDougall, Angus MacPhail and occasional 'interlopers' such as Harry Kurnitz and Walter Meade. See Burton and O'Sullivan (2009: 322–7).

9 At this time, Tynan was film critic on *The Evening Standard* before moving later to *The Observer.* He was later to co-script *Nowhere to Go* (1958), the penultimate Ealing film – not a comedy – and he also wrote an early study of Alec Guinness (1953), who was later to refute the suggestion that he had modelled aspects of his persona as the character Professor Marcus in *The Ladykillers* (especially the protruding teeth) on Tynan.

10 See Harper and Porter (2003: 61–2) for a more sympathetic account of the film.

11 Philip Kemp provides a most carefully researched and written account of *The Maggie* (1991: 89–109) and other Mackendrick films in his important study.

12 For a critical reading of *The Maggie* and *Whisky Galore*, see McArthur (1982).

13 Landy (2000: 68) provides an insight into how Ealing comedies were reviewed and received in America.

14 Of course, the reference here is to Durgnat's (1970) engaging, always rewarding if slightly maverick study. See also Rolinson (2003).

15 For instance, Clarke's rapid shift from his work on *Pool of London* (1951) to *The Lavender Hill Mob*. See Clarke (1974: 165–6).

16 See Harper and Porter (2003: 57–73), who note that Ealing films of the period did not fit easily into the formats of predictable genres, with consequent problems for marketing and profitability. Rather, they suggest that this generic 'slipperiness' was supplanted by a cross-cutting focus on certain themes, the most significant of which – even in comic mode – concerned 'the social process that ratifies notions of right and wrong' (60).

17 Clarke (1974: 159) suggests that the 'what if' formula – the bizarre introduction, suspension or reversal of existing rules and normality – was a key basis for many of his scripts. See Muir (2010: 74).

18 See Ritchie (2010: 33–5) for a broader but related discussion.

19 For development of these metaphors see the analysis presented by Williams (1992: 95–105, and 2000: 163–70).

20 Geraghty (2000) has initiated valuable inroads into this rather neglected dimension of 1950s British films. Charles Crichton in a later interview noted that Balcon had decided views on sex in the Ealing universe: 'Sex was a big problem. I do think he knew how babies were born but it was not a subject we were allowed to treat on the screen.' In a BBC (1986) *Omnibus: 'Made in Ealing'*, interview, cited in Muir (2010: 94).

21 Porter (2001: 92) in an analysis which skirts Ealing comedy output argues that: 'To be successful, a film subtly had to appeal, both to the traditional values of the old order and those that were emerging from the younger generation.'

22 See Burton and O'Sullivan (2009) for more detailed discussion and analysis of these two films.

Bibliography

Armes, R. (1978) *A Critical History of British Cinema*, Oxford and New York: Oxford University Press.

Balcon, M. (1969) *Michael Balcon Presents … A Lifetime of Films*, London: Hutchinson.

Barr, C. (1977) *Ealing Studios*, London: David & Charles. Revised (1993) Studio Vista.

Brown, M. (2011) 'Ealing Comedy *The Ladykillers* reborn on the stage', *The Guardian*, 6 June.

Burton, A., O'Sullivan, T. and Wells, P. (eds) (1997) *Liberal Directions: Basil Dearden and Postwar British Film Culture*, Trowbridge: Flicks Books.

Burton, A. and O'Sullivan, T. (2009) *The Cinema of Basil Dearden and Michael Relph*, Edinburgh: Edinburgh University Press.

Chapman, J. (1997) 'Films and flea-pits: *The Smallest Show on Earth*', in A. Burton, T. O'Sullivan and P. Wells (eds), *Liberal Directions: Basil Dearden and Postwar British Film Culture*, Trowbridge: Flicks Books.

Chapman, J., Glancy, M. and Harper, S. (eds) (2007) *The New Film History: Sources, Methods, Approaches*, London: Palgrave Macmillan.

Clarke, T.E.B. (1974) *This Is Where I Came In*, London: Michael Joseph.

Curran, J. and Porter, V. (eds) (1983) *British Cinema History*, London: Weidenfeld & Nicolson.

Dennison, M. (2009) 'A movie to mock morality', *The Daily Telegraph*, 10 July.

Dixon, W.W. (ed.) (1992) *Re-Viewing British Cinema, 1900–1992*, New York: SUNY Press.

Durgnat, R. (1970) *A Mirror for England: British Movies from Austerity to Affluence*, London: Faber & Faber.

Geraghty, C. (2000) *British Cinema in the Fifties: Gender, Genre and the 'New Look'*, London and New York: Routledge.

Gilligan, A. (2011) 'The gentle, trusting Britain that lives forever in an Ealing Comedy', *The Daily Telegraph*, 29 July.

Green, I. (1983) 'Ealing: In the comedy frame', in J. Curran and V. Porter (eds), *British Cinema History*, London: Weidenfeld & Nicolson.

Harper, S. and Porter, V. (2003) *British Cinema of the 1950s: The Decline of Deference*, Oxford: Oxford University Press.

Kemp, P. (1991) *Lethal Innocence: The Cinema of Alexander Mackendrick*, London: Methuen.

Landy, M. (1991) *British Genres: Cinema and Society, 1930–1960*, New Jersey: Princeton University Press.

——(2000) 'The other side of paradise: British cinema from an American perspective', in J. Ashby and A. Higson (eds), *British Cinema: Past and Present*, London: Routledge.

Linehan, G. (2011) 'My *Today* programme ambush', *The Guardian*, 8 June.

Mackillop, I. and N. Sinyard (eds) (2003) *British Cinema of the 1950s: A Celebration*, Manchester: Manchester University Press.

Macnab, G. (2011) 'The shadow cast by Ealing comedies is no laughing matter', *The Independent*, 15 July.

McArthur, C. (ed.) (1982) *Scotch Reels: Scotland in Cinema and Television*, London: British Film Institute.

Medhurst, A. (2007) *A National Joke: Popular Comedy and English Cultural Identities*, London and New York: Routledge.

Muir, S. (2010) *Studying Ealing Studios*, Leighton Buzzard: Auteur.

Patterson, J. (2004) 'The Coen Brothers should have left *The Ladykillers* alone', *The Guardian*, 29 March.

Perry, G. (1981) *Forever Ealing: A Celebration of the Great British Film Studio*, London: Pavilion/Michael Joseph.

Porter, V. (2001) 'The hegemonic turn: Film comedies in 1950s Britain', *Journal of Popular British Cinema* 4: 81–94.

Pulleine, T. (1997) 'A song and dance at the local: Thoughts on Ealing', in R. Murphy (ed.), *The British Cinema Book*, London: British Film Institute.

Richards, J. (1997) *Films and British National Identity: From Dickens to Dad's Army*, Manchester: Manchester University Press.

Ritchie, C. (2010) 'England? Whose England? Selling Albion in comic cinema', *Comedy Studies* 1.1: 33–42.

Rolinson, D. (2003) '"If they want culture, they pay": Consumerism and alienation in 1950s comedies', in I. Mackillop and N. Sinyard (eds), *British Cinema of the 1950s: A Celebration*, Manchester: Manchester University Press.

Stokes, J. (1999) *On Screen Rivals: Cinema and Television in the United States and Britain*, London: Macmillan.

Sweet, M. (2011) 'Parochial? Watch again … ', *The Guardian*, 22 July.

Tynan, K. (1951) 'Film Review', *The Evening Standard*, 9 September.

—— (1953) *Alec Guinness*, London: Rockliff.

—— (1955) 'Ealing: The studio in suburbia' and 'Ealing's way of life', in *Films and Filming*, November and December.

Williams, T. (1992) 'The repressed fantastic in *Passport to Pimlico*', in W.W. Dixon (ed.), *Re-Viewing British Cinema, 1900–1992*, New York: SUNY Press.

—— (2000) *Structures of Desire: British Cinema 1939–55*, New York: SUNY Press.

6   'From adolescence into maturity'

The film comedy of the Boulting brothers

Alan Burton

> The Boulting Brothers are specialists in irreverence. For film-makers it is a very healthy
> specialisation and they have done well with it.
>
> (*The Manchester Guardian* 15 August 1959)

Identical twin brothers John and Roy Boulting were an important independent force in
British cinema from the late 1930s through to the mid-1970s. In a famous assessment,
critic Raymond Durgnat labelled the brothers 'earnest evangelicals', their serious wartime
films *Pastor Hall* (1940), *Thunder Rock* (1942), *Desert Victory* (1943) and *Journey Together*
(1945) displaying a progressive idealism, with later post-war features such as *Fame is
the Spur* (1947), *The Guinea Pig* (1948) and *Seven Days to Noon* (1950) continuing to
function as moral dramas (Durgnat 1970: 234).[1] In the mid-1950s, after a period of
working for other producers on pictures such as *High Treason* (1951), *Singlehanded*
(1953) and *Seagulls Over Sorrento* (1954), the Boultings returned to independence and
artistic freedom, once again settled in their own Charter Productions, announcing they
were 'in the mood for comedy' ('Boulting Brothers prefer private progress', *Films and
Filming*, December 1955: 21). However, they didn't turn their back on significant
themes, declaring:

> We have sung our film 'songs of social significance' with a dreadful seriousness
> and, in the process, discovered, with Bernard Shaw, that the force most destructive of
> injustice and ignorance and pomp, is wit. You may call our comic style, then, a
> movement from adolescence into maturity.
>
> (Conrad 1959: 7)

The reference to Shaw is apposite, both in the sense that much of the comedy of the
Boultings is informed by a social purpose *and* derived from a literary tradition which
found some of its most eloquent expressions on the stage. The first half of the 20th
century, especially since 1920, has been appreciated as a Silver Age for theatrical
comedy, a period in which playwrights such as Somerset Maugham, Noël Coward and
Terence Rattigan recaptured the great English comic tradition established during
the Restoration. The over-riding style was a comedy of manners blended with satire,

located in sophisticated society, and described by one theatrical historian in the following terms:

> Its ideas are frequently very amusing, its situations resulting from clash of character highly diverting, its plots hilarious and its lines smoothly slick as the cocktail lounges and London flats in which so much of it takes place.
>
> (Reynolds 1949: 161)

The fundamental approach of stage comedy of the interwar period is thus discerned as a 'stream of clever talk flowing over the river-bed of an adroitly managed intrigue', and found at its most successful in Merton Hodge's *The Wind and the Rain* (1933), Rattigan's *French Without Tears* (1936) and Coward's *Easy Virtue* (first staged in London in 1926) and *Blithe Spirit* (1941) (Reynolds 1949). The stage farce, a strong influence on the Boultings, also belonged to this tradition, and occupied the same space in the social spectrum; but while spectacularly commercial at its best, as with *Tons of Money* (1922), *Rookery Nook* (1930) and *Banana Ridge* (1938), lacking clear social commentary, the farce failed to attract as much attention from serious drama critics.[2]

The comedy films of the Boulting brothers, in their interweaving of satire, social comment and farce, conform to an established literary tradition. This distances them from an alternative vulgar, Music Hall tradition which was prominent in British film comedy in the 1930s, but was disappearing in its purest form from British screens in the 1950s when veteran performers such as Frank Randle, Arthur Lucan's Old Mother Riley and The Crazy Gang were completing the last of their films.[3] However, as disappointed critics often complained, many of the Boulting comedies leavened the supposed sophistication with large doses of physical comedy and simple innuendo in an effort to broaden the appeal of the films. This of course was part of the structure and identity of farce and largely responsible for steering the drama critic from taking this form too seriously; a situation echoed in the critical response to many of the Boulting pictures. It has in fact become commonplace to claim the Boultings as makers of satirical comedies, but this distorts the picture, overemphasising the satirical thrust of many of their films, ignoring the centrality of other styles of 'sophisticated' comedy, and wilfully leaving out the sex comedies that occupied the Brothers in the latter years. The following survey restricts itself to an examination of the contemporary critical reception of the Boulting comedies. There is insufficient space to interrogate closely any individual film or group of films; rather the intention is to reveal the critical ambivalence regarding the nature and identity of the brothers' approach to humour in the cinema: a cinema in which satire was seen to have played a far less pronounced role than is often credited.

First, though, a necessary observation. Several writers have argued for the ideological nature of British screen comedy in the 1950s. The war film and the comedy are commonly appreciated as the two main popular genres and Vincent Porter has pointed to the 'comparative absence of contemporary dramas and melodramas among Britain's most popular films' in this decade, which 'suggests that audiences came to terms with the new values of the post-war consensus by absorbing them obliquely from comedies and war films' (Porter 2001: 81). The Boulting films of the 1940s were supportive of the wartime consensus and the comedies, in their turn, can be understood in terms of the impact of modernising tendencies in the 1950s and 1960s on the social and political ideals thrown-up in the immediate post-war settlement. Christine Geraghty has seen British film comedies of the period as broadly resisting modernity, exhibiting the 'curious quality of being both stultifying and rebellious and that, when faced with the conflict between the traditional and the modern, they revert to the traditional in a way that blocks off the challenges and risks that comedy can present' (Geraghty 2000: 56). Dave Rolinson has observed an opposing tendency, suggesting the defining theme of 1950s comedy to be 'consensus and its breakdown through the alienating individualism of consumerism', wherein 'consumerism is the enemy of consensus, an alienating presence impinging on the value of work and, through the individualising agency of television, the domestic space' (Rolinson 2003: 87 and 88). In these terms, Boulting comedy films such as *Private's Progress* (1956) and *Rotten to the Core* (1965) make a nostalgic yet complex reference to an idealised wartime experience; while films such as *I'm All Right Jack* (1959) and *Heavens Above!* (1963) strive to expose the empty sham of the materialist 1950s and 1960s, indexed through such consumerist devices as advertising and television.[4] It is in such social-historical terms that the Boultings' films have been largely understood, and in turn lending a greater emphasis on the place of satire in their cinema.

The three 'biggest box-office attractions' in Britain in 1954 were the comedies *Doctor in the House*, *Trouble in Store* and *The Belles of St. Trinian's* (*Kinematograph Weekly*, 16 December 1954), and the following year the brothers embarked on a long run of humorous pictures.[5] Between 1955 and 1974 the Boultings made 13 comedies out of a total of 16 productions across the period. While never observing a pure style, the films covered the range of farce, satire and sex comedy, and drew some cohesion through casting regular star performers like Ian Carmichael, Terry-Thomas and Peter Sellers, and character players such as Ian Bannen, Miles Malleson, Raymond Huntley, Thorley Walters, Cecil Parker, Irene Handl, Victor Maddern and Kenneth Griffith. Regular contributors to the script, alongside the two brothers, were Frank Harvey and Jeffrey Dell. As they had done throughout their careers, John and Roy alternated the roles of director and producer, with Roy taking responsibility for shooting the films which lent most towards farce and sex comedy, and John directing the bulk of the productions that were characterised by satire. The uncompromising Boulting brothers, in their own admission 'bloody-minded', had always raised eyebrows with their film-making and courted controversy, and this persisted with their comedies, several of which led to disputes, legal wrangles and press interest.[6]

The entry into comedy for the Boultings came with *Josephine and Men*, released in November 1955, directed by Roy and starring Glynis Johns, Donald Sinden, Peter Finch and veteran performer of stage and screen Jack Buchanan. The screenplay was provided by Nigel Balchin from his own story, with additional material from Roy Boulting and Frank Harvey. The drama and presentation closely approximated to the sophisticated stage comedies of the period, dealing with the romantic complications arising from the heroine's love of two men. While finding the picture 'an amusing evening's entertainment', the critic at *Films and Filming* alluded to the style's dated theatrical origins (December 1955: 17). The reviewer at *The Times* was even less forgiving, believing the farce too restrained, the audience left patiently waiting 'for someone to lose his trousers', the whole 'untidy, unresolved, amusing and entertaining in fits and starts' (14 November 1955). While *Monthly Film Bulletin* found nothing to amuse it in the film, declaring the script 'limp', the direction lacking sparkle and the performances 'dogged' (December 1955: 181). The modern viewer is unlikely to quibble with these views when confronting what is a mannered and old-fashioned comedy-drama. The brothers returned to this traditional style of comedy some years later with *Happy is the Bride*, released in February 1958 and starring Ian Carmichael, Janette Scott, Cecil Parker and Terry-Thomas. This was adapted by Roy Boulting and Jeffrey Dell from the classic stage comedy *Quiet Wedding*, written by Esther McCracken and filmed expertly by Anthony Asquith and released in 1941. The comedy dealt with a young couple caught up in the ever-escalating arrangements for their wedding. The reviewer at *The Times* appreciated a 'number of humorous moments, and a few very funny ones' (24 February 1958); but *Monthly Film Bulletin* remained hostile to Roy Boulting's handling of this type of traditional material, finding the film a 'badly managed affair, lacking real wit, style or grace', merely a 'frantic remake [with] only a fraction of the earlier film's virtues' (February 1958: 21). The final film before the Boultings gave up for good on this type of comedy was *A French Mistress*, released in September 1960 and self-described in the credit sequence as a 'romp'. Set in a boy's public school and dealing with the disruption on both pupils and masters wrought by the arrival of a young and pretty new teacher of French, the film was based on a popular stage play by Robert Monro and dealt with conventional farcical material centred on mistaken identities and cross-purposes.[7] Starring Agnès Laurent, Cecil Parker, James Robertson Justice and Ian Bannen, the film was again scripted by Roy Boulting and Jeffrey Dell who appeared dogged in their determination to succeed with this style of humour. The review in *The Times* was supportive, finding *A French Mistress* a 'Good Farcical Comedy' (3 September 1960); however, other viewpoints were more critical, with *The Guardian* dismissing the film as a 'predictable little frolic' (3 September 1960), and Dai Vaughan at *Films and Filming* also yawning in boredom at its conventional handling of sex business and foreigners in a story that wavered between the 'feeble and the offensive' (October 1960: 29).[8] The reviewer in *Monthly Film Bulletin*, while finding the picture 'a mildly amusing, quintessentially English farce, with stock material and jokes', bemoaned the lack of any genuine relation to real life, noting the time had come 'to pension off, even in farce, these phoney English public schools, fire-eating colonels, bird-watching vicars, sporty cane-brandishers and all the other dearly loved images of "the English as they see themselves"' (October 1960: 142). It was advice which, for the time being, the Boulting brothers heeded.

Of course, by the time of the release of *A French Mistress*, the Boultings had already achieved considerable success with comedies that did connect with contemporary British life, in what have been perceived as popular satirical pictures that took a swipe at national institutions such as the Army, the diplomatic service, and industrial relations. Interviewed in 1959, the brothers alluded to the commercial failure of *Josephine and Men*, acknowledging the film's 'high comedy' as 'just a little bit too sophisticated, a little bit too remote from the understanding of a mass cinema audience', and subsequently recognising the need within a story for 'a field of reference with which a mass audience is immediately familiar' (Conrad 1959: 7). This type of thinking was first applied to *Private's Progress*, a military comedy set during the Second World War, directed by John Boulting and scripted by John with Frank Harvey from a story by Alan Hackney. It starred Ian Carmichael, Richard Attenborough, Dennis Price and Terry-Thomas, was released in February 1956, achieved great commercial success in Britain and did well overseas. In explaining this, the Boultings pointed to the shared experience of military life for the many that had served in the war or subsequently completed national service, and for whom 'No comic absurdities could be too far-fetched' (Conrad 1959). In effect, this meant a significant shift in comic approach, whereby the intention became 'the use of *satire* within a frame of *broad* comic constructs' (Wells 2000: 49, italics in original). Reviews were decidedly mixed and the critical response did not match the popular enthusiasm for the film. A very short review in *Films and Filming* lumped *Private's Progress* in with routine service comedies such as *Worm's Eye View* (1951), *Dry Rot* and *Sailor Beware* (both 1956) (April 1956); while an even briefer piece in *The Manchester Guardian* complained of a shuffling central performance from Carmichael (17 April 1956). More considered criticism complained about the uneven structure and tone of the film. 'Inconsistent in mood, untidy in form, restless and possessed of the urge to cram in any number of inconsequent scenes and characters' was how *The Times* saw it (20 February 1956). In a common assessment, the dominant comedic style of the film was appreciated as farce, overbearing a note of 'satirical mockery'; an approach later neatly described as 'the familiar Boulting Brothers' formula of uninhibited contemporary satire' (*Monthly Film Bulletin*, April 1959: 42). Gavin Lambert acknowledged the material's opportunity for 'real satire', but 'writing and direction choose the less demanding level of affable farce' (*Monthly Film Bulletin*, April 1956: 44). Lambert pursued the same line in *Sight and Sound*, believing the comedy 'too mild, even too affectionate, for satire. Some of it amuses; none of it cuts deep' (April 1956: 199). It would become standard for contemporary reviewers to assert that any genuine satire in the comedies was lost to broader styles of humour, dinting claims for seriousness and sophistication.[9] As expressed by Wilfred Sheed, it was the Boultings' practice 'never to pass up a laugh however much it weakens the film as a whole' (1963, quoted in Wells 2000: 48).

Signed to a six-picture contract, Carmichael, as well as several others from the previous film, was put into the next two 'satirical' comedies in quick succession. *Brothers in Law* directed by Roy was released in March 1957 and adapted by Roy Boulting, Frank Harvey and Jeffrey Dell from the novel by Henry Cecil. *Lucky Jim* was directed by John and released in August 1957, adapted by Patrick Campbell and Jeffrey Dell from the popular novel by Kingsley Amis. The dominant note in both films was once again farce, something which at this early stage in the Boulting comedies readily attached itself to Carmichael's comedic style and persona, 'a kind of sophisticated intimate revue butt' as Gavin Lambert put it after witnessing his performance in *Private's Progress* (*Sight and Sound*, April 1956: 199). The source novel for *Brothers in Law* itself was of the mildest satire, described in one review as offering 'gay and entertaining reading' (*Times Literary Supplement*, 25 February 1955), and the film version, in detailing the privileged upper-middle-class world of the law courts in which young professional men about town could unselfconsciously utter, without irony, such phrases as 'Gosh! Jolly good, bags of briefs', retained this affec- tionate tone. Roy explained at the time that *Private's Progress* was basically a 'satire with a helping of slapstick', while *Brothers in Law* was 'pure comedy' ('Law and laughter with the Boultings', *Kinematograph Weekly*, 5 July 1956: 45). The critic at *The Times*, while claiming with a banner headline a 'Film satire at the expense of the law', conceded in the body of the review that the comedy was drawn from the 'physical mishaps of farce'

(4 March 1957). Penelope Houston writing in *Sight and Sound* found the treatment only 'mildly iconoclastic', matching the book's quality of 'urbane extravagance, its appreciation of the jarring encounters between the perfectly regulated legal machine and the fallible individual' (Spring 1957: 212). *Monthly Film Bulletin* found *Brothers in Law* 'the most enjoyable British comedy for some time', with script and performances 'unusually sophisticated'. The review noted though Carmichael's 'tendency towards theatrical, rather than cinematic mannerisms' and predictably decried the presence of slapstick in which the lead character was too often called upon to 'stumble and tumble pointlessly' (April 1957: 42). This was a typical critical attitude towards farce, but, relatively untainted by the lowest forms of humour, reviewers were pleased to acknowledge *Brothers in Law's* 'persistent good taste' (*The Manchester Guardian*, 2 March 1957). *Lucky Jim* derived from a more bitingly satirical novel about a young probationary academic caught up in the atrophied attitudes of academia; however, once again the Boultings tended to dampen the satire in favour of farce and the contrast is therefore particularly illustrative of the film-makers' approach to comedy. The film had its *première* as the opening event at the Edinburgh Festival, where the reporter for *The Manchester Guardian* witnessed 'the satire of Kingsley Amis's novel [waging] a losing battle against the conventions of British film comedy', and, echoing other reviews, claiming a reprehensible degeneration into the 'broadest farce' (20 August 1957). The report of the *première* in *The Times* found Ian Carmichael's characterisation of Jim Dixon 'more likeable – but less interesting – than the original'; the film as a whole 'more farcical and less bitter than the book' (23 August 1957). Penelope Houston writing in *Monthly Film Bulletin* felt the film 'broadens the comedy into farce ... turns the whole thing into an amiable joke', adding significantly, 'from the screen version, with its thoroughly traditional humours, one would never suspect that the novel had become the symbol of a new movement in English fiction' (November 1957: 135).

A clearer, surer turn to satire came in the next comedy, *Carlton-Browne of the F.O.*, released in March 1959, although it was Roy who was mainly involved in the creative side of its production, co-writing and untypically co-directing the film with Jeffrey Dell. The topicality of the film's comedy – the world's imperial powers are focused on the tiny island of Gallardia which has discovered it is mineral rich – had the result of bringing the political dimension into sharper focus and made the satire more apparent. However, Roy claimed no more for it than a 'gentle dig at some of our modern stupidities' (*The Times*, 27 June 1959). *Monthly Film Bulletin* still bemoaned the odd 'lavatory joke' and 'some facile caricature', but acknowledged that the targets of Cold War *realpolitik* and post-Suez colonialism were subjects that could not easily be dismissed (April 1959: 42). *Carlton-Browne of the F.O.* was the first Boulting comedy since *Josephine and Men* in 1955 not to star Ian Carmichael, giving the lead role over to Terry-Thomas, in the view of *Monthly Film Bulletin* a 'subdued, neatly-timed performance' (April 1959: 42), and who endowed the diplomatic servant with a sharper, caddish edge, in place of the former's bumbling naivety. A minor diplomatic incident occurred when *Carlton-Browne of the F.O.* was selected by the British Film Producers' Association and the Federation of British Film Makers for screening at the Moscow Film Festival. The view of the Foreign Office was sought, which, in a clumsy expression, 'thought it was not very good acceptable material'. John and Roy were livid, questioning whether 'there is in fact a Carlton-Browne at the Foreign Office?' (*The Manchester Guardian*, 27 June 1959). As a result the film was withdrawn from the festival, and the brothers regarded the approach to the Foreign Office a 'gross impertinence' (*The Manchester Guardian*, 29 June 1959).

Peter Sellers made his first appearance for the brothers in *Carlton-Browne of the F.O.*, playing the self-serving Prime Minister of Gallardia. He made a more significant impact in the next Boulting comedy *I'm All Right Jack*, released in August 1959 and more widely received as a genuine satire.[10] The film was a direct descendant of *Private's Progress*, with the same writing team of John Boulting, Frank Harvey and Alan Hackney, with John once again directing, and Ian Carmichael, Terry-Thomas, Richard Attenborough, Dennis Price and Miles Malleson reprising their characters from the earlier film. The setting was switched from the Army to a factory, the target of the film became trade unions and big business, and the Boultings enjoyed just as big a hit. Declaring the brothers' films as 'lightly satirical explorations of the contemporary scene', the critic in *The Times* assured his readership that *I'm All Right Jack* was 'thoroughly good-natured, verging on farce but generally stopping just short' (17 August 1959). Most reviews accepted the evenness of the film, balancing 'the restrictive practices of trade unions' with 'the folly of the employers' (*The Manchester Guardian*, 15 August 1959). This was certainly the intention of the film-makers, who were out to tar everyone with the same brush, and declared it with a touch of hyperbole 'the most cynical film ever made' (*The Manchester Guardian*, 7 January 1959).[11] An inkling of trouble to come for the Boultings manifested itself early in January 1959 when the production of the film was suspended following claims by the Association of Cinematograph, Television and Allied Technicians that the Boultings were in arrears with their union dues. A temporary settlement to the dispute was reached and the film was completed. However, the Boultings found themselves in four years of legal wrangles, centring on the issue of whether the brothers, in their capacity as managing directors of a film production company and therefore employers, could be compelled to be members of the trade union. John and Roy did not believe that it was a coincidence that the makers of *I'm All Right Jack* were targeted on this matter when film-makers such as Herbert Wilcox, Ian Dalrymple and Michael Powell who served in a similar capacity had no pressure brought to bear on them (*The Times*, 18 June 1960). The case was eventually decided in the High Court against the Boultings, who later lost an appeal. Prepared to take the matter to the House of Lords, a settlement was eventually reached whereby the union accepted that those serving an executive producer function could suspend their membership. John declared this a 'victory for commonsense' (*The Guardian*, 20 January 1964).[12] The whole complicated saga was a curious coupling of *Brothers in Law* with *I'm All Right Jack*.

Sellers earned great plaudits for his performance as the idealistic but blinkered shop steward Fred Kite in *I'm All Right Jack*, winning Best British Actor at the annual British Film Academy Awards. Critics were less impressed with the actor's contribution in the next Boulting comedy *Heavens Above!*, in which he played a wrongly assigned vicar who brings primitive Christianity to a traditional English parish. The film was released in May 1963, written by Frank Harvey and John Boulting from an idea by Malcolm Muggeridge, and, unusually, co-directed by John and Roy. Expecting a sharper critique in the mould of *I'm All Right Jack*, reviewers were disappointed. *Monthly Film Bulletin* declared the new film 'Way off target as a satire', and once again found fault with 'the amount of schoolboy smut it manages to incorporate', all pointing 'to real desperation' (July 1963: 95). The film critic at *The Times* chose to head his column 'A serious film

Figure 6.1   Peter Sellers on the picket line in *I'm All Right Jack* (1959). Image courtesy of Canal + Image UK.

comedy goes wrong', going on to deny the film's validity as satire and decrying an 'irrelevant plunge into farce' (23 May 1963). Similar sentiments attached themselves to *Rotten to the Core*, directed by John, written by Jeffrey Dell, Roy Boulting, John Warren and Len Heath, and released in July 1965. Taking some inspiration from the 1963 'Great Train Robbery', the film was a caper comedy detailing an attempt by a gang of crooks to steal an Army payroll. The film contained many familiar faces from the Boulting stock company and featured newcomers Anton Rodgers and Charlotte Rampling as the gang leader and his girl.[13] *Rotten to the Core's* limited claim for satire came from the gang's efforts to apply Prime Minister Harold Wilson's modernising rhetoric regarding the 'White Heat of Technology' to the business of crime, with additional swipes at James Bond and the emerging mod scene in Britain in the mid-1960s. *The Times* found the film little more than a 'desperate collection of crime-comedy clichés'; 'a rather alarming offering from what has for so long been Britain's foremost comedy team' (15 July 1965). Ian Wright at *The Guardian* found it a 'poor successor to "I'm all right, Jack"' [sic], 'a rag-bag of humorous and satirical material' (16 July 1965). It was pointed out in more than one review that the Boultings' film failed to rise above the routine standard of recent British crime comedies such as *Two Way Stretch* (1960) and *The Wrong Arm of the Law* (1963), which at least had the advantage of starring Peter Sellers. The main problem for these later Boulting comedies was that satire had moved on considerably in Britain since the 1950s when the brothers had established their loose approach to the comedic style. In his review of *Heavens Above!*, critic Raymond Durgnat pointed to the 'meaner, sharper jabs of TWTWTW', against which 'the Boultings' farcical tone has a slightly old-hat feel' (*Films and Filming*, July 1963: 23).[14]

In their final three comedies, all awarded 'X' certificates restricting audiences to adults only, the Boultings turned away from any obvious satire and embraced the new trend for sex themes, which had been generated in the 'sexual revolution' of the mid-1960s. Especially in the latter two pictures, this allowed the brothers to be uninhibited in their engagement with farce and related comic styles, and ultimately proved to be the swansong for their joint filmmaking. *The Family Way*, released in December 1966, was co-produced and co-directed by John and Roy, with a screenplay by Bill Naughton from his original stage drama *All in Good Time*, and additional writing credits for Roy and Jeffrey Dell. In a curious blend of Northern working-class realism, (the film is set in Bolton), and swinging 1960s permissiveness, it dealt with a honeymooning young couple's inability to consummate their marriage while temporarily residing in the home of his parents. Reviews were respectful. Finding it a 'sincere' and 'sympathetic' film, critics were sometimes surprised that the Boultings, usually associated with irreverence, had managed an 'understated' treatment of a delicate theme (*Monthly Film Bulletin*, February 1967: 26). Some thought the film 'stodgily made' (*The Times*, 22 December 1966), even 'stagey' (*The Guardian*, 17 December 1966), but there was widespread praise for the performances, especially John Mills and Marjorie Rhodes as the groom's parents who have surprising revelations about their own honeymoon.[15] It was a considerable return to form for the Boulting brothers who subsequently moved onto the hip scene unfolding in London in the later 1960s with another adaptation of a hit play, Terence Frisby's *There's a Girl in My Soup* (1970).[16] The film was directed by Roy, co-produced by John and the American Mike Frankovich, with a screenplay by Frisby. Where the approach had seemed fresh and restrained in *The Family Way*, it now felt forced, and not a little embarrassing for critics to witness Peter Sellers as an aging Casanova become smitten by a 1960s 'chick' in the delectable form of Goldie Hawn. Once more, Roy's direction was criticised for being 'stodgy' (*The Times*, 24 December 1970), and, in reference to an extended sequence set in France, more 'suet pudding' than 'soufflé' (*The Observer*, 3 January 1971). Margaret Tarratt at *Films and Filming* was turned off by the 'laboured farce' and 'lavatorial innuendo', believing 'the sex comedy genre does not sit easily in an English setting' (June 1971: 68). Accommodatingly, the Boultings switched the location, for what would be their final comedy, wholly to France. *Soft Beds, Hard Battles* was released in January 1974, directed by Roy and co-written with Leo Marks, who had previously contributed to the controversial script for the Boultings' thriller *Twisted Nerve* (1968). It was a troubled production: almost abandoned in the face of a blacking threat from the trade union following the Boultings' role in the sale of British Lion and the consequent jeopardy to Shepperton Studios; and with additional problems arising from a reluctant star, Peter Sellers, who was scheduled to play six roles in the picture and around whom the film was built ('Boulting threat to halt films', *The Guardian*, 19 March 1973; Roy Boulting, 'What happened after the cliffhanger', *Films and Filming*, March 1974: 24–5). The picture when it eventually appeared was described by the Boultings as 'the bawdiest film we've ever made' (*The Times*, 26 January 1974). Set in a Parisian brothel during the Second World War in which the Madame and her girls are recruited into the Resistance,[17] it attracted a predictable response from critics who found in it a new low in the preferred humour of the brothers. For Gordon Gow at *Films and Filming* it was 'quite awful, not to say ghastly'

(June 1974: 52); David McGillivray at *Monthly Film Bulletin* warned his readers that 'anyone hoping for even a dash of the comic brilliance of *I'm All Right Jack* will be sadly disappointed' (February 1974: 33); Derek Malcolm at *The Guardian* found it 'dreadful': 'I can't think how it happened' (24 January 1974); while *The Times* pronounced that 'low comedy comes no lower' (1 February 1974). It was an ignoble end for the Boultings to two decades of making comedy pictures.

In a generous view of satire in popular cinema, Raymond Durgnat makes the distinction between 'superior' and 'defensive' forms. The former appeals to a social snobbery, was derived from traditions of the comedy stage, could be accepted as wit and tended to be preferred by critics for its 'sophistication'. The latter drew on a broader comedic style which to the 'unattuned critic' could be mistaken for 'ordinary humour or knockabout'. Despite a limited persistence with the 'sophisticated' approach in *Josephine and Men*, *Happy is the Bride* and *A French Mistress*, and arguably unrecognised as such in *Brothers in Law*, the Boultings found greater success with the 'defensive' mode, put to best commercial advantage in *Private's Progress* and *I'm All Right Jack*. For Durgnat, such an approach is a 'benevolent' form of satire in which the audience 'recognises itself, and laughs at itself' (1965: 10, 14); evidence for which is offered in the numerous letters the Boultings received following the release of *Private's Progress*, claiming the producers must have been thinking of 'their particular unit' while writing the script (Conrad 1959: 7). To engage the popular audience, the Boultings imported less sophisticated forms of comedy into their films, but in nature and presentation derived from the marginally superior style of farce rather than Music Hall. This was consistently alluded to in the reviews, usually as an element of impurity undermining the more acceptable and serious satire. Virtually a lone voice, film director J.P. (Paddy) Carstairs was prepared to accept a synthesis, finding *Private's Progress* 'broad but wonderfully sophisticated' (1958: 9). In a more stringent contemporary view of British film comedy, Ian Johnson assessed satire 'as a form of humour which is a means of escaping or lessening a threat by ridiculing the threat itself'. In applying this test to the recent 'satirical romps' of the Boultings, he asked himself: 'How many people snug in their two-and-sixpenny stalls are concerned about the army (these days), the law, the universities, or even diplomacy?' For Johnson, such subjects lacked popular political relevance. In his view, *I'm All Right Jack* was in fact the only properly satirical film of the period as it touched a 'truly controversial nerve' (1963: 52, 53).[18] In their defence, the Boultings made no great claims for a satirical cinema, suggesting nothing more than a 'dislike for cant, humbug and hypocrisy' (Conrad 1959: 31), and as such their comedies work on the level of deflating pomposity, of exposing self-interest and of puncturing privilege. Neither did John and Roy claim any special insight into the national sense of humour, professing not to know 'what makes the British laugh'. Instead, their approach to comedy was dependent on a modest, simple fact: 'We only know what makes the Boulting Brothers laugh' (Conrad 1959: 7).

Notes

1 *Pastor Hall*, *Thunder Rock*, *Desert Victory*, *Journey Together*, *Fame is the Spur* and *Seven Days to Noon* all receive critical attention in Burton, O'Sullivan and Wells (2000); while *The Guinea Pig* is discussed in Aldgate (1983).

2 The first two farces were filmed in 1930, and the latter followed in 1942, all by the famous Aldwych team.

3 For Richard Dacre (1997), the literary and Music Hall make up the twin traditions of British screen comedy. In a class-inflected reading of British film comedy, Ian Johnson (1963: 50) claimed that a proletarian tradition was losing out to 'lower-middle or upper-working-class suburban subjects'. The Boultings claimed not to like British film comedy of the 1930s, finding it 'too broad for our own taste' (Conrad 1959: 31).

4 In his political capacity as an active Liberal, John Boulting regarded the main task of radicals being 'to reconcile the benefits of the Welfare State with the rights of the individual' (*The Guardian*, 6 July 1960).

5 In explaining their decisive shift to comedy, the Boultings put it this way: 'Our invasion of the comedy field was only a response to a challenge: we were tired of hearing, "Yes, the Boultings know their stuff, but they're so intense, too serious – no sense of humour!"' (Conrad 1959: 31).

6 In a late interview, John was reported as saying: 'Our chief source of pride is that we've managed to aggravate, provoke, irritate, annoy and perhaps stimulate practically every side of the business' (*The Times*, 26 January 1974).

7 In his discussion, Wells (2000: 51) treats *A French Mistress* as a satire.

8 It was becoming common for British comedies to import continental actresses to exude sexiness and Ian Johnson blamed this for the 'comic film's lewd descent in recent years' (1963: 52). The issue of 'foreignness' in *A French Mistress* is explored in Allen (2010).

9 The most recent analysis of the film sees it as a parody and satire of 'national mythologies enshrined in the British cinema of the Second World War' (Landy 2000: 176).

10 Sellers contracted to the Boultings in January 1959 to make five pictures (*The Times*, 7 January 1959).

11 In a later observation, Kenneth Tynan saw this even-handedness as a weakness: 'What vitiates their films as satire is their determination to play both ends against the middle, and call the result integrity' (*The Observer*, 18 July 1965).

12 In the various reports of the court proceedings, it was revealed that union disputes, usually centring on demarcation, had affected the production of *Seven Days to Noon* and *Josephine and Men*. For later assessments of *I'm All Right Jack* see Aldgate (1983) and Stead (1996).

13 In the film, Rodgers is called upon to play several masquerades, a spy chief, a German general, and – in an effective in-joke – a principal doctor at a health clinic made up to look like a Boulting.

14 'TWTWTW' was the acronym for *That Was The Week That Was*, the popular and controversial weekly satirical show broadcast on British television in 1962–3. Stanley Kubrick's British-made *Dr. Strangelove or: How I Learned to Stop Worrying and Love the Bomb* (1964) would also establish a new standard for satirical cinema. Durgnat returned to reconsider *Heavens Above!* a quarter of a century later (see Durgnat 2000).

15 Issues of adaptation, censorship and reception of *The Family Way* are treated in Aldgate (2000).

16 By the time shooting on the film began, the play had been on stage in the West End for four years.

17 Leo Marks had been a code-breaker in World War II and was intimately acquainted with the European Resistance.

18 In his survey of British film comedy, Ian Johnson sees farce as a popular 'lower-middle/middle-middle class entertainment' (1963: 50).

Bibliography

Aldgate, A. (1983) 'Vicious circles: *I'm All Right Jack*', in J. Richards and A. Aldgate, *Best of British. Cinema and Society 1930–1970*, Oxford: Basil Blackwell.

——(2000) '"Obstinate humanity": The Boultings, the censors and courting controversy in the late-1960s', in Burton, A., O'Sullivan, T. and Wells, P. (eds) *The Family Way: The Boulting Brothers and Postwar British Film Culture*, Trowbridge: Flicks Books.

Allen, A. (2010) 'A French exchange: education as the cultural Interface in British comedies', *Journal of British Cinema and Television*, 7:3: 439–58.

Burton, A., O'Sullivan, T. and Wells, P. (eds) (2000) *The Family Way: The Boulting Brothers and Postwar British Film Culture*, Trowbridge: Flicks Books.

Carstairs, J.P. (1958) 'British laughter-makers', *Films and Filming*, January 1958: 9–10.

Conrad, D. (1959) 'What makes the British laugh?', *Films and Filming*, February: 7, 31.

Dacre, R. (1997) 'Traditions of British comedy', in R. Murphy (ed.), *The British Cinema Book*, London: BFI Publishing.

Durgnat, R. (1965) 'Raymond Durgnat's World of Comedy', in *Films and Filming*, August: 10–15.

——(1970) *A Mirror For England: British Movies from Austerity to Affluence*, London: Faber & Faber.

——(2000) 'St. Smallwood: Or, left of *Heavens Above!*', in A. Burton, T. O'Sullivan and P. Wells (eds), *The Family Way: The Boulting Brothers and Postwar British Film Culture*, Trowbridge: Flicks Books.

Geraghty, C. (2000) *British Cinema in the Fifties: Gender, Genre and The 'New Look'*, London: Routledge.

Johnson, I. (1963) 'Have the British a sense of humour?', in *Films and Filming*, March: 48–53.

Landy, M. (2000) 'Nation and imagi-nation in *Private's Progress*', in A. Burton, T. O'Sullivan and P. Wells (eds.), *The Family Way: The Boulting Brothers and Postwar British Film Culture*, Trowbridge: Flicks Books.

Porter, V. (2001) 'The hegemonic turn: Film comedies in 1950s Britain', in J. Chapman and C. Geraghty (eds), *Journal of Popular British Cinema*, 4: 81–94.

Reynolds, E. (1949) *Modern English Drama. A Survey of the Theatre from 1900*, London: George G. Harrap.

Richards, J. (1983) 'Old school ties: *The Guinea Pig*', in J. Richards and A. Aldgate, *Best of British. Cinema and Society 1930–1970*, Oxford: Basil Blackwell.

Rolinson, D. (2003) '"If they want culture, they pay": Consumerism and alienation in 1950s comedies', in I. Mackillop and N. Sinyard (eds), *British Cinema of the 1950s: A Celebration*, Manchester: Manchester University Press.

Stead, P. (1996) 'I'm All Right Jack', *History Today*, January: 49–54.

Wells, P. (2000) 'Comments, custard pies and comic cuts: The Boulting brothers at play, 1955–65', in A. Burton, T. O'Sullivan and P. Wells (eds), *The Family Way: The Boulting Brothers and Postwar British Film Culture*, Trowbridge: Flicks Books.

7   Margaret Rutherford and comic performance

Sarah Street

> There is something exhilarating about film-making because although the technique differs so much from the stage it has an intimate magic of its own. Unlike a play, in which you can grow into the part during rehearsals, in a film your reactions and emotions must be instantaneous. You must be precise and economical in your expressions remembering that fleeting changes of light and shade on the features are visible to everyone and not merely to the first row of the stalls.
>
> (Rutherford 1972: 80)

Commenting on the craft of film acting, Margaret Rutherford highlighted the need for precision and economy, attributes which might appear to be at odds with the larger-than-life, eccentric characters she often portrayed. For many years she was one of Britain's most respected character actresses on stage and screen, and this minute attention to the details of expression and gesture was at the heart of her iconic comic performances in many significant British films including *Blithe Spirit* (1945), *Miranda* (1948), *Passport to Pimlico* (1949), *The Happiest Days of Your Life* (1950), *The Importance of Being Earnest* (1952), *An Alligator Named Daisy* (1955), *I'm All Right Jack* (1959), and a series of films produced in the UK by MGM in the early 1960s in which she played Agatha Christie's Miss Marple (*Murder She Said* (1961), *Murder at the Gallop* (1963), *Murder Most Foul* and *Murder Ahoy* (both 1964)).

Until the Marple films, Rutherford was not identified with a particular British film comedy institutional brand or series. *Passport to Pimlico* was her only Ealing comedy; *The Happiest Days of Your Life* was her only Launder and Gilliat film, and *I'm All Right Jack* was her sole appearance in a Boulting brothers' film. Anthony Asquith, the director she worked with on five films (*Quiet Wedding* (1941), *The Demi-Paradise* (1943), *While the Sun Shines* (1947), *The Importance of Being Earnest* and *The VIPs* (1963)), was not particularly known for a consistent comic approach, and the films were spread over many years. Yet she was a quintessential British character actress whose theatre performances often led to the same parts in screen adaptations and whose performance style often combined contradictory elements that made good roles exceptional and contributed to a comic persona that transcended individual films. She found success on the screen when middle-aged. Physically quite large with a small mouth, large eyes and fleshy jowls, she was often cast as a spinster who was enthusiastic about a cause, activity or her profession, be it as a clairvoyant, professor, magistrate, governess or aunt. These roles provided scope for embellishment, at which Rutherford excelled in terms of inserting distinguished touches of lightness and shade to connote eccentricity, vulnerability or sensitivity. As Harper notes, along with actresses including Edie Martin, Katie Johnson, Joyce Grenfell and Irene Handl, Rutherford 'had more room for technical manoeuvre than the sexpots, whose narrative function was fixed' (2000: 99).

After directing Rutherford in *The Happiest Days of Your Life*, Frank Launder commented that she was an actress capable of creating 'great moments' on screen, transforming scripted lines in such a way that the hilarious impact on audiences exceeded all expectation (Rutherford 1972: 90). While her individual performances were exquisitely crafted, she frequently worked in productive symbiosis with celebrated British comedians including Alastair Sim, Robert Morley, Frankie Howerd, Peter Sellers and Norman Wisdom. The tradition Rutherford inhabited was a very British celebration of eccentricity. Comic theorist Henri Bergson (1956) characterised laughter and comedy in terms of providing a function of social correction, by working to restrain eccentricity through ridicule. What is notable about Rutherford is that on the contrary, rather than present eccentricity to be humiliated through laughter, her performances instead generate more positive affectionate, endearing attitudes towards her characters and as a key element of her appeal. This chapter will analyse particular comic 'moments' which exemplify the specificity of her sense of comic timing, gesture and the use of her body and voice to produce an expansive, affectionate portrayal of eccentricity. Clayton (2011) observes that 'an intention to amuse' is central to performances we recognise as 'comedic'. Rutherford's delivery of dialogue, her execution of physical comedy and response to other actors, exemplify that the essence of a comic performance is located in the specifics of its execution. The consequences of contradictory elements contained within the characters played by Rutherford, such as their association with disruption, anarchy, morality, eccentricity and stability, will also be explored in an attempt to place her roles and persona in a broader context, considering her brand of comic performance in relation to contemporary issues of gender, femininity, class and national identity.

Rutherford's first film role was in *Dusty Ermine* (1936) and she appeared in character roles in several subsequent films including *The Demi-Paradise*, *The Yellow Canary* (1943) and *English Without Tears* (1944). After working with her on *The Yellow Canary*, a spy thriller, Herbert Wilcox admired how she embellished her small, cameo part as an interfering passenger on an ocean liner by 'bringing light and shade into an ordinary situation and gave a very dramatic story the touch of lightness that it needed … You made a whimper and a sniff your own comment on a situation. I have never met anyone in my long experience so completely camera and audience unconscious' (Wilcox, quoted in Rutherford 1972: 83). In essence, Rutherford's tendency towards embellishment enhanced her command of the spaces in which her comic performances took place. Much in the spirit of Manny Farber's notion of the 'termite' actor (1962–3) who was able to carve out space from within, she enlivened even the most unpromising bit parts with delightful comic flourishes.

The first major role that fully distinguished her as a comic film actress was as Madame Arcati, a medium invited to an author's house to conduct a séance in *Blithe Spirit*, a role she had performed on stage with great success in Noël Coward's play which first opened in 1941. Although Madame Arcati is to some extent an eccentric figure of fun and is exploited by the sceptical author Charles Condomine (Rex Harrison) to provide him with material for one of his books, Rutherford brought out the integrity of her convictions, of her belief in the afterlife. In this role she developed key techniques of her comic performance style for the screen which involved combining physicality, precisely executed facial expression and expressive intensity. In spite of the temptation to play Madame Arcati simply as caricature, Rutherford gains comic effect from such elements while at the same time indicating that there is an essential goodness about her that exposes other characters' moral weaknesses and exploitative motives. This works in particular contradistinction to Charles who blatantly uses Madame Arcati but is forced to accept the reality of the spirit world when the ghost of his first wife materialises.

We hear about Madame Arcati before we see her when Charles advises Ruth (Constance Cummings), his second wife, to repress her laughter when Madame Arcati is conducting the séance to take place that evening in their house: 'You must be dead serious and if possible, a little intense. We can't hurt the old girl's feelings however funny she is.' The scene is followed by Madame Arcati cycling purposefully to the house, dressed in a plaid cape and red dress as she nods cheerfully to people she recognises on the route. The musical accompaniment creates a jaunty tone of comic expectation. These impressions are reinforced by comments made by Charles's friends whom we see in their car as they pass Madame Arcati on her bicycle on their way to the séance. One of them comments: 'She certainly is a strange woman. The vicar told me he saw her up on the Knowle on Midsummer Eve dressed in some sort of Indian robes. Apparently she's been a professional in London for years.' From this expansive introduction, a combination of dialogue description and the image of Madame Arcati cycling fast with her cape flying behind her, a particular tone of comic expectation is created around an eccentric 'professional' who is larger than life. This is further confirmed when she arrives at the house to conduct the séance, surprising them when she appears from the garden, using an unconventional entrance. She greets them breezily, and then her jaw drops quickly and closes in a fashion which was a typical Rutherford facial movement. The subsequent exchanges demonstrate her quick, animated facial expressions as she directs her attention to each person conveying a wide-eyed, intense yet caricatured persona of the exuberant, eccentric and enthusiastic medium. Pitted against Charles, Ruth and their guests who we know are all sceptical about the existence of an afterlife, Charles at one point saying that Madame Arcati must be a 'charlatan', Rutherford's performance immediately establishes the desired impression of someone who defies convention but in this situation is permitted to take control.

During the séance, Madame Arcati transforms herself into the medium in action, the role requiring Rutherford not only to be physical with her performance as she strides around the room in an assertive manner, with hands on hips and then arms above her head as she assesses how to create the best conditions for attracting spirits, but also to speak with very precise, authoritative diction. She turns off the lights so that the firelight creates flickering shadows on the back wall. As she moves out of view to the other side of the room, her own shadow forms a large silhouette on the wall; her corporeality has been transformed into a dark, spectral vision in seconds. In this way, as her red dress changes into a black shape looming large on the wall, her performance is expanded quite literally into another dimension. This uncanny, spectral 'doubling' also takes place in an aural sense. As she says a rhyme to attract the 'control', the dead child Daphne through whose agency she contacts spirits, the performance becomes further exaggerated, even sinister, as the séance develops and the 'control' delivers a rhyme through Madame Arcati. The sound of the child's voice coming from her lips creates a strange spectacle that borders on the grotesque. Since Rutherford's voice was very much an integral aspect of her comedic persona the intrusion of an 'unnatural' presence in this way seems incongruous. It creates a kind of odd break in the scene which combines comedy with horror. As Charles, Ruth and their guests become more and more drawn into the séance, their scepticism begins to dissolve, and the compelling nature of Rutherford's performance creates a cumulative effect of comic suspense for the characters as well as the audience. The stark contrast between her general domination of the scene through such movements and gestures, and the increasingly passive, incredulous characters witnessing the spectacle of the séance, serves to highlight the specificity of Rutherford's performance. Indeed, the success of her acting, the quality of her diction and the sparkling dialogue written by Coward conspire to produce an affectionate, comedic engagement with spiritualism. As I have argued elsewhere, this was all the more fascinating for contemporary audiences in the context of the Second World War (Street 2010: 37–38).

A comedy in which Rutherford plays a far less assertive character was Oscar Wilde's *The Importance of Being Earnest*. She had played Lady Bracknell in John Gielgud's stage production which toured Canada and then went to New York in 1947, but in the film she was cast as Miss Prism, Cecily's governess, who has a pivotal role at the end in unravelling the mystery around the real identity of Earnest. Miss Prism is played as a governess with a strong sense of duty and seriousness to make sure Cecily (Dorothy Tutin) is suitably instructed, while Rutherford's performance indicates that she is also a likeable, somewhat vulnerable figure with romantic longings that prompted her in the past to write a melodramatic novel. We gain a visual sense of this when we are first introduced to her as she calls for Cecily in the garden. We see her dropping her books and later fumbling with her pince-nez, gestures which indicate a lack of co-ordination but are an endearing counterpoint to the rigorous teaching regime she aspires to share with her pupil. The role is a much gentler one than Madame Arcati, even though the same respect for professionalism is maintained. This characterisation is further developed in Miss Prism's interactions with Dr. Chasuble (Miles Malleson), in whose company she becomes almost flirtatious as their admiration for each other becomes apparent, a situation which Cecily, who is clearly fond of Miss Prism, encourages. Touches such as the somewhat incongruous floral hat Miss Prism wears in some of the scenes demonstrate how costume is used to embellish character as her role as governess is tempered by a gentle, undemonstrative demeanour with an occasional flourish of abandon.

In the final 'where is that baby' scene, when Lady Bracknell (Edith Evans) confronts Miss Prism about the baby she lost when its perambulator was found containing the manuscript of Miss Prism's novel (described by Lady Bracknell as 'of more than usually revolting sentimentality'), she looks genuinely horrified at the memory of events 28 years ago. Her trauma continues as she confesses to having mistakenly placed the baby in a handbag, the manuscript in the perambulator and then leaving the handbag (containing baby Earnest) at Victoria Station. In all of this, Rutherford's performance exhibits many of the 'fleeting changes of light and shade' she considered to be integral to film acting (1972: 80), including the delight she expresses when the handbag is presented to her that switches to horror when Earnest, throwing his arms around her, mistakenly believes her to be his mother and she exclaims: 'I am unmarried!' Pitted against Lady Bracknell's bullying authoritarianism in this final scene Rutherford's performance brings out greater depths to Miss Prism as she confronts a past mistake with affecting remorse.

Other performances demonstrate a similar achievement of nuance within roles that might on first glance appear to offer limited scope for manoeuvre. The situations within which the characters were placed of course influenced the extent to which this was possible. The existence of Dr. Chasuble in *The Importance of Being Earnest* created an unusual romantic interest for a character played by Margaret Rutherford. In most of the other roles she is 'married' to her profession or enthusiasm and we hear little or nothing of her past life. The relative brevity of some of her scenes means that her performances are assisted by visual details that suggest complexity to roles that might otherwise appear stereotypical. Rutherford's only appearance in an Ealing comedy was in *Passport to Pimlico* as Professor Hatton-Jones, the historian who confirms the authenticity of a document discovered with ancient treasure in a bomb crater in Pimlico. The original casting was Alastair Sim as the professor, with only one word of dialogue being altered by the screenwriter when Rutherford took the role instead (Harper 2000: 59). Her performance involves a combination of techniques that are displayed in the scene in which the professor testifies in court that the document is a Royal Charter which means that the area belongs to the Duchy of Burgundy. Her long, confident speech exudes the authority of the expert completely absorbed in her subject as she presents the established historical facts and how the document is an extra-ordinary find that will change history and the lives of those who live in Pimlico. Her strong voice, clear diction and swaying body movements that become more exaggerated as the account becomes increasingly compelling, communicate her enthusiasm for history combined with a pedagogic seriousness that does not patronise the audience. Her character 'whose intellectual fervour is vitiated by battiness' (Harper 2000: 59), is further embellished with strategic elements of costume and accessories including a hat, cloak, large brooch and a watch on a chain that inexplicably chimes as she begins to make her case. Unperturbed by this momentary interruption, she proceeds to deliver her speech as a parson from a pulpit. These are markers of eccentricity, traits which recur in her subsequent appearances in the film as she is completely caught up by the monumental historical discovery she is witnessing and in her great delight on meeting a descendant of the Duke of Burgundy visiting from Dijon who serves as a romantic interest for one of the other, younger female characters. Rutherford's portrayal thus combines the historian's professional expertise with light touches of naïve enthusiasm which communicate affection for the character.

The role of Miss Whitchurch, the headmistress in *The Happiest Days of Your Life*, presented Rutherford with another character in education but from a very different perspective, described by Harper as 'a marvel of doggedness' (2000: 87). The film was an adaptation of a play, and in the film she was paired with Alastair Sim as Wetherby Pond, headmaster of the boys' school which is forced to share facilities with Miss Whitchurch's evacuated girls' school. This situation provides an excellent example of how Rutherford excelled at being part of a double-act as produced by the volatile relationship between the two characters. Their sparring exchanges, particularly early in the film when each resents the other's presence in the school, rely on quick-fire dialogue and shocked, angry facial expressions, particularly from Rutherford, as the impossible situation unravels. The reliance on this kind of visual comedy is also present on other occasions, for example, when Miss Gossage (Joyce Grenfell) and Miss Whitchurch first see the school motto, 'Guard Thine Honour', not a word is spoken between them. A close-up of Rutherford's face shows her read the words, purse her lips in surprise as she takes in the meaning which in the context of her believing that she is in a girls' school acquires a sexual connotation. She clears her throat and glances at a similarly dismayed Gossage who also looks deeply embarrassed. Such 'great moments', admired by the film's director Frank Launder, demonstrate her precision and timing in generating comedic impact from minute facial expressions, knowing glances and gestures. This was extremely well suited to Launder and Gilliat's brand of ironic and satirical comedy. Character actors such as Rutherford were very important in creating the necessary mix whereby: 'The eccentricity of their characters is heightened by the contrast between the familiar situations in which they are placed and their own idiosyncratic behaviour' (Landy 1991: 363). Rutherford commented on the importance of her facial expressions: 'I have always been told that I can manipulate each part of my face with

Figure 7.1 Margaret Rutherford, a shocked Joyce Grenfell and Alastair Sim in *The Happiest Days of Your Life* (1950). Image courtesy of Canal + Image UK.

precision while the rest remains homely and normal. That is true, because like any trained and experienced actress I do have every twitch and ripple of my body under control' (quoted in Merriman 2009: 139). Movements of her face and eyes are indeed keys to conveying comic intention as with a rolling of the eyes to convey an ironic comment on a situation as with the 'Guard Thine Honour' moment discussed above.

As well as being capable of sophisticated visual comedy, Rutherford's voice was a distinctive aspect of her craft. Early in her career she taught elocution, and alongside theatre and film she often did radio work. She would typically deliver lines of dialogue with excessive precision, emphasising particular words as if she were teaching a class and as appropriate to the authoritarian roles in which she was often cast as a governess, headmistress, professor or spinster aunt. Comic impact was further accentuated with lines invested with innuendo and double entendre when characters respond to situations such as when Miss Whitchurch and her female staff examine the school common room which contains fishing trophies, risqué books and magazines that belong to the masters but which they persist in believing are the property of strange female staff. She comments, 'We are descending into a spiral of iniquity' as the women's responses to the incongruity of the possessions being found in a girls' school create the comedy while the audience knows the truth of the situation. This is sustained by Rutherford's intrigued and shocked expressions in her attempts to find rational explanations for the puzzling discoveries. Rutherford's craft can be related to her stage roles and overtly 'theatrical' verbal traditions of comic performance which involved the coupling of florid, verbose language with precise diction. Her delivery of lines often communicated a sagacious, ironic perspective on a situation that sounded erudite and often with an air of camp bravado.

A scene from *The Importance of Being Earnest* when Miss Prism and Dr. Chasuble go for a walk in the garden demonstrates the range of techniques applied by Rutherford. The scene combines gentle double entendre with gestures and expressions that convey the slow unravelling of a romantic attachment for two people who would not normally engage in flirtatious behaviour. The staging of the scene is complicit with declaring Miss Prism as the dominant figure in a relatively short scene. She agrees to accompany Dr. Chasuble on a stroll in the garden and as she fastens her hat with a pin her figure assumes centre-frame position, with Dr. Chasuble in the background and Cecily on the right, her face mostly turned away from the camera. This provides one of the commanding spaces often occupied by characters played by Rutherford, even though Miss Prism is hardly a domineering figure. Her placement in the frame however accentuates the impact of Wilde's lines as she instructs Cecily to study political economy, but to omit the chapter on 'The Fall of the Rupee' as 'somewhat sensational … even these metallic problems have their melodramatic side'. The idea of something greater beyond the confines of the scene makes it memorable visually and aurally, a 'termite' performance indeed.

A little earlier in the scene, Dr. Chasuble comments that if he were Miss Prism's pupil he would 'hang from her lips', quickly adding 'my metaphor was drawn from bees', to deflect any sexual connotation these words may unwittingly have implied. This begins a gentle, flirtatious see-saw between the pair as Miss Prism sees an opportunity to convey something of her attraction towards Dr. Chasuble while remaining cautious about being too explicit. The risqué implications of Wilde's lines are enhanced by

Rutherford's gestures and facial expressions as she comprehends how what she has said might be interpreted. When she comments that Dr. Chasuble should get married her voice is raised to a slightly higher pitch as she smells a rose and slowly draws it to her cheek. For a brief moment she is engulfed in a romantic reverie before being momentarily emboldened to comment that single men can be a 'permanent temptation', and that 'a man should be more careful or he may lead weaker vessels astray'. As she delivers the word 'astray' her eyes are cast downwards giving the impression that it is she who might be led astray. She further makes the most of her secluded moment with Dr. Chasuble with another comment that we immediately link with her own predicament: 'Maturity can always be depended on. Ripeness can be trusted. Young women are green.' After a momentary pause and as Dr. Chasuble is on the point of interrupting, to deflate any sexual inference suggested by the comment she adds: 'I speak horticulturally. My metaphor was drawn from fruits.' Again an attempt is made to counter the sense of risk the lines have conveyed by adding an intellectual comment. The comedic effect is created by it being too late to withdraw the risqué sentiments that have been suggested. In fact the reverse occurs because the absurdity of intellectualising the comment highlights the sexual implications even more. Rutherford's combination of timing, gesture, facial movements (especially her eyes) and changes in the pitch of her voice are deployed in an astute and precisely measured way so that the comic possibilities of Wilde's lines are fully expressed and expanded by the execution of the performance.

One of Rutherford's most famous roles, as Agatha Christie's Miss Marple, came fairly late in her career. She was first offered the part in December 1955 when a BBC radio producer sent her a script of *Death by Drowning* but she did not take up the offer. She overcame her reluctance to play the part late in 1960 when director George Pollock and her friends persuaded her that Miss Marple 'was not so much concerned with crime, even though she was an indomitable sleuth always one stage ahead of the police, but that she was more involved in a game – like chess – a game of solving problems, rather than of murder' (Rutherford 1972: 176). It was important to Rutherford that her character possessed her own sense of moral integrity which, as we have seen, inflected many of her previous roles. The series of films were popular box-office successes and they rescued Rutherford from her personal financial difficulties. The Marple formula was simple, summarised by critic Alexander Walker writing about *Murder She Said*: 'With chin wagging like a windsock in an airfield and eyes that are deceptively guileless, she clumps her way through the lines, situations and disguises that would bunker an actress of less imperial aplomb' (quoted in Merriman 2009: 225). A.H. Weiler of the *New York Times* also refers to her 'prognathous jaw jutting determinedly, Miss Rutherford dominates most of the scenes with a forceful characterization that enhances the humour of her lines and the suspense in this murder' (quoted in Merriman 2009: 225).

In *Murder at the Gallop*, the second film in the series, the comedy depends on the gap between the audience's knowledge of Miss Marple as the super-sleuth and the police inspector's scepticism about her theory on the cause of an old man's recent death. Miss Marple contends that it was murder, perpetrated by someone who knew that the victim had a pathological fear of cats and so made sure the man was frightened to death by one. The interview again shows Rutherford's face doing all the work as she looks at the inspector intently but intermittently looks down as she is delivering a line of dialogue to convey careful thought and concentration. The camera angles would mostly appear to privilege the inspector's viewpoint by adopting a high angle as he sits on his desk, bearing down on her as she sits in the chair and as his scepticism borders on dismissive interrogation. Yet the lighting which highlights her face with the light from the window facing her, combined with her performance and the audience's knowledge of Miss Marple's intelligent sagacity, pushes at the boundaries of an otherwise constraining cinematographic strategy. The inspector is incredulous when she tells him her theory and recommends that the police force should read Agatha Christie novels in which such occurrences are abundant. He advises that she should read instead a 'nice, soothing' love story to get rid of such fantastical ideas. When he dismisses her ideas she resolves to investigate the mystery herself, striding out of the room, flinging her cape around her in defiance and with aplomb. Rutherford often wore elaborate layers of clothing that she was able to incorporate into her performances in this way. This scene is typical of the basic premise of many of the Marple mysteries with comedy being created from situations which arise from the gap between the audience's knowledge of her skills and intelligence, and characters who assume she is an elderly busybody with little better to do with her time than meddle in affairs that are none of her business. When Marple proves, as she invariably does, that this impression is false, the audience's superior knowledge is validated. This type of comic vehicle was therefore perfect for Rutherford since many of her previous roles similarly played on questioning stereotypes and exploring complexities that lie beneath superficial appearances: the emotionally vulnerable governess, the clairvoyant with integrity or the elderly lady with a razor-sharp mind. As noted earlier, this ebullient, affectionate presentation of eccentricity is at odds with Bergson's notion of its function in comedy as social correction.

The subtle nuances of character that were conveyed by Rutherford's performances were often contained within the confines of small parts. These include the nurse sympathetic to the mermaid in *Miranda* (1948) or the conservative, dowager aunt in *I'm All Right Jack* (1959) who finds unexpected commonalities with the shop steward's wife. The disruptive, anarchic effect of Madame Arcati on the Condomine household in *Blithe Spirit* is perhaps an unusual instance of how the actions of a character played by Rutherford could unleash repressed desires and determine the direction of the entire narrative. More typically her characters acted in symbiosis with others and would appear more than once as often she contributed to their creative development. Sometimes referred to as 'sexless' (Babington 2003: 583) her gender was nevertheless important particularly in films such as *The Happiest Days of Your Life* that was awash with sexual innuendo, or even in *Blithe Spirit* when the intensity of Madame Arcati's physical reactions during the séance borders on sexual arousal as the spirit establishes contact. Comedic effect was on occasion achieved by undermining the authoritative positions held by her characters by adorning them with eccentric costumes and accessories, typically hats, jewels and enveloping capes; she may be a professor but her clothes make her look ridiculous. As previously noted, her characters also reproduced stereotypes of women in authority, as with the tweed-suited headmistress in *The Happiest Days of Your Life* or the booming voice of Professor Hatton-Jones in *Passport to Pimlico*. She rarely appeared in completely different clothes from the suits, tightly-buttoned, puff-sleeved patterned blouses, pince-nez and voluminous capes but when she did, as in a sequence in *Murder at the Gallop* when she wears an evening dress and dances the twist, a strange spectacle results from the incongruity of seeing her thus displayed. But as noted earlier, Rutherford's embodiment of eccentricity tended on the whole towards an affectionate, rather than a satirical or grotesque portrayal.

In terms of class, Rutherford typically played aristocrats, upper-middle-class and middle-class women and could range between them; on stage she took the part of Lady Bracknell but she was Miss Prism in the film of *The Importance of Being Earnest*. She plays a pet shop owner in *An Alligator Named Daisy* (1955)and an employee in a cinema in *The Smallest Show on Earth* (1957). While her characters were often unconventional the 'types', she played veered towards humanist conservatism in their values. Her distinctive voice was a constant – she never put on accents – and her career as a stage actress was a crucial professional training, particularly regarding the importance of diction. Her place as an English actress can be identified with West End traditions of popular theatre which she adapted for her film and radio work. The ensemble practices of theatre and film suited her very well resulting in performances that are distinguished even when taken out of their immediate narrative context. Some critics regretted the fact that many of her film appearances were relatively small comic roles. Assessing her career in the mid-1950s, Eric Kneown believed her talents had not been exploited to the full:

> Somebody by now should surely have had the vision to give her a central dramatic part that would have extended all her capacity to be funny and moving at the same time. … Whatever the film kings may think, their public is not so moronic that it will walk out simply because at last she has been allowed to reveal herself to them in a full-size part as an actress of depth and subtlety. Others denied such equipment are fully up to the task of stealing toy trains and using an umbrella as a cosh.
>
> (Kneown 1956: 67–8)

Perhaps sharing this sentiment Orson Welles cast her as Mistress Quickly in *Chimes at Midnight* (1965). Yet the comic character roles should not be underestimated for their particular blend of depth and subtlety. As this chapter has demonstrated her command of the expansive capacity of 'comic moments' within sequences embodied a tradition of British character acting that celebrated idiosyncratic, unconventional behaviour while generating humour, gentle affection and even admiration. In this, and many other respects, Margaret Rutherford contributed immensely to a tradition of central importance in British cinema history.

Acknowledgement

I would like to thank Alex Clayton for his insightful comments on this essay.

Margaret Rutherford filmography and roles

1936: *Dusty Ermine* (Evelyn Summers aka Miss Butterby); *Talk of the Devil* (Housekeeper)
1937: *Beauty and the Barge* (Mrs. Baldwin); *Big Fella* (Nanny – uncredited); *Catch as Catch Can* (Maggie Carberry); *Missing, Believed Married* (Lady Parke)

1941: *Quiet Wedding* (Magistrate); *Spring Meeting* (Aunt Bijou)

1943: *The Demi-Paradise* (Rowena Ventour); *The Yellow Canary* (Mrs Towcester)

1944: *English Without Tears* (Lady Christabel Beauclerk)

1945: *Blithe Spirit* (Madame Arcati)

1947: *Meet Me at Dawn* (Madame Vernorel); *While the Sun Shines* (Dr. Winifred Frye)

1948: *Miranda* (Nurse Carey)

1949: *Passport to Pimlico* (Professor Hatton-Jones)

1950: *The Happiest Days of Your Life* (Miss Whitchurch); *Her Favourite Husband* (Mrs. Dotherington)

1951: *The Magic Box* (Lady Pond)

1952: *Curtain Up* (Catherine Neckwith/Jeremy St. Claire); *Castle in the Air* (Miss Nicholson); *Miss Robin Hood* (Miss Honey); *The Importance of Being Earnest* (Miss Prism)

1953: *Innocents in Paris* (Gwladys Inglott); *The Runaway Bus* (Cynthia Beeston); *Trouble in Store* (Miss Bacon)

1954: *Aunt Clara* (Clara Hilton); *Mad About Men* (Nurse Carey)

1955: *An Alligator Named Daisy* (Prudence Croquet)

1957: *Just My Luck* (Mrs. Dooley); *The Smallest Show on Earth* (Mrs. Fazackalee)

1959: *I'm All Right Jack* (Aunt Dolly)

1961: *Murder She Said* (Jane Marple); *On the Double* (Lady Vivian)

1963: *The Mouse on the Moon* (Grand Duchess Gloriana XIII); *Murder at the Gallop* (Jane Marple); *The VIPs* (Duchess of Brighton)

1964: *Murder Most Foul* (Jane Marple); *Murder Ahoy* (Jane Marple)

1965: *The Alphabet Murders* (Jane Marple – uncredited); *Chimes at Midnight* (Mistress Quickly)

1967: *A Countess from Hong Kong* (Miss Gaulswallow); *Wacky World of Mother Goose* (Mother Goose – voice); *Arabella* (Princess Ilaria)

Bibliography

Babington, B. (2003) 'Margaret Rutherford', in B. McFarlane (ed.), *Encyclopedia of British Film*, London: BFI and Methuen.

Bergson, H. (1956) *Laughter: An Essay on the Meaning of the Comic*, New York: Doubleday Anchor Books.

Clayton, A. (2011) 'Play-acting: A theory of comedic performance', in Aaron Taylor (ed.), *Screen Acting: Theory and Philosophy*, Detroit: Wayne State University Press.

Farber, M. (1962–3) 'White elephant art vs. termite art', *Film Culture*, 27, Winter.

Harper, S. (2000) *Women in British Cinema: Mad, Bad and Dangerous to Know*, London and New York: Continuum.

Kneown, E. (1956) *Margaret Rutherford*, London: Rockliff Publishing.

Landy, M. (1991) *British Genres: Cinema and Society, 1930–60*, Princeton: Princeton University Press.

Merriman, A. (2009) *Margaret Rutherford, Dreadnought with Good Manners*, London: Aurum Press.

Rutherford, M. (1972) *An Autobiography*, London: W.H. Allen.

Street, S. (2010) '"In blushing Technicolor": Colour in *Blithe Spirit*', *Journal of British Cinema and Television*, 7. 1.

8   A short history of the *Carry On* films

James Chapman

It is no longer the case that the *Carry On* films are a neglected or despised tradition of British cinema. Arguably they never were. The critical reception of the films was patronising but never demonstrated the 'fear and loathing' that Julian Petley has identified as a characteristic of responses to other examples of the 'lost continent' of British cinema (Petley 1986: 98). In fact the *Carry On*s have long since ceased to be regarded as the embarrassing distant relation of British cinema and have become a cherished and much-loved national institution. They are celebrated for their irreverence towards authority and respectability, for their gleeful parody of genre conventions and for their unashamed embracing of a tradition of vulgar comedy. Their place in British film culture is best summarised by Andy Medhurst: 'If I had to think of one reason why the *Carry On*s matter so much, it's because they really aren't recuperable for proper culture … they display a commitment to bodily functions and base desires that will always render them irreducibly vulgar, inescapably Not Art' (Medhurst 1992: 19).

Critical discussion of the *Carry On* films has focused hitherto on their employment of stereotypes (Jordan 1983), on their qualities as 'camp' (Medhurst 1992), their exploration of queer identities (Anderson 1998) and their representation of Britishness (Cull 2002). This chapter approaches them from the perspectives of industry and agency. It draws upon the production records and scripts of the films in the papers of their director Gerald Thomas to examine how the *Carry On*s came to be a continuous presence in British cinema for two decades. It argues that the longevity of the series was due in large measure to the production team's ability to negotiate the changing economic and cultural landscape of British cinema between 1958 and 1978. This differs from other critics who see the *Carry On* formula as static and repetitive. That position is exemplified by Jeffrey Richards, who writes: 'The "Carry On" series … allegedly included twenty-nine films, but in fact were the same film made twenty-nine times' (Richards 1997: 165).

There are three distinct phases in the history of the *Carry On* series. The first, from 1958 to 1962, is characterised by a broadly social realist mode of comedy and by a largely consensual outlook that challenges but ultimately preserves social structures and institutional values. It is no coincidence that one writer, Norman Hudis, was responsible for all these early films, from *Carry On Sergeant* (1958) to *Carry On Cruising* (1962). The second phase, from 1963 to 1968, sees a shift in the content and style of the films towards genre parodies and costume spoofs. The humour becomes coarser, fantasy replaces realism as the dominant mode of comedy, and the films become more transgressive in their social and gender politics. This shift was due in large measure to the replacement of Hudis by Talbot Rothwell as the series' principal writer. The third and final phase, from 1969 to 1978, is less stable, as the films alternate between the realist and fantasy modes. Nevertheless there is an underlying trend throughout the later films as they respond to the new culture of permissiveness emerging in the 1970s. The over-riding theme throughout the series – characteristically for British comedy – is that that of class.

1958–62: Hudis, realism and the comedy of consensus

The *Carry On* films emerged at a time of significant institutional and cultural change in the British film industry. The late 1950s saw a precipitous decline in the cinema audience and a process of structural reorganisation that ended the duopoly of the Rank Organisation and the Associated British Picture Corporation. A consequence of the fragmenting of a homogenous audience was the emergence of new forms and genres that ranged from the social realism of the British new wave to the melodramatic excesses of Hammer horror. The *Carry On* series was one of these new forms born during a period of institutional transition.[1]

The production history of *Carry On Sergeant* demonstrates that the origin of the *Carry On* series was largely the outcome of a series of coincidences. In 1955, Sydney Box had approached novelist R.F. Delderfield 'to write an original story and screenplay' about a 'National Service subject'.[2] The project was abandoned within a few weeks – Box produced the thrillers *Lost* and *Eyewitness* for the Rank Organisation instead – but was revived early in 1957 as a project for Box's newly formed Beaconsfield Films. Delderfield was contracted to write 'an original screenplay in master scenes' under the working title of *The Bull Boys*.[3] At this stage, the intention was that the film would be an ensemble drama about a group of young National Servicemen drawn from a variety of social backgrounds. Delderfield delivered a treatment that he described as 'one-third laughter, one-third documentary, one-third exciting incident building up to the climax'. He wanted to explore 'how these men feel about an alien institution like conscription in peacetime'. Delderfield was particularly interested in the role of National Service in promoting shared values ('the great compensating factor for enforced discipline is the comradeship it engenders') and in education ('a modern army training can be an important educational factor in the lives of underprivileged men'). The film was to show how by the end of their training the conscripts have 'all acquired a sort of naive pride in their regiment and uniform'.[4] In this regard the planned film might be seen as a sort of peacetime equivalent of Carol Reed's *The Way Ahead* (1944).

However, the project was quickly overtaken by events. The Defence White Paper of April 1957 proposed drastic reductions in the size of the British armed forces and paved the way for the abolition of National Service. The need to promote the value of National Service had passed. The answer instead was to produce a film that poked fun at the institution. There were precedents for this in the wartime films of Frank Randle and the cycle of Second World War service comedies in the 1950s such as *Worm's Eye View* (1951) – coincidentally adapted from a successful stage farce by Delderfield – and *Private's Progress* (1956).[5] However, it was the success of Granada Television's *The Army*

Figure 8.1 National Service *Carry On* style in *Carry On Sergeant* (1958). Image courtesy of Canal +
Image UK.

Game that evidently persuaded Box and his brother-in-law Peter Rogers, the manager
of Beaconsfield Studios, to follow the comedy route. *The Army Game*, which began in
1957 and ran for 154 episodes, focused on a group of malcontents and ne'er-do-wells
in an ordnance depot at Nether Hopping. It perfectly caught the mood of resentment
that unwilling National Servicemen felt against the petty regulations of the peacetime
army. In 1955, for example, a committee chaired by Sir John Wolfenden had found that
'with few exceptions the National Service man regards his period of service as an
infliction to be undergone rather than a duty to the nation' (Weight 2002: 308).

Box turned to John Antrobus, one of the writers of *The Army Game*, to script the
film now entitled *Carry On Sergeant*.[6] Antrobus refashioned the material in the style of
The Army Game, focusing on a new intake of National Servicemen and the training
sergeant assigned to whip them into shape. His script followed the platoon through
training with a series of comic mishaps, but maintained Delderfield's dramatic climax
wherein they prove themselves in an emergency when a fire breaks out in a nearby
town.[7] However, this did not satisfy Peter Rogers, now the designated producer of the film,
who felt that it lacked sufficient visual humour, remarking that 'what he [Antrobus]
wrote was really a radio script'.[8] Norman Hudis was brought in to revise it. Hudis
developed the part of the platoon sergeant, introducing the idea that he was in charge

of his last intake and determined to win the prize for star platoon that has so far eluded him. 'From this point,' Hudis suggested, 'the film can naturally resolve itself into a series of comedy sequences – *but* because there is a central idea, each situation and character can be related, however lightly, to the basic story of Grimshawe [*sic*], and the film cannot fall into the trap of being an unrelated play-off of Army-life sketches'.[9] Hudis changed the ending so that instead of a dramatic action sequence the film shows how the men pull together to win the platoon prize for Sergeant Grimshaw. Hudis would receive the screenplay credit on the film, with Antrobus credited for 'additional material' as some of his lines and characters remained in the finished film.

Carry On Sergeant provides a revealing case study of the complex political economy of the British film industry by the late 1950s. It was supported by the National Film Finance Corporation, which agreed a loan for half the cost of the film provided the total budget did not exceed £80,000.[10] The remainder was advanced by the distributor Anglo-Amalgamated Films, who raised their half of the finance through a loan from the National Provincial Bank.[11] It had been planned to shoot at Beaconsfield, but with the studio full the production moved to Pinewood Studios, which would remain the base of the *Carry On* films. Rogers handed the directing duties to his protégé Gerald Thomas.[12] *Carry On Sergeant* was evidently produced under conditions of strict economy. The film's production discourse made a virtue of this by asserting 'that here was an opportunity for everybody concerned to see that pictures can be produced on a low budget'.[13] In the event Rogers and Thomas brought it in considerably under budget: the final audited cost was £68,714.19*s*.[14]

The tone of *Carry On Sergeant* is gentle and good-natured: the gruff sergeant turns out to be not such a fearsome tyrant and the film concludes on a sentimental note as the platoon present him with a cigarette lighter ('To Sergeant Grimshaw – from the boys'). Much of the comedy arises from recognisable situations. Hudis drew upon his own experience of National Service. In his script notes, for example, he wrote: 'Bayonet training. This could make Horace sick. (It did make *me* sick.)'[15] The film endorses collective action: the motley assortment of misfits finally succeeds in passing out as the star platoon through their own determination. In this sense the theme of *Carry On Sergeant* is much the same as *The Way Ahead*: the men come to accept the army and the comradeship it offers.

It is difficult to explain the success of *Carry On Sergeant* as anything other than a happy accident. Critics did not recognise it as anything special. The *Monthly Film Bulletin*, for example, called it a 'conventional farce, in which all the characters come from stock'.[16] The casting of William Hartnell, who played Sergeant-Major Bullimore in *The Army Game*, as Grimshaw no doubt helped, but Bob Monkhouse, the only other performer with separate billing, could hardly be considered a box-office draw. While several future *Carry On* regulars appear – principally Kenneth Connor, Kenneth Williams, Charles Hawtrey and Hattie Jacques – audiences at the time would not have recognised them as such. Nevertheless *Carry On Sergeant* became the third most successful British film of 1958.[17] Released during the traditionally quiet summer months, its success has been attributed in some measure to the wet weather experienced in many seaside towns (Harper and Porter 2003: 263).

There was nothing accidental, however, about the success of *Carry On Nurse* (1959), which topped the box office the following year.[18] It was with *Carry On Nurse* that the series' formula began to take shape. Rogers and Thomas kept together most of their ensemble cast – Hartnell and Monkhouse were those who bowed out – and Hudis wrote an original screenplay based around the personalities established in the previous film.[19] It was during production of *Carry On Nurse*, furthermore, that Rogers began to map out the future of the series. In November 1958, he wrote to the National Film Finance Corporation (NFFC):

> Since 'Carry on, Sergeant' and my present production 'Carry on, Nurse' it has become increasingly evident that the 'Carry Ons' will depend more and more for their success upon a handful of feature Artistes. These feature Artistes, by virtue of the success of the 'Carry Ons' – if this success is maintained – are fast becoming stars of a new and different kind. It has always been difficult in this country to pin down successful players to a definite date for a film as they are in more demand than so-called stars. In order, therefore, to maintain the success of the 'Carry Ons' it is essential to my mind, to keep the present team of comics together and the only way to do this is to offer them some kind of contract or promise for their services at some future date.[20]

Rogers predicted that 'by the time the October "Carry on" is made these Artistes will be as famous as such comedy teams as The Crazy Gang and the Marx Brothers' and requested an advance from the NFFC to secure their services. In the event, however, the advance was not forthcoming and the practice of contracting the actors a film at a time would continue.

Carry On Nurse is a more episodic narrative than *Carry On Sergeant* – the absence of an equivalent of Hartnell's character means there is no thematic axis – but this allows space for the personalities of the *Carry On* regulars to develop, particularly Kenneth Williams's intellectual egghead and Charles Hawtrey's childish eccentric. Joan Sims joined the cast as the hapless Nurse Dawson, while Hattie Jacques was handed her defining role as the fearsome Matron. *Carry On Nurse* is generally regarded as the most realistic of the *Carry Ons*: according to the publicity, Hudis had been hospitalised with appendicitis shortly before working on the film, and based many of the incidents on his observations of hospital life. The decision to adhere to a realist mode is also revealed in the fact that the finished film omits a fantasy sequence that appeared in the first draft of the screenplay where Ted York (played by Terence Longdon in the film), under anaesthetic, dreams about a pretty girl 'in idealised, scant and diaphanous harem costume' who transforms into a nurse: their embrace is rudely interrupted by the ward sister 'dressed in jodphurs [sic] and roll-neck sweater' and wielding a whip![21]

After *Nurse*, Hudis scripted another four films – *Carry On Teacher* (1959), *Carry On Constable* (1960), *Carry On Regardless* (1961) and *Carry On Cruising* – after which he decamped to Hollywood to work in US television (Ross 1996: 34). The *Carry On* formula was still evolving in these early films. *Teacher* was a vehicle for radio comedian Ted Ray, whose one appearance in the series it would be. *Constable* marked the first appearance in the series of the walnut-faced Sidney James, though his character is not yet the Cockney lothario he would become in later films. It also included the first instance of what would become a recurring motif in the series as two of the recruits

(Kenneth Williams and Charles Hawtrey) appear in drag. *Regardless* is the most episodic of all the films, amounting to little more than a series of sketches linked by the Helping Hands odd-job agency. *Cruising* was the first film in colour and the first without Charles Hawtrey, whose role went to Lance Percival.

With the partial exception of *Regardless*, the Hudis-scripted films largely adhere to the same conventions. The films are characterised by institutional settings (hospital, school, police station, cruise ship) and are broadly realist in content. To some extent they can be seen as comedy variations on the conventions of British social-realist film-making in the 1950s. *Nurse*, for example, offers a more light-hearted look at the National Health Service (still a relatively young institution) than earnest hospital dramas such as *White Corridors* (1951); *Teacher* foreshadows *Spare the Rod* (1961) with its clash between unruly pupils and their harassed teachers; and *Constable* is nothing if not a comedy variant of *The Blue Lamp* (1950) and its BBC television spin-off *Dixon of Dock Green*. The theme of each film (again *Regardless* is a partial exception) is the conflict between institutional authority and a group of unruly misfits. It has been suggested that these early *Carry Ons* represent 'a rejection of the old deferential structures' (Harper and Porter 2003: 194). However, in each case the resolution of conflict emerges through consensus and collective action. Thus the platoon wins the award for their retiring instructor (*Sergeant*), pupils and teachers jointly foil the attempt to close the school by inspectors (*Teacher*), the new police recruits capture a dangerous criminal gang and see their sergeant promoted to inspector (*Constable*), and the efforts of the eager-to-please crew persuade their captain to stay rather than fulfil his dream of taking charge of an ocean-going liner (*Cruising*). To this extent, the early *Carry Ons* demonstrate consensual social politics characteristic of British cinema: individual differences are overcome, authority figures and institutions are humanised, and normal social relations are preserved.

1963–8: Rothwell, fantasy and the comedy of transgression

The realist mode of the early *Carry Ons* can be seen in relation to the prevailing discourses of British cinema in the late 1950s and early 1960s. This was the time of the new wave, the cycle of 'kitchen sink' dramas that were seen as bringing a new degree of realism to British cinema in their representation of working-class experience and their frankness in relation to sex. Like all such movements, however, the British New Wave was short-lived. There is a neat congruence in the fact that the last recognised New Wave film, Lindsay Anderson's *This Sporting Life*, was released the same year (1963) as the last (for the time being at least) of the realist *Carry Ons*. *Carry On Cabby* marked the debut of a new writer, Talbot Rothwell, though other than a stronger emphasis on gender politics – the neglected wife of the owner of a taxi firm establishes a rival firm called 'Glamcabs' staffed by attractive female drivers – *Cabby* is largely indistinguishable from the Hudis films. This changed with the next entry, *Carry On Jack* (1963), the first costume spoof. Talbot Rothwell's agent had sent the original outline, entitled *Poop-Decker, RN*, to Rogers with a note saying: 'It strikes me that this could be a completely new look for the "Carry On" gang, and I hope it will amuse you.'[22] While *Jack* was far from being the best of the *Carry Ons* – for the first time neither Sid James nor Kenneth Connor appeared – it turned the series in a new direction.

Carry On Spying (1964) is a good example of the changes to the series' formula. This had originally been slated to follow on from *Cruising*, and Norman Hudis wrote a screenplay early in 1963 based on his usual formula of a team of new recruits fresh from training who are assigned to an important mission. It envisioned roles for Sid James (Agent Fearless), Joan Sims (Agent Valiant), Kenneth Connor (Agent Bold), Hattie Jacques (Agent Dauntless) and Charles Hawtrey (Agent Intrepid).[23] The twist ending was that the assignment has all along been a test. As the Director of BOSH (British Operations Security Headquarters) tells them: 'At the end of your theoretical schooling, we must find out if you can apply what you have learned practically … An initiative test – with the vital difference that *you* think it's *genuine*.'[24] A later screenplay, unattributed but apparently also by Hudis, introduced a role for Kenneth Williams as suave secret agent Peter Bull who recruits a team of operatives from different walks of life to counter an enemy who plots to blow up a nuclear research facility. It has a more serious tone than other scripts. The early 1960s was the height of support for the Campaign for Nuclear Disarmament and the script includes an implicit critique of the policy of nuclear deterrence. Amelia Barley (a role written specially for Esma Cannon, a specialist in playing dotty spinsters) is horrified by the idea of deliberately causing a nuclear explosion: 'If you merely want to stop an invading army using this plant – why obliterate not only the plant – but all those pretty villages for miles around – killing our own people? … I mean – the advantage of having an ordinary war'll be rather lost on them if, the second there's an invasion they're wiped out by a nuclear catastrophe caused by our own side.'[25]

Clearly this was not what the producers wanted. *Carry On Spying* was rewritten from scratch by Rothwell – working for the only time with another writer (Sid Colin) – and became a parody of the genre. It retained the motif of a group of new recruits, pitting them against the sinister organisation STENCH (Society for the Total Extermination of Non-Conforming Humans) but, in a major shift from the Hudis films, the authority figure (Williams's Desmond Simkins) is even more hapless and incompetent than his team. Hudis's films had challenged authority but had not subverted it: Rothwell's films would represent authority as ridiculous and would take every opportunity to mock it. Thus the film concludes with the destruction of secret service headquarters when STENCH headquarters, directly beneath it, blows up. Jim Dale and Barbara Windsor became the last of the *Carry On* regulars to join the cast.[26]

For the rest of the 1960s, the *Carry On* series mined a rich seam of genre parody. *Carry On Cleo* (1964) was a deliciously funny spoof of the Ancient World epic, *Cleopatra* (1963) in particular, notable for some inspired puns ('Infamy! Infamy! They've all got it in for me!') and for a scene-stealing performance by Amanda Barrie as a coquettish Cleopatra. Other targets included the Western (*Carry On Cowboy*, 1965), Hammer horror (*Carry On Screaming!*, 1966), *The Scarlet Pimpernel* (*Don't Lose Your Head*, 1966) and *Beau Geste* (*Follow That Camel*, 1967). The last two films were originally released without a 'Carry On' prefix as in 1966 the series changed distributor to the Rank Organisation. Here there is some evidence of muddled thinking within the production team. Before starting *Don't Lose Your Head*, Rogers had 'wondered whether the words "carry on" need be used in the picture. He thought that as the film was more visual than previous "Carry On" productions it could stand on its own without any reference to "carry on".[27] However, Thomas wished to emphasise the 'Carry On' connection: he suggested the promotional line 'It's the "Carry On" team again – sticking its neck into the French Revolution'.[28] The familiar prefix was restored for *Carry On Doctor* (1967), marking a return to the institutional comedy. In November 1967, Rogers suggested a British Empire spoof entitled *Up the Khyber* to Rank: this time the addition of the 'Carry On' prefix was at the suggestion of Rank's managing-director John Davis.[29]

The production of the *Carry On* films was nothing if not streamlined.[30] Their success was due in large measure to Rogers' ability to deliver the films economically and with low overheads. Even so there was mounting concern throughout the 1960s over the rising costs. *Carry On Spying* was the first to run over budget due to accidents to Hawtrey and Williams necessitating overtime payments to the cast and crew and a greater than anticipated spend on set construction.[31] The budgets increased when the series moved to Rank, but this was due as much to inflation as an investment in production values. Rogers explained that the estimated budget of *Don't Lose Your Head* (£249,538) was nearly 30 per cent more than *Carry On Cleo* (£194,323) – 'made exactly two years ago with the same cast and schedule' – because of the rising costs of unit salaries, artistes, studio facilities and set construction.[32] John Davis nevertheless felt that 'you put in some pretty good production values at a viable figure'.[33] The crisis point, however, came with *Carry On ... Up the Khyber*. Rogers's initial budget of £228,512 was rejected by Rank: 'Frankly the Board will not accept this figure on the score that it is uneconomic and cannot but show a loss situation. The maximum we are prepared to put up is £200,000.'[34] This would suggest that the films were made on extremely narrow margins and were vulnerable to the continuing decline in cinema attendances. In the event, Rogers put up a personal guarantee to cover the additional spend in return for a percentage of the profits: the final cost of *Carry On ... Up the Khyber* was £235,637. 2s. 1d.[35]

There is a marked shift in both the style and the tone of the Rothwell-scripted films. Most obviously they are laden with innuendo: for this reason, from *Carry On Jack*, they were deemed 'A' rather than 'U' certificate films by the censors. Sometimes the censors did not appreciate the double entendres. Gerald Thomas wrote an amusing note to BBFC secretary John Trevelyan concerning a line in *Carry On Again Doctor* (1969):

> Your examiners' words 'May the God of fertility suck your coconuts', are very amusing and probably better than the original dialogue and I can see this reason for objecting to it. However, the dialogue in the picture is 'May the fertility of Sumaka swell your coconuts' and I am sure this is only referring to an abundant harvest of coconuts.[36]

It was Rothwell, too, who introduced punning character names into the series. Among the more inspired were Daphne Honeybutt (*Spying*), Hengist Pod and his wife Senna (*Cleo*), the Rumpo Kid and Marshal P. Knutt (*Cowboy*), Sergeant Bung (*Screaming*), Sir Rodney ffing ('two small fs') and Citizens Camembert and Bidet (*Don't Lose Your Head*), Sergeant Nocker, Commandant Burger and Captain Le Pice (*Follow That Camel*), Dr. Tinkle (*Doctor*), and the Khasi of Kalabar, Princess Jelhi, Bunghit Din and Private Widdle (*Up the Khyber*).

The Rothwell films mark the transition of the *Carry On* series from a realist mode of comedy to a fantasy mode. Whereas the Hudis films were rooted in shared social experiences such as hospitals and schools, Rothwell's points of reference are mostly cinematic. The films are no longer set in recognisable social spaces (*Cabby* and *Doctor* excepted) but in a world of film genres. This usually involves displacing protagonists from their home: a recurring motif is the hero finding himself in unfamiliar surroundings. Thus a wheel-maker from Ancient Britain is transported to Rome where he unwittingly earns a reputation as a fearsome warrior (*Cleo*), a sanitary engineer is mistaken for a Wild West sharpshooter (*Cowboy*) and a young English aristocrat joins the Foreign Legion when he is falsely accused of cheating at cricket (*Follow That Camel*). Rothwell delights in sending up genre conventions for all they are worth. In particular the conventions of heroism and melodrama are mocked. The films include spoofs of the death of Nelson at Trafalgar (*Jack*), Sidney Carlton's noble sacrifice in *A Tale of Two Cities* (*Don't Lose Your Head*) and the heroic battlefield death scenes of imperial adventure films (*Up the Khyber*). It is perhaps no coincidence that this tendency in the series coincided with the satire boom of the 1960s in television shows such as *That Was The Week That Was* and *The Frost Report* that symbolised the end of a culture of deference.

The humour of the *Carry Ons* becomes more transgressive in the Rothwell films. This takes several forms. On a basic level it involves subverting traditional ideas of class: only in a *Carry On* film could working-class Cockney characters called the Ruff-Diamonds be cast as the Governor of the Northwest Frontier Province and his wife. On another level Rothwell sets out to undermine social conventions. In particular the sanctity of marriage can no longer be taken for granted. The first draft of *Carry On Cleo*, for example, had Hengist Pod (Kenneth Connor) returning home after five years to discover his wife has two additional children: 'He looks thoughtful, does a little count on his fingers, then looks into camera and shrugs.'[37] In the event this was not used in *Cleo*, but the motif of the cuckolded husband turned up at the end of *Follow That Camel* when it is revealed that the baby of the married Bo West and Lady Jane (Angela Douglas) is the spitting image of Commandant Burger (Kenneth Williams). And normal social relations are subverted. At the end of *Screaming*, for example, Sergeant Bung (Harry H. Corbett) is content to leave his harridan of a wife (Joan Sims) as a waxwork while the sexy Valeria (Fenella Fielding) moves in as his mistress.

The *Carry Ons* can hardly be claimed as sites of progressive social politics: Medhurst observes that the series is characterised by 'ceaseless sexism' and displays moments of both 'appalling racism' and 'callous homophobia' (Medhurst 2007: 142). (And some of the draft scripts are even worse: *Cleo* included the line 'Oh shut up, you old faggot!' and a character in *Khyber* called the Khasi of Kalabar a 'brown-job'.) Rather than dismissing them as entirely reactionary, however, the 'non-PC' aspects of the *Carry Ons* are perhaps best understood as exploring anxieties around the issues of gender, sexuality and race. *Khyber*, for example, includes a joke about the social problems of immigration: Afghan rebel Bunghit Din (Bernard Bresslaw) fires at British with the line 'That'll teach them to ban turbans on the buses!'. While heterosexual male desire is accepted as entirely normal, female desire is presented as problematic. This is best expressed in *Doctor* where the sexually frustrated Matron attempts to seduce a terrified Dr. Tinkle. Above all – and somewhat bizarrely given that the regular cast included several known gay artistes – the films demonstrate a sense of acute anxiety about male homosexuality. Several of the films – including *Spying*, *Cleo*, *Follow That Camel* and *Khyber* – include scenes where male protagonists find themselves disguised in drag (typically as harem girls or vestal virgins) and desired by the villain. And the plot of *Khyber* revolves around the threat represented by the male body. The fearsome reputation of the 3rd Foot and Mouth Regiment (known as 'the devils in skirts') is based on wearing nothing beneath their kilts. This reputation is undermined when a photograph reveals them all to be wearing longjohns. The Afghan tribes, no longer in fear of the devils in skirts, rebel and lay siege to the British Residency. The regiment lines up and lift their kilts to prove they are no longer wearing undergarments, whereupon the rebels flee in terror.[38]

1969–78: Censors, realism again, and the comedy of permissiveness

Carry On … Up the Khyber is held by many aficionados to represent the high water mark of the series. Robert Ross, for example, considers it 'the one *Carry On* that almost gets its foot in the door of respectable British cinema' (Ross 1996: 73). It was the top British box-office attraction of 1968: its success suggested that the series was in rude health as it reached its tenth anniversary.[39] Behind the scenes, however, all was not well. The Rank Organisation continued to exert pressure to keep costs down. The decision to make the next film *Carry On Camping* (1969) seems to have been an economic decision – it was shot mostly in fields close to Pinewood – but even so its budget of £208,354 was questioned by the Rank accountants. This prompted an extraordinary letter from Peter Rogers:

> Now, in spite of the increased costs of so many of the facets of film production, you will see from the enclosed breakdown of comparative figures that I am, by my own peculiar method of production, devising a means of presenting each subject more economically than the last – this in spite of the fact that I am neither a magician nor a mathematician nor a company secretary nor one in a position to impose charges for imagined increases of otherwise normal facilities. I am a writer first and a producer second.[40]

Carry On Camping was another popular success: it was the highest-grossing film in the series since *Carry On Nurse*.[41] But Rank had hesitated over the next film, *Carry On Again Doctor*, telling Rogers that his proposed schedule 'is far too close to comfort to what would be the latest release'.[42] Rogers again provided a personal guarantee to cover any spend over Rank's maximum of £205,000 in return for an increased share of the profits. He nearly severed his connection with Rank over the same film: 'A film is a film and a promise is a promise and if you are not prepared to honour such a promise then I have no intention of continuing with the film and reserve the right, even at this date, to offer it to another distributor'.[43] It is clear, then, that the position of the *Carry On* series was far from secure as it entered the 1970s.

The production strategy of 1970s *Carry On* would suggest, on the face of it, that the series was uncertain about what direction to take. The last three genre parodies – *Carry On Up the Jungle* (1970), *Carry On Henry* (1971) and *Carry On Dick* (1974) – alternated with more hospital farce in *Carry On Matron* (1972) and the return to a realist mode of

Figure 8.2 No expense was spared for *Carry On Camping* (1969), shot in the fields around Pinewood. Image courtesy of ITV Studios Global Entertainment

comedy in *Carry On Loving* (1970), *Carry On At Your Convenience* (1971), *Carry On Abroad* (1972), *Carry On Girls* (1973), *Carry On Behind* (1975) and *Carry On England* (1976). It would be fair to say that these later films were inconsistent in quality and tone. They suffered from the fragmentation of the core *Carry On* cast: Charles Hawtrey made his last appearance in *Abroad*, Sidney James in *Dick*, and Hattie Jacques's appearances were reduced due to illness. *Carry On Dick* would be Talbot Rothwell's last *Carry On* film. On this occasion he rewrote a script by two other writers, Lawrie Wyman and George Evans, which included a great deal of crude material.[44] The following films by Dave Freeman (*Behind*) and David Pursall and Jack Seddon (*England*) were to all intents and purposes remakes of *Camping* and *Sergeant* (with a Second World War setting). Kenneth Williams bemoaned the declining quality of the scripts. He felt that *Carry On Loving* 'seems to be the bottom of the barrel, but for Talbot Rothwell bottoms are capable of infinite variety' (Davies 1993: 371). *Carry On Dick* prompted the remark: 'The script is utterly banal. It is incredible that human minds can put such muck on to paper' (Davies 1993: 466). As for *Carry On Behind*: 'It is the *worst* I've ever read. The part for me, Roland Crump, is small, it is unfunny, and is mostly concerned with heavily contrived slapstick. Don't know why on earth they offer it to me' (Davies 1993: 487).

The conventional view of the later *Carry On* films is that they struggled to adapt to the social and cultural climate of the 1970s. In particular they are seen as having lost ground to a new style of 'X'-certificate sex comedies such as the *Confessions* and

Adventures series. Sarah Street, for example, writes that the *Carry On*s became 'increasingly out of kilter with the perceived demand for nudity and sexual explicitness' (Street 1997: 97). And for Steve Gerrard the films were 'failing to adapt to the changing tastes of both audiences and film distributors' (Gerrard 2008: 43). However, the 1970s *Carry On*s were arguably more in touch with the *zeitgeist* than at any time since *Carry On Sergeant*. They began to address topical issues such as trade union militancy (*Carry On At Your Convenience* focuses on industrial relations in – appropriately – a toilet factory) and even feminism (*Carry On Girls* takes place against the background of a beauty contest in a run-down seaside town). *Carry On Matron* concerns the attempts of a gang of bungling crooks to steal a supply of contraceptive pills (not available on the National Health Service until 1973) from a maternity hospital. In the first draft it was cocaine they were stealing, but this would seem to have been *too* realistic.[45] Norman Hudis had been approached to write *Matron*, but was prevented from doing due to a problem over his membership of the Writers' Guild of America.[46]

There are two notable trends in 1970s *Carry On*s. The first is the shift towards more permissive content. This is sometimes traced back to a moment in *Carry On Camping* where Barbara Windsor's brassière springs off during a series of energetic physical jerks – though in fact the first naked breasts to appear in a *Carry On* were in the naturist documentary (*Nudist Paradise*) at the beginning of the same film. In the 1970s, the film-makers started to push the boundaries of what was acceptable for an 'A' certificate, particularly in relation to female nudity. The censors required cuts to *Carry On Matron* to 'remove all shots in which [a] girl's naked breasts are seen in bath'. The new BBFC secretary Stephen Murphy wrote: 'As you will know we try to keep nudity to an absolute minimum in "A" pictures: can you help us a little more in this Reel?'[47] *Carry On Dick* prompted a long 'exceptions list' including much 'dubious dialogue' and 'Quick flash of Barbara Windsor's tits as her blouse buttons burst.'[48] *Carry On Girls* only narrowly escaped with an 'A': on this occasion the offending scene was a cat-fight between rival glamour girls Hope Springs (Barbara Windsor) and Dawn Brakes (Margaret Nolan) where they nearly spill out of their bikinis. *Carry On England* was the first to warrant a more restrictive 'AA' certificate due to its shots of bare-breasted female soldiers. It was also the first outright box-office failure. The producers resubmitted the film with cuts for an 'A', but the reissue did nothing to help its reputation (Gerrard 2008: 43).

The other trend in 1970s *Carry On*s is the prominence of leisure as a theme. The early *Carry On*s had been set in the world of work. In later *Carry On*s the settings are campsites (*Camping, Behind*), seaside resorts (*Girls*) and package holidays (*Abroad*). Rogers had long been resistant to the idea of locating a contemporary *Carry On* film abroad. He had rejected Rothwell's first treatment for *Camping* 'because I was taking the campers abroad mainly'.[49] The seaside has long been associated as a site not only of leisure but also of permissiveness: its pleasures offer a temporary release from normal social constraints. Even a workplace film such as *Carry On At Your Convenience* – whose working titles included *Carry On Comrade* and *Carry On Worker* – includes an extended sequence of a works outing to the seaside town of Brighton. This is a recurring motif of British comedy, from the Blackpool sequences of the Gracie Fields film *Sing As We Go* (1934) to the Margate episode of *Only Fools and Horses* ('Jolly Boys' Outing'). The spaces of leisure are classless: they break down the hierarchical and social structures of the workplace. This shift from the spaces of work in the institutional *Carry On*s to the spaces of leisure brings about a significant shift in the sexual politics of the films. *Carry On Girls*, for example, is the first contemporary *Carry On* in which the middle-aged male lothario succeeds in getting 'it' with the nubile young female of his desire.

In his study of British low culture of the 1970s, Leon Hunt argues that the later *Carry On*s exemplify 'permissive populism': the permeation of the values of the permissive society into residual forms of popular culture (Hunt 1998: 19). The same outlook is evident in much 1970s comedy, especially television comedy, such as *On the Buses* or *The Benny Hill Show*. This would suggest that the 1970s *Carry On*s, rather than failing to adapt to changing popular tastes, were in fact representative of those tastes. It could be argued, in fact, that in the 1970s the *Carry On*s became more central to British film culture than at any point in their history. The low-budget comedy was the only genre to hold its own at the box office during the 1970s as cinema attendances continued their seemingly inexorable decline and the quantity of domestic production fell. Hammer's *On the Buses* was the leading British box-office film of 1971, Columbia's *Confessions of a Window Cleaner* in 1974. *On the Buses* was a spin-off of a popular television series, but in tone and content it could almost have been released with a 'Carry On' prefix. And the *Carry On* films continued to hold their own at the box office until the failure of *Carry On England*. What finally killed the *Carry On*s was not the rise of the sex comedy – in fact neither the *Confessions* (1974–7) nor the *Adventures* (1975–8) series outlived the *Carry On*s – but rather the combination of inflationary production costs and declining box-office revenues that effectively killed off all low-budget British films in the 1970s. And even then the *Carry On*s would enjoy a successful afterlife on television where in the 1970s screenings attracted audiences of 20 million (Hunt 1998: 29).

Postscript

There are few if any examples of cycles of popular cinema that end on a high note. Certainly this is not the case with the *Carry On* series. *Carry On Emmannuelle* (1978) was the last of the continuous series that had begun with *Carry On Sergeant* 20 years before. After the box-office failure of *Carry On England*, the Rank Organisation had finally cut its ties with the series. Rogers raised the finance for *Carry On Emmannuelle* from a City investment firm called Cleves Investments which put up the £350,000 budget in return for 40 per cent of the gross receipts.[50] With an 'AA' certificate the film fell between two schools: it did not reach the traditional family audience for the *Carry On*s but at the same time it was not racy enough to appeal to audiences of the sort of soft-core sex films it rather lamely spoofed. *Carry On Columbus* (1992) was a belated coda to the series. This marked a return to the tradition of the costume spoof and was intended to do for the two Columbus epics of 1992 – *Christopher Columbus: The Discovery* and *1492: Conquest of Paradise* – what *Carry On Cleo* had done for Fox's *Cleopatra*. Perhaps the best that can be said for it is that it is better than *England* and *Emmannuelle* – though only marginally so. With most of the original *Carry On* cast now deceased – Jim Dale, as Columbus, is the one regular to appear – the film has to recruit from the ranks of so-called 'alternative' comedians such as Alexei Sayle, Julian Clary, Keith Allen and Rik Mayall. Given that alternative comedy emphasises its non-discriminatory, non-racist, non-sexist credentials, the presence of these performers in a *Carry On* film is incongruous to say the least. While a film of *Carry On London* has been announced several times since the mid-1990s, it remains unrealised. Like all popular culture, the *Carry On* films were of and for their time. They belong to the period of mid-20th-century Britain that witnessed the transition from the consensual social politics of the 1950s to the permissive populism of the 1970s. They can be seen both as an agent and a reflection of that process. The fact that they endured for so long is testimony to the producers' knack for judging popular taste, to the quality of the writing and performances at their best, and to the enduring appeal of the tradition of vulgar humour in British popular culture.

Notes

1 The *Carry On* films ran in parallel to the Hammer films in several ways. They emerged at the same time – *The Curse of Frankenstein*, the first of Hammer's Gothic horrors, was released in 1957 – and both would endure throughout the 1960s until they simultaneously ran out of economic and cultural energy in the mid-1970s.

2 British Film Institute Special Collections Unit Gerald Thomas papers (hereafter BFI GT) GT/26/13: Joyce Briggs to Hugh Parton, 29 August 1955.

3 Ibid: Felix de Wolfe to Sydney Box, 4 January 1957.

4 BFI GT/26/2: 'Preliminary treatment of National Service film, provisionally entitled *The Long and the Short and the Tall* or *The Other Side of the Ocean* by R.F. Delderfield'.

5 Mancunian comedian Frank Randle starred in a series of wartime comedies – including *Somewhere in England* (1940), *Somewhere in Camp* (1942), *Somewhere on Leave* (1943) and *Somewhere in Civvies* (1943) – that can be seen as precursors of the *Carry On* films in their vulgar humour and cheap production values.

6 The title may have been inspired by a film called *Carry On Admiral* (Val Guest 1957) which has no connection with the *Carry On* series other than a small role for Joan Sims.

7 BFI GT/26/4: *Carry On Sergeant*. Screenplay by John Antrobus, n.d.

8 BFI GT/26/13: Peter Rogers to Beryl Vertue, 31 March 1958.

9 BFI GT/26/1: *Carry On Sergeant!* 'First Treatment and Development Ideas', NH [Norman Hudis] for Beaconsfield Films Ltd, 27 January 1958.

10 BFI GT/26/11: A. J. Buck to Insignia Films, 3 March 1958.

11 BFI GT/26/14: Contract between Anglo-Amalgamated Film Distributors, Sydney Box and the National Film Finance Corporation, 31 March 1958.

12 Gerald Thomas was the younger brother of Ralph Thomas, who had formed a successful director-producer team with Betty Box, sister of Sydney Box and wife of Peter Rogers.

13 BFI GT/26/14: Minutes of Pre-Production Meeting for *Carry On Sergeant* at Pinewood Studios, 20 March 1958.

14 BFI GT/26/10: P. H. Grislingham (NFFC) to Anglo-Amalgamated Film Distributors, 7 January 1959.

15 BFI GT/26/1: *Carry On Sergeant!* 'First Treatment and Development Ideas'.

16 *Monthly Film Bulletin* 25: 296 (September 1958: 6).

17 *Kinematograph Weekly*, 18 December 1958: 6.

18 *Kinematograph Weekly*, 17 December 1959: 6.

19 At one point Box indicated 'that the film will be based on a play by Patrick Cargill and Jack Beale'. He had paid £1,000 for the film rights to their play *Ring for Catty* in 1956 (BFI GT/23/6: Sydney Box to Bernard Main, 3 October 1958). However, the first draft of *Carry On Nurse*, dated 18 June 1958, states 'Original Story and Screenplay by Norman Hudis' and is very close to the finished film in incident and characterisation (GT/23/1).

20 BFI GT/23/6: Peter Rogers to John Terry, 26 November 1958. Rogers identified the next films as being 'Teacher', 'Constable', 'Regardless' and 'Perhaps?'

21 BFI GT/23/1: *Carry On Nurse!* Original Story and Screenplay by Norman Hudis.

22 BFI GT/20/9: Kevin Kavanagh to Peter Rogers, 25 June 1962.

23 Hawtrey was the only one of those five actually to appear in *Carry On Spying.*

24 BFI GT/27/2: *Carry On Spying.* Screenplay by Norman Hudis, 20 February 1963.

25 BFI GT/27/3: *Carry On Spying.* Screenplay, 19 June 1963. (Amelia is an ex-army officer whom the villains, masquerading as British agents, attempt to embroil in their plot.)

26 Dale had appeared in a bit part in *Carry On Jack* but this was his first substantial role.

27 BFI GT/14/9: Minutes of the Pre-Production Publicity Meeting for *Don't Lose Your Head*, 1 September 1966.

28 Ibid: Minutes of the Post-Production Meeting for *Don't Lose Your Head*, 1 February 1967.

29 BFI GT/30/7: John Davis to Peter Rogers, 1 December 1967. *Don't Lose Your Head* and *Follow That Camel* were also reissued with the 'Carry On' prefix in 1968.

30 It is an indication of the streamlined nature of their film-making that Rogers and Thomas also turned out several non-*Carry On* comedies including *Please Turn Over* (1960), *No Kidding* (1961), *Watch Your Stern* (1961), *Raising the Wind* (1961), *The Iron Maiden* (1963), *Nurse on Wheels* (1963) and *The Big Job* (1965).

31 BFI GT/27/9: Peter Rogers to Stuart Levy, 29 April 1964.

32 BFI GT/14/9: Peter Rogers to F.L. Thomas, 22 August 1966.

33 Ibid: F.L. Thomas to Peter Rogers, 30 December 1966.

34 BFI GT/30/7: F.L. Thomas to Peter Rogers, 11 March 1968.

35 BFI GT/30/6: Peat, Marwick, Mitchell & Co to Peter Rogers, 28 July 1969.

36 BFI GT/2/8: Gerald Thomas to John Trevelyan, 6 June 1969.

37 BFI GT/7/1: *Carry On Cleo.* A Funny Sort of Screenplay by Talbot Rothwell, First Draft.

38 The first draft of *Carry On ... Up the Khyber* had a different ending. In this version Sir Sidney Ruff-Diamond faces the Burpas alone and drops his trousers to reveal he is wearing 'a startling pair of brilliant red bloomers, rather baggy, the leg ends gathered just above the knees with cute white satin bows. It is too much for the KHASI even. He shudders, turns and runs for it.' Sid remarks: 'They belong to the Memsahib.' Captain Keene: 'But didn't you see, sir? They all turned and ran!' 'So did I when I first saw her in 'em!' BFI GT/30/2/: *Carry On ... Up the Khyber* by Talbot Rothwell, January 1968.

39 *Kinematograph Weekly*, 18 December 1968: 5.

40 BFI GT/6/7: Peter Rogers to Graham Dawson, 23 September 1968.

41 Ibid: F. S. Poole to Peter Rogers, 27 October 1969.

42 BFI GT/2/8: F. L. Thomas to Peter Rogers, 12 November 1968.

43 Ibid: Peter Rogers to F. L. Thomas, 13 March 1969.

44 BFI GT/12/1: *Carry On Dick* by Lawrie Wyman & George Evans, n.d. This included jokes about male rape ('Right lads! Rape the men and rob the women!') and auspices and horse pisses. Lines such as Twirpin's comment (to buxom Gladys): 'With your bum and your boobs, who needs somebody with a brain!' are lacking in the usual innuendo.

45 BFI GT/22/1: *Carry On Matron* by Talbot Rothwell. First Draft, n.d.

46 BFI GT/22/8: Christopher Grimes to Peter Eade, 6 February 1970:

47 BFI GT/22/7: Stephen Murphy to Gerald Thomas, 30 December 1971.

48 BFI GT/12/11: Stephen Murphy to Gerald Thomas, 23 May 1974.

49 BFI GT/30/7: Talbot Rothwell to Peter Rogers, 13 June 1968.

50 BFI GT/15/11 L. S. Lee to Gerald Thomas, 25 January 1978.

Bibliography

Anderson, M. (1998) '"Stop messing about!": The gay fool of the *Carry On* films', *Journal of Popular British Cinema*, 1: 37–47.

Cull, N. J. (2002) 'Camping on the borders: History, identity and Britishness in the *Carry On* costume parodies, 1963–74', in C. Monk and A. Sargeant (eds), *British Historical Cinema*, London: Routledge.

Davies, R. (ed.) (1993) *The Kenneth Williams Diaries*, London: HarperCollins.

Gerrard, S. (2008) 'What a Carry On! The decline and fall of a great British institution', in R. Shail (ed.), *Seventies British Cinema*, London: Palgrave Macmillan/British Film Institute.

Harper, S. and Porter, V. (2003) *British Cinema of the 1950s: The Decline of Deference*, Oxford: Oxford University Press.

Hunt, L. (1998) *British Low Culture: From Safari Suits to Sexploitation*, London: Routledge.

Jordan, M. (1983) 'Carry on ... follow that stereotype', in J. Curran and V. Porter (eds), *British Cinema History*, London: Weidenfeld and Nicolson.

Medhurst, A. (1992) 'Carry on camp', *Sight & Sound*, New Series, 2: 4 (August): 19.

——(2007) *A National Joke: Popular Comedy and English Cultural Identities*, London: Routledge.

Petley, J. (1986) 'The lost continent', in C. Barr (ed.), *All Our Yesterdays: 90 Years of British Cinema*, London: British Film Institute.

Richards, J. (1997) *Films and British National Identity: From Dickens to 'Dad's Army'*, Manchester: Manchester University Press.

Ross, R. (1996) *The Carry On Companion*, London: B.T. Batsford.

Street, S. (1997) *British National Cinema*, London: Routledge.

Weight, R. (2002) *Patriots: National Identity in Britain 1940–2000*, London: Macmillan.

9 'Gird your armour on'

The genteel subversion of the *St. Trinian's* films

Andrew Roberts

A point-of-view-shot through a windshield of a bus shows the inhabitants of a typical small market town that might have been used for a Group Three or late Ealing comedy, fleeing in utter terror – the opening shot of one of Frank Launder and Sidney Gilliat's finest films, *The Belles of St. Trinian's* (1954). It is a film that is as cynical a view of the British class system as *The Rake's Progress* (1945) and as visually stylish as their comedy film noir *Green for Danger* (1946) – and one of the few British pictures of the 1950s to have an idiosyncratically positive view of the popular new folk devil, the teenager.

St. Trinian's is a girls' school with desperate aspirations to be considered 'public' – as in those establishments that were so named as being open to the paying public, unlike religious schools. The boy's public school flourished as a means of inculcating the value system of the British Empire in the minds of young Victorian upper-class males. In the 19th century, such institutions were typically the repository of the sons of middle-class businessmen, the landed gentry and colonial administrators, who sent their boys back to the mother country to be educated in the ways of a gentleman: Greek, Latin, etiquette and, of course, sportsmanship ('It's not whether you win or lose, it's how you play the game').

Yet the plays, films and comics inspired by such places transcended the barriers of class and gender; the 1939 film adaptation of *Goodbye Mr. Chips* was one of the major commercial and critical successes for MGM-British and in the following year George Orwell wrote of the popularity of the comics the *Gem* and the *Magnet*:

> I have known them to be read by boys whom one might expect to be completely immune from public-school 'glamour' … I have seen a young coal miner, for instance, a lad who had already worked a year or two underground, eagerly reading the *Gem*. Recently I offered a batch of English papers to some British legionaries of the French Foreign Legion in North Africa; they picked out the *Gem* and *Magnet* first.
>
> (Orwell 1940).

From the early 1900s, narratives centred upon boys' schools were augmented by the new genre of the 'girls' school story', following the rise in educational opportunities for middle-class girls. At the beginning of the 20th century, less than a quarter of all British girls aged between 12 and 18 attended any kind of school, but by 1920, the number receiving a secondary education had risen from 20,000 in 1897 to 185,000 by the beginning of the 1920s (Kamm 1971: 113). Reflecting this change were the stories of Angela Brazil, whose 1906 *The Fortunes of Phillipa* is heralded as the beginning of the genre's mass popularity amongst younger readers:

> Angela Brazil broke deliberately with tradition, by expressing the girls' attitudes from the inside. Instead of boring her readers with a long-winded narrative view of events, she adopted as far as possible their vocabulary and their viewpoint, to achieve a zest and immediacy which the Edwardian schoolgirl must have relished. Her girls can be ruthless, stupid, vain or pig-headed without incurring overt narrative disapproval; the issue is rather the girls' tolerance of one another, than the author's concern to instruct her readers (though that of course is implicit in the stories' outcome, and occasionally *does* obtrude).
>
> (Cadogan and Craig 1986: 180)

Brazil went on to write almost 50 more girls' stories before her death in 1947 and by the 1920s her chief rival was Elinor M. Brent-Dyer's *Chalet School* series. After the end of the Second World War, Enid Blyton's *Malory Towers* series continued the genre at a time when more British girls had the opportunity of at least an approximation of a public school education via the 1944 Education Act, which ensured free secondary education for all up until the age of 15. Section 3 of the Act determined that entrance to a state grammar school would now be determined only by the pupils' academic ability in the form of 'passing' the Eleven Plus examination and not by parental financial ability to pay.

Although grammar school pupils were always in the minority of children to benefit from the Act – around 20 per cent attended such schools whilst the vast majority were enrolled in a Secondary Modern School – it did give thousands of students an opportunity to attend schools that deliberately modelled themselves upon boarding establishments in terms of curriculum and dress.

But in addition to venerable grammar schools and those establishments that were signed to the Headmasters' Conference for Leading Independent Schools, there also existed the privately-run institutions that offered teaching staff of dubious or no academic achievement, very reasonable fees and the sense of middle-class respectability, at least in terms of outward appearance. Just as the advent of the 1944 Act did not abolish the public school, nor did it bring about the demise of those establishments described by Orwell as 'the schools that are designed for people who can't afford a public school but consider the Council schools "common"' (Orwell 1940) – schools such as the defunct Belmont College in Devon that expelled a young John Osborne. In pre-war British cinema these were the seats of learning presided over by Will Hay in *Boys Will Be Boys* (1935) and *Good Morning Boys* (1936), a world of seedy pedagogues who kept order via a mixture of desperation and cunning – a world eminently familiar to any reader of Ronald Searle's cartoons.

Searle's first St. Trinian's cartoon appeared in *Lilliput* magazine in 1941 but it was not until after the Second World War, during which Searle had been a prisoner of the Japanese for three years, that the drawings of demonic, gin-swigging boarding-school girls took on their iconic form. The name of the school was derived from a real 'progressive' girl's school called St. Trinnean's in Edinburgh but much of Searle's inspiration for the drawings derived from Searle's own depictions of his prison camp guards and as Kaye Webb, his former partner, noted:

> [I]t was inevitable that the débacle [Searle] had just witnessed, the atmosphere of cruelty and the smell of death in which he and his companions existed for ... four years, should permeate his drawings so that the next two schoolgirl jokes took on their first flavour of violence. It hardly seems necessary to mention that Searle does not really think of schoolgirls as murderous little horrors. But unconsciously he was seeking to reduce horror into a comprehensible and somehow palatable form.
>
> (Searle 1959: 16)

The cartoons began appearing in book form – *Hurrah for St. Trinian's!* in 1947, followed by *The Female Approach* (1949), *Back to the Slaughterhouse* (1951) and *Souls in Torment* (1953). These all depicted a world diametrically opposite to that of *Malory Towers* – wherein Enid Blyton keeps in vigorous circulation the great myths of boyish manliness, the efficacy of individual action, the great solidarities of friendship, the joys of spontaneous freedoms innocent of all authority, except a moral law – or *Girl Magazine*, with its many articles on how to darn with verve and aplomb. Instead Searle's pictures celebrated the general absence of team spirit, standards of uniforms and jolly hockey sticks:

> For every girl whose uniform never fitted, whose hat looked permanently on loan, whose mother worried silently and sighed audibly, whose report commented on Absence of Team Spirit, whose arrival was marked by a volley of sharp reports as elastic burst in all directions, whose appearance suggested an abandoned Christmas parcel on which the temporary staff at Mount Pleasant had worked off their grief and frustrations, Searle came as a prophet of liberty and new self-respect.
>
> (quoted in Searle 1959: 23)

And it was Launder's daughter who informed her father that all of her classmates were vast fans of the St. Trinian's books – 'Sidney agreed that it sounded like a good basis for a comedy and we negotiated the rights with Ronald Searle, including an agreement on his part to provide the background to the credits and the posters' (Brown 1977: 134), although Searle had actually killed off his characters via a nuclear explosion in *Souls in Torment*. Heading the cast would be Alastair Sim as headmistress Miss Fritton, the very embodiment of shabby gentility, and it is a testament to Sim's vast talent's that Miss Fritton does not actually appear as grotesque, especially in comparison with her staff.

Nor, unlike Will Hay's Dr. Twist, does Miss Fritton have to resort to bluster to achieve her frequently nefarious goals. In British cinema of the 1930s, an alternative to Hay's shambolic establishments was provided by the benevolent traditionalism of MGM-British's *Goodbye Mr. Chips*. After the Second World War, it was not only in actual boarding school narratives that public school values found cinematic expression, however. From 1950's *The Wooden Horse* onwards, the 'people as hero' theme current in World War II films was replaced by a celebration of individual heroism, usually of public-school-educated men. So many British films of this era were dominated by headmaster-like commanding officers exercising stern benevolence towards prefect-style officer cadets. From horseplay – 'Come chaps, off with their trousers!' in *The Dam Busters* (1955) – to reticence in the face of danger, the sporting and social ethos of the public schools permeated the screen.

The parallels are most notable in films set in the enclosed world of the prisoner-of-war camp – as in *The Wooden Horse* or *The Colditz Story* (1955) – but the analogy can be extended to movies about civilian life such as *Doctor in the House* (1954) in which Dirk Bogarde and his chums indulge in all manner of joshing under the eye of James Robertson Justice's Chief Surgeon, Sir Lancelot Spratt, one of British cinema's most prominent curmudgeonly yet benevolent patriarchs. The difference here between St. Swithun's training hospital and the ethos of St. Trinian's, is the antithesis of the community virtues that won us the war and a total lack of the idea that the young should ultimately defer to the established system.

As for the actual school narratives in mainstream British films made after the Second World War, the cosiness of *Goodbye Mr. Chips* was sometimes replaced with cynicism and human despair. The Boultings' adaptation of *The Guinea Pig* (1948), concerning how a lower-middle-class scholarship boy, under the short-lived Fleming Scheme,[1] learns to love cold baths, may have been as conformist as the 1951 adaption of *Tom Brown's Schooldays*. But in *Mr. Perrin and Mr. Traill* (1948) and *The Browning Version* (1951), the central characters are 'Elderly failures, unloved, pedantic disciplinarians with tormented private lives. Their schools are joyless prisons, Perrin's Benfield being described by one character as a "decaying tooth"' (Richards and Aldgate 1983: 91).

And there was Launder and Gilliat's 1950 adaptation of John Dighton's 1948 West End farce *The Happiest Days of Your Life*, which introduced a welcome note of cynicism, with Nutbourne College portrayed as a haven of mediocrity in the midst of Attlee's England. When the Ministry of Education billets St. Swithin's School for Girls at Nutbourne, Alastair Sim's ambitious headmaster, Wetherby Pond, is confronted by the seemingly ferocious Miss Muriel Whitchurch (Margaret Rutherford), head of an organisation that's not quite top-drawer, a school that specialises in 'girls whose parents are from the Colonies'. Meanwhile the future of his own hallowed institution seems precarious: 'The school goes back to 1830 and if Pond doesn't keep up the payments it goes back to the bank,' muses Arnold Billings, the cynical maths master.

Despite the ivy-wreathed school grounds – Alton in Hampshire – Pond's establishment is looking increasingly threadbare in a post-war England where certain sectors of the middle classes were starting to consider their position. David Cannadine noted:

> [N]otwithstanding all of the forebodings in 1939 and again in 1945 that civilisation as they knew it was coming to an end, and there would be a 'decline in the value formerly placed on hierarchy and deference', the fact is that many Britons continued to see their society in this way and from this perspective.
>
> (Cannadine 2000: 155)

When *The Belles of St. Trinian's* entered production in early 1954, many traditional middle-class Conservative voters, in the words of a Tory Central Office report to Sir Anthony

Eden, felt as though 'they have not had a square deal and are looking for somewhere else to go' (Cannadine 2000: 152). It was this sense of clinging to middle-class status with a minimum of means that pervade *The Belles of St. Trinian's* where the staff are obliged to consort with book-makers and Spivs in order to maintain their dubious – and even spurious – sense of respectability. As Cadogan observes, the film's plot involving 'switched race horses was a virtual inversion of typical girl's comic strip involving ... mystery and detection, exploits of gypsies in disguise, poor little rich girls and rich little poor girls' (Cadogan and Craig 1986: 233).

It is the depiction of St. Trinian's undisciplined but highly intelligent and pro-active sixth form that marks a contrast with much British cinematic output of the 1940s and 1950s. Aside from The Children's Film Foundation, which produced films specifically for juveniles' matinees, mainstream British cinema during this period provided very few films in terms of child- or teenager-centred narratives where the narrative resolution would be provided by the young people themselves. Two early examples of films centred around the teenager are Basil Dearden's *I Believe In You* (1952), in which Joan Collins' Norma needs to be guided away from Laurence Harvey's subterranean world of jazz dens by the probation service towards a respectable future with Harry Fowler, and in Lewis Gilbert's *Cosh Boy* (1953) where the post-war juvenile delinquency problem can apparently be dealt with by the judicious application of a damned good thrashing.

Both films displayed working-class male youth as a monochrome vision of sideburned delinquents, mooching among the bombsites and threatening any decent respectable lady. A further common denominator was the need for control, a theme that echoed reams of memos from the Youth Club Association and various educational bodies discussing the merits, or otherwise, of cinema going for young people. In the words of Alan Burton:

> Unease was shown following the findings of the Social Service Division of the Central Office of Information and its report on children's leisure, and observers were left with the impression that some out of school activities like the popular cinema clubs 'would be better suppressed not developed'.
>
> (Burton 2005: 55)

National Service for young men continued until 1963 and, in 1960, the Government published the Arblemarle Report on Youth Clubs:

> To offer individual young people in their leisure time opportunities of various kinds, complementary to those of home, formal education and work, to discover and develop their personal resources of body, mind and spirit and thus the better equip themselves to live the life of mature, creative and responsible members of a free society.
>
> (Ministry of Education 1960: 36)

The release of *The Belles of St. Trinian's* also coincided with the media attention focusing upon Britain's first post-war teenage cult, the Teddy Boys, resulting in a spate of films à la *My Teenage Daughter* (1956), a searing drama of how Sylvia Syms' 17-year-old Janet leaves business college in order to spend all her time with Kenneth Haigh's Tony; a homicidal Teddy Boy. But worse, far worse, than the alcohol and the (not very) wild parties is the dance-hall where Shelia learns how to jive, thereby destroying her moral compass. Rock 'n' roll, being a sensual form of music, would obviously cause problems for many a British film-maker of this period and so the solution was either to neuter the performers beyond all recognition or to use jiving Teddy Boys as folk-devils of the post-war age. Occasionally these scenes would bear a sub-text that was evidently not envisaged by the director. *Violent Playground* (1957) had Stanley Baker's juvenile liaison officer witnessing David McCallum, Freddie Starr and sundry other Teds engage in a bout of dancing that positively crackles with homo-erotic charge. As Christine Geraghty noted of official responses to the Teddy Girl phenomenon:

> In so far as young women entered the picture, it was as adjuncts who attached themselves to such youths; and while there was concern about their sexuality there was also the feeling that young women could, through their desire for home and family, be part of the process of settling their boyfriends down.
>
> (Geraghty 1997: 154)

British cinematic role models for the sixth formers, those women who did not wish to 'settle down' in any way, shape or form, were rare indeed. The Gainsborough Gothic heroines may have been mad, bad and dangerous to know but they all too often seemed

Figure 9.1 George Cole as Flash Harry the Spiv in *The Belles of St. Trinian's* (1954). Image courtesy of

to crave a thrashing at the hands of James Mason. A later Gainsborough heroine, Jean Kent in *Good-Time Girl* (1948), learnt the lesson that the System can be inherently oppositional to a bright, vulnerable teenager from a working-class background.

By the 1950s, the vibrancy of Diana Dors was frequently demonstrated to be in need of strong control or even punishment: *Dance Hall* (1950) provides an early glimpse of La Dors as an intelligent, witty, buxom and openly sexual leading lady, but five years later that would have mutated into an ersatz-Marilyn Monroe, caked in studio make-up and forever photographed at 'Personal Appearances' in suburban Odeons. Her performance in the anti-capital-punishment drama 1956's *Yield to the Night* may have been genuinely Oscar-worthy but it also highlighted the fact that the qualities Dors displayed in her best films – i.e. that sex was very enjoyable and intelligence and individuality were to be encouraged – were subconsciously deserving of punishment. This fate will never overtake Miss Fritton's graduates, none of whom could you ever imagine becoming the insipid ingénues of *Father's Doing Fine* (1952) or *For Better, For Worse* (1954), and all of whom most probably took their cue from La Dors' spirited disobedience of the central rule in 1950's *Dance Hall* – 'No Jiving'.

But *The Belles of St. Trinian's*, in addition to being able to make mincemeat of any drape-jacketed would-be suitor, are essentially middle-class delinquents who operate in a world of ostensible tradition – a further vexed issue for several British comedy films of this era. In *The Titfield Thunderbolt* (1953), the natural order is that of a traditional village hierarchy presided over by the steam-train-loving village squire and with any outside commercial interests – in the form of the Pearce & Crump Bus Company. Here the Squirearchy successfully attempts to keep all visible signs of the post-war world out of a rural arcadia for as long as possible. But whilst the Victorian Titfield is apparently under siege from the post-war world, with John Gregson's Squire railing against the prospect of 'traffic lights' and 'zebra crossings!', St. Trinian's own great heritage, despite all appearances, merely dates back to the late 1920s.

Or, in the words of Miss Fritton: 'When poor Freda and I started this school during the General Strike of 1926, we vowed to make it the happiest carefree establishment in the whole of Britain.' By 1954, Miss Fritton is reduced to pawning the school trophies and bemoaning the lost 'gay Arcadia of childhood it was until the war broke out and people with money lost it', echoing the cynicism of William Rose's screenplays for *Genevieve* (1953) and *The Ladykillers* (1955), where tradition is seen to be only as good as those who maintain it.[2]

In *Genevieve*, John Gregson and Dinah Sheridan may have a 1904 Darracq in their garage but they also have a modern kitchen with every mod con, and their rage at the incompetence of Joyce Grenfell's aspidistra-infested hotel is seen to be wholly justified. In the latter film, Victoriana, initially seeming innocuous, or even quaint, is still capable of the dead weight of tradition – 'We'll never be rid of her, Louis,' moans Alec Guinness of the redoubtable Mrs. Wilberforce. 'We'll be with her forever and ever and there's nothing we can do about it.'

As the reviewer from *Time* (7 February 1955) succinctly put it, St. Trinian's is 'a finishing school with a difference; it is not the students but the staff who are finished'. St. Trinian's attempts a veneer of respectability when the staff lack food let alone wages and just as Stanley Windrush in *Private's Progress* (1956) was to discover a new world of corruption and sheer boredom during his wartime military service, the staffroom at Miss Fritton's establishment emphatically does not boast a kindly house mistress who is keen to show the new bugs the ropes.

But, compared with Diana Dors or indeed Jean Kent in *Good Time Girl*, the St. Trinian's inmates do not have to suffer lectures concerning tradition, save for Miss Fritton's introduction to the school's philosophy – 'in other schools, girls are sent out quite unprepared into a merciless world, but when our girls leave here, it is the merciless world which has to be prepared'. Nor are they punished for their individuality, intelligence and keen sense of enterprise.

This sense of aggressive individuality is reflected in Launder's direction of *The Belles of St. Trinian's* where, as with Searle's own drawings, every corner of the screen was filled with surreal imagery such as a blankly menacing first former with bird's-nest hair, or a fiendish 'innocent' peering through banisters as a form of uniquely British grotesque Greek chorus. George Cole has stated that his body language as Flash Harry was directly inspired by the actual cartoon character: 'It was all there in Ronald Searle's cartoons. That character of Flash Harry was in the cartoons. Ronald Searle has him coming around the wall at an angle that is physically impossible to do – worse than forty-five degrees' (quoted in Macfarlane 1997: 134). However, several critics complained that there was not enough of Searle's menacing viewpoint in the finished film – 'but if good money's worth it's not Searle and not nearly as much fun as that other frolic ... *The Happiest Days of Your Life*' (*New Statesman*, 9 October 1954) and 'This is not darkest St. Trinian's but – in spirit and soul – an Angela Brazil high school on an end of term rampage' (*Daily Sketch*, 1 October 1954).

But compared with other British comedy films centred on the world of the school, *The Belles of St. Trinian's* was indeed different. *Top of the Form* (1953) was an updating of Will Hay's *Boys Will Be Boys* as a post-war vehicle for Ronald Shiner, and *Fun at St. Fanny's* (1956) was merely an example of how British second-feature producers could occasionally lose their minds.[3] It would not be until as late as 1959 that British cinema made a Secondary Modern set comedy with *Carry On Teacher*, three years after ABPC's commercial success with *It's Great to be Young!* (1956), a major colour comedy-musical.

Unlike fortress St. Trinian's, the world of *It's Great to Be Young!* is that of a grammar school in middle-middle-class suburbia – 'Angel Hill Grammar School boasts venerable, ivy-covered, buildings, masters in gowns and mortar boards and white-flannelled cricketers at play on lazy summer afternoons' (Richards and Aldgate 1983: 91). Still, the narrative was focused upon the genuinely young cast who retained an engaging Nigel Molesworth[4] attitude towards authority as filtered through vibrant Eastmancolor and suffused with quasi-Hollywood dance numbers, even if the *Monthly Film Bulletin* (July 1956) did grumble: 'The dubbing of the musical numbers by professional groups is quite efficient, though the sugary, American-style songs strike an alien note in such emphatically British surroundings.'

But, as with so many other British films, authority in *It's Great to be Young!*, in the form of Cecil Parker's headmaster, is seen to be ultimately professional and benign whereas the staffroom of St. Trinian's is peopled by vamps, gin-addicts and mistresses who merely keep a nervous eye out for a police Wolseley clanging up the driveway. Presiding over this strangely appealing ménage is Alastair Sim's Miss Fritton, who regards her charges with a justifiable pride and takes their extra-curricular activities with amiable equanimity; her response to discovering that the school's one-time Boot Boy is now the campus's resident Wide-Boy is more one of horror at his choice of hair cream than shock at his new role in the school.

As for the middle-class authority figures outside of St. Trinian's gates, HM School Inspectorate in the form of Richard Wattis is both incompetent and impotent, with two of his former number 'gone native' in the school grounds. Joyce Grenfell's Sergeant Ruby Gates, operating undercover as the games mistress 'Miss Crawley', is a truly inept overgrown sixth former, a cruel parody of an Enid Blyton heroine in middle-age ('We're all Girl Guides, aren't we?', she implores Miss Fritton at one point, only to receive the withering response, 'Are we? Some of us may have aspired beyond that happy state, Miss Crawley') and her Superintendent, played by Lloyd Lamble, is the epitome of smoothly-bland, time-serving incompetence. Meanwhile, the fact that the ostensibly respectable parents, seen in the final reel, have clearly chosen the cheapest boarding school in England puts them as little better than Sid James's crooked bookie and henchmen.

The commercial success of the *Belles* resulted in a sequel two years later, *Blue Murder at St. Trinian's*, which tellingly dropped the girls' parents who would no longer appear, unless they were used as plot devices to introduce a further note of the outside adult criminal world into the school grounds. The sole conduit between school and the out-side world is Flash Harry, who by *Blue Murder* had modified his Spiv outfit into a complete Teddy Boy outfit; his return to the school at the wheel of his Heinkel Cabin Cruiser bubble car captures the late 1950s *zeitgeist*. But compared with the first film, the narrative emphasis was now upon mockery of post-war institutions such as the Civil Service, the police and the Army rather than a deliberate inversion of girls' schools stories.

The main focus of satire was now upon the adult characters instead of girls, who were described by Searle as 'would-be sadistic, cunning, dissolute, crooked, sordid, lacking morals of any sort and capable of any excess. [They] would also be well-spoken, even well-mannered and polite, sardonic, witty and very amusing. [They] would be good company. In short: typically human and, despite everything, endearing' (quoted in Davies 1990: 101–2). However, not only were the adults played with sublime comic timing by Cole, Grenfell, Lamble, Terry-Thomas and Lionel Jeffries, they were even less trustworthy than the grown-ups in the first film. Terry-Thomas's Captain Romney Carlton-Rickets, a bankrupt wartime Army officer reduced to maintaining standards amongst the exceedingly dead fleet of 'The Dreadnaught Motor Traction Company', encapsulates the post-Suez malaise writ large, and a second new development was the greater narrative emphasis upon the sixth formers, who were now far more ready to use their sex appeal in Flash Harry's matrimonial bureau and in tormenting both the police and the Army.

There was also the addition of the school song to the strains of Malcolm Arnold's theme song which encapsulated the St. Trinian's ethos[5] and the inmates were taken away from the familiar surroundings of Oakley Court in Windsor to Italy. According to Launder: 'The location in Rome had Italian schoolgirls playing St. Trinian's girls and their uninhibited behaviour matched that of our British girls. We got permission to shoot a chase through the Forum and Coliseum on the grounds that the film was a "cultural documentary"' (Brown 1977: 142).

By 1960, the girls' roles in the plot of *The Pure Hell of St. Trinian's*, the film that Launder regarded 'as perhaps the most intellectual of the St. Trinian's films ... the jokes tended to be fractionally more subtle' (Brown 1977: 150), had been even further reduced, Miss Fritton was nowhere to be seen and the adults are even less trustworthy, with an Honorary British Consul having to double as a Hotpoint dealer to make ends meet and cynical Majors commanding a Mobile Bath Unit in an increasingly bleak post-Suez world. Most of the scenes taking place in Cobham Common doubling as an 'Arabian' state are at the expense of the titular characters, whose sixth form spent far too much screen time trapped in a not terribly plausible 'harem'.

Launder and Gilliat's concerns with other films such as *Only Two Can Play* (1962) and their heavy involvement with the management of the British Lion production company meant that the final entry in the original St. Trinian's canon was not released until as late as 1966 in the form of *The Great St. Trinian's Train Robbery*. By this time, British cinematic comedy was undergoing several challenges, or to quote Robert Murphy: 'Writing the history of British comedy in the 60s is like reviewing a play in which the actors have walked out halfway through the performance, leaving a cast of cleaners, stagehands and volunteers from the audience to stagger through the remains of the play' (Murphy 1992: 236). The world of bellowing patriarchs as played by James Robertson Justice was on the wane and familiar staples of institutional comedy such as the army film had declined in popularity as the end of National Service in 1963 rendered the experience of life in uniform once more the province of the minority – Michael Winner's *You Must Be Joking!* and the Boultings' *Rotten to the Core*, both shot in black and white and released in 1965, were the last of their genre. Even the British wartime military ethos had been comprehensively subverted by Basil Dearden's *The League of Gentlemen* (1960), with Jack Hawkins' retired Colonel presiding over a less than magnificent septet of cashiered officers.

Of the St. Trinian's erstwhile box-office rivals, Norman Wisdom made his last mainstream family comedy, *Press for Time* (1966), in the same year that Leslie Phillips attempted to go 'mod' in *Doctor in Clover*, displaying a palpable sense of unease with the world outside of Pinewood Studios in the process. As for the *Carry On* films, after 1963's *Cabby* they rarely strayed outside of institutional and genre parody – the spectacle of the 'hippie rave' in 1969's *Camping* merely highlighted the film's middle-aged paranoia with youth culture. St. Trinian's also seemed ill-at-ease in the context of late-1960s Britain. *Train Robbery* shows a British comic landscape in transition. Unlike the previous two films, much of the narrative takes place in the school – there is even a parents' day – but several of the trains attacked by the girls are now diesel-powered and Flash Harry now drives a Sunbeam Alpine and (unwisely) affects Ray Davies-length hair, but the girls still wear a parody of a public school uniform and the police still arrive in their bell-ringing black Wolseleys.

Launder may have stated that last of the classic St. Trinian's was 'the first in colour, and topping all of the others at the box office' (Brown 1977: 152) but his subsequent remarks about Howerd and Bryan – 'a couple of good natured stars' – demonstrates how much the focus has shifted from the girls themselves to the adult farceurs. By now, the connection to the original cartoons is limited to the theme song whilst most of the actual students are mere extras populating their runaway trains. Sim, Grenfell and Lamble are very conspicuous by their absence and the charming whimsy of the first film – Miss Fritton summonsing Flash Harry and being enchanted to discover that she can whistle in the process – is replaced by clod-hopping slapstick and dismal racist sight-gags.

The world which St. Trinian's was definitely opposed to was starting to disappear; by 1967, the Empire had diminished to the stage that the Colonial Office had ceased to be a separate entity and the traditional 'girl's stories' were moving into the realm of nostalgia.[6] Royston Lambert's classic survey into British boarding schools in the late 1960s may have demonstrated that there remained plenty of comic mileage in the genre – 'Tea is over. I have got detension [sic]. At least I think so, for chucking a piece of bread, soaked in tea, across the table' – remarked one potential St. Trinian's inmate (quoted in Lambert 1968: 246), but although *The Great St. Trinian's Train Robbery* may have succeeded at the box office, in the words of Murphy: 'Like 1960s town planning, which pulled down friendly terraces and replaced them with shopping precincts and high rise flats, it now seems a dreadful mistake' (Murphy 1992: 252).

The Great St. Trinian's Train Robbery was the last film to bear the Launder and Gilliat logo; for several years, the pair now being heavily engaged in the politics of British Lion films. An attempt to revive the series with 1980's *The Wildcats of St. Trinian's* met with extremely well-deserved obscurity. The series would not be revived until *St. Trinian's* (2007), a loose remake of *Belles*, and its sequel, *St. Trinian's 2: The Legend of Fritton's Gold* (2009), which provided a timely rejoinder to the curiously retro-1950s world of the *Harry Potter* films but could not hope to approach the deceptive subversion of the original film.

After *The Belles of St. Trinian's* there would not be as corrosive a view of school life and the British establishment until Lindsay Anderson's *If* ... (1968), with its inept staff and power-crazed sixth form. Maybe Malcolm McDowell's Mick Travis even took inspiration from the wise words of Sirrol Hugh-Jones: 'St. Trinian's is English womanhood – plain, imprisoned, disguised according to Regulation Uniform Lists as trolls, demons, scarecrows, and under-privileged gargoyles – against the world' (Searle 1959: 22).

Notes

1 Named for the Scottish judge Lord Fleming, which enabled talented boys from state schools to attend public schools such as Winchester, Rugby and Eton, paid for by their counties. The scheme ran for about 30 years from 1947.

2 Dinah Sheridan's character Wendy in *Genevieve* is probably a St. Trinian's graduate. Kay Kendall's Rosalind almost definitely is.

3 What other explanation could there be for a film that combined the talents of Cardew 'The Cad' Robinson, Freddie Mills and Francis Langford's Singing Scholars?

4 Created by Geoffrey Willans and illustrated by Ronald Searle, as any fule kno.

5 'Maidens of St. Trinian's, gird your armour on. Grab the nearest weapon, never mind which one,' complete with lyrics accompanied by a bouncing ball.

6 Although the last *Chalet School* story was published as late as 1970.

Bibliography

Brown, G. (1977) *Launder & Gilliat*, London: BFI.

Burton, A. (2005) *The British Consumer Co-Operative Movement and Film, 1890s–1960s*, Manchester: Manchester University Press.

Cadogan, M. and Craig, P. (1986) *You're A Brick, Angela! The Girls' Story 1839–1985*, 2nd edn, London: Victor Gollancz.

Cannadine, D. (2000) *Class in Britain*, London: Penguin.

Geraghty, C. (1997) 'Women and 60s British cinema: The development of the "Darling" girl', in R. Murphy (ed.), *The British Cinema Book*, London: BFI.

Kamm, J. (1971) *Indicative Past: A Hundred Years of the Girls' Public Day School Trust*, London: George Allen and Unwin.

Lambert, R. (1968) *The Hothouse Society*, London: Weidenfeld & Nicolson.

Macfarlane, B. (1997) *An Autobiography of British Cinema*, London: Methuen.

Ministry of Education (1960) *The Youth Service in England and Wales*, London: Her Majesty's Stationery Office.

Murphy, R. (1992) *Sixties British Cinema*, London: BFI.

Orwell, G. (1940) 'Boys' Weeklies', *Horizon*, March.

Richards, J. and Aldgate, A. (1983) *Best of British – Cinema & Society 1930–1970*, Oxford: Basil Blackwell.

Searle, R. (1959) *The St. Trinian's Story*, London: Penguin, 1959.

10 Norman Wisdom

Rank Studios and the rise of the Super Chump

Richard Dacre

It is surprising, especially given the number of great clowns who emerged in the wake of World War II, that only one was to make a significant and lasting impact in British cinema and that was Norman Wisdom. Others shone as character comedians, and yet others developed their careers on stage, radio and television, but only Wisdom lasted the course in the cinema with a series of films built around the comic character that he had developed while working on the stage and on television and which he named the Gump.

Norman Wisdom was born in Paddington in 1915 to a seamstress and a chauffeur. He and his elder brother had a horrendous childhood. Their parents split up when they were young and the two children were forced to fend for themselves while their alcoholic, often violent father would leave them alone for days on end. A spell in foster homes followed before, at the age of 14, having acquired little education, Norman talked his way into the Army as a boy bandsman. This changed his entire life – companionship, regular meals, discipline and the learning of musical and gymnastic skills which would hold in him in good stead for the rest of his life. He was soon performing in Army concert parties, playing instruments, dancing and singing. He gradually incorporated comedy into his act, and continued to entertain his service comrades before and during the war. With demobilisation, he chose to go professional and was soon getting the occasional spot on variety bills throughout the country.

By 1948, Wisdom was being noticed. He found himself Billy Marsh, an agent at the powerful Bernard Delfont Agency; an association which would prove to be mutually beneficial and would propel them both to the top of their respective professions. Marsh brought Wisdom to the prestigious London Casino when he heard that his rival Val Parnell was interested in booking him for the Palladium – an indication of Wisdom's growing status. Wisdom triumphed in his West End debut, but both Marsh and Wisdom knew there was still a lot to learn, and Wisdom was despatched to the provinces to gain more experience.

In the summer of 1948, Wisdom was booked for the season at Scarborough which required him to develop different material for each week of its six-week run. This was a tough regime and one of Wisdom's fellow performers, conjuror David Nixon, asked Wisdom to help him out by coming on stage as a planted stooge from the audience. Wisdom decided that a distinctive costume was required to differentiate this conjurer's stooge from the characters he was playing in his solo turn. With an eye on budget, he went out and, for 30 shillings, purchased an ill-fitting suit and cap, little knowing that they would soon become his trademark.

What started out as a way to differentiate his guest role from his central performance ended up dominating his solo act and his career. As the Gump gradually took centre-stage, so Wisdom built up the character, tailoring his existing comic persona of the accident-prone simpleton to fit the man in the deficient suit. The main components of the Gump played on Wisdom's diminutive five-foot three-inch form. He was the little man who wanted to be accepted and his eagerness to make friends was expressed through a deep-seated compulsion to entertain. Wisdom's gymnastic skills were mainly put to the service of the falls for which he was already known, resulting either from incompetence, bad luck, or the hostility of others. He was a firm believer in the infectiousness of laughter and the sight of him collapsing helplessly in mirth was a familiar one. This, combined with Wisdom's skills as musician developed through his years as a boy bandsman, plus a pleasing singing voice, would make him a major power on the variety stage.

The year 1948 continued to be a key one in Wisdom's career, not only did he create the Gump but he also made his first headline television show – *Wit and Wisdom* (tx 18 October 1948) – and had his big screen debut, albeit only a 13.5-second cameo, in *A Date with a Dream* (1948), directed by Dicky Leeman. Brief thoughts of a double-act with Nixon were discarded, and Wisdom continued to make his name through touring and a series of prestigious Derek Salberg Pantomimes in the Midlands which helped Wisdom expand his theatrical reach and introduced him to Eddie Leslie who played the Dame in a number of these. Wisdom soon teamed up with Leslie to write sketches and work with him on stage, with Leslie becoming his first regular straight man.

By 1951, Wisdom's breakthrough to the top of his profession was confirmed when he returned to the capital for the starring role in an ice show, *London Melody*, at Earls Court's Empress Hall. The Gump had been perfected and the show was a phenomenal success leading directly to a guest spot Stateside on Ed Sullivan's *Toast of the Town* (tx CBS, 11 November 1951).

It was inevitable that the film industry would show an interest. ABC were already making enquiries, but it was Rank who got the signature after head of production Earl St John chanced on Wisdom in a television special *Christmas Party* (tx 25 December 1951) and successfully argued the case for how well Wisdom would fit into Rank's production plans.

At the time Rank were struggling to maintain their position as Britain's dominant cinema force. They were still recovering from a period of near-bankruptcy following an over-ambitious production programme intended to fill the gap caused by Hollywood's embargo on exporting films to Britain. The embargo had arisen as a result of the Government's misguided imposition of a 75 per cent levy on imports in 1947. Rank's patriotic attempt to fill British exhibition schedules was undermined almost immediately by the Government's hasty capitulation to American pressure, which allowed a backlog of top American products into the market in time to compete with Rank's overstretched and thus under-resourced home product. This put Rank in an impossible position of either playing their own films and risking the well-being of their cinemas, or playing as many Hollywood films as possible and writing off much of their production

Figure 10.1 Norman Wisdom as the classic Gump in a publicity shot. Image author's own.

expenditure. Additionally, there was the continuing problem of the excessive and dis-
criminatory levels of Entertainment Tax on cinema ticket prices which undermined
exhibition viability. It would take several years of belt-tightening under a conservative
regime put into place by Chief Executive John Davis for them to recover from a
position, which at its worst saw Rank with a £16 million overdraft. The thrust of this
recovery was to limit the Organisation's involvement in film production to that which

was necessary to supply the required quota of British films to be shown in their cinemas; now set at 30 per cent. These films were made to strictly controlled budgets with a maximum spend of £150,000. This process of reducing production expenditure, backed up by cutting overheads and selling-off everything superfluous to making immediate profit, was remarkably successful in terms of financial recovery but also marked a decisive switch from the wartime years that had seen Rank as the champion of artistic film making. The films they now wanted to make were uncontroversial fare for the family audience. The business emphasis was more on marketing and maximising ancillary sales at front-of-house. It is not surprising that St John saw Wisdom as the perfect fit.

But St John was not the one who faced the responsibility of turning this plan into a reality. Once Wisdom was signed to Rank, the issue facing them was to take the Gump into feature-length narratives while retaining the key elements which had made the character such a success in other media. This is not an easy process, as evidenced by the paucity of clowns who have made a successful transfer to the big screen. Indeed Rank were saddled with memories of their shambolic failure to make the transfer with the great Sid Field only a few years earlier. It is an instructive failure which had nothing to do with resources, money was lavished on the Technicolor showcase *London Town* (1946). Field was a brilliantly instinctive comic who had dominated London's comedy stage throughout the war. For the film, he played a version of himself, a provincial comic coming to London to make his name. The sentimental storyline of the film is interrupted during its more than two-hour running time with straightforward recordings of some of Field's great stage sketches. While this has proved a boon to present-day historians, it proved a disaster for contemporary audiences, Field's strength as a comic counted for nothing in this anaesthetised format, and audiences stayed away.

Rank's worries were only compounded by Wisdom's post-signature screen-test directed by Ronald Neame, which was deemed unsatisfactory. As a result, Neame and producer John Bryan abandoned what was meant to be Wisdom's first film which had been scripted by Jill Craigie. In what could have had a devastatingly negative effect on his career, Rank offered Wisdom a buy-out from the contract, but Wisdom's difficult upbringing had helped to make him extremely resilient and he declined. Rank paid him as per contract for the first year without making a film. As the second year progressed, Wisdom was farmed out to Ealing for *Meet Mr Lucifer* (1947), a rather overwrought satire on the evils of television. Wisdom was to be seen on the box, being watched by a young couple and the girl joins him in the television studio in a fantasy sequence. This cameo – with Eddie Leslie, Peggy Cummins and Jack Watling – was shot, but was cut pre-release when Rank finally came up with a starring project for Wisdom and did not want its impact diminished.[1]

By now, Rank had put a new team in place to support Wisdom consisting of producer Maurice Cowan, comedy specialist director John Paddy Carstairs and writer Ted Willis. In association with Wisdom and Leslie they built on Jill Craigie's original script which, in her own words, was 'a satire on a big store in rather a Chaplinesque vein, with plenty of scope for slapstick',[2] to produce *Trouble in Store* (1953). The new team took the basic setting of the department store and simplified the storyline. Wisdom was to play an accident-prone stockroom boy who dreams of being a window dresser and getting the girl. The simplicity of the storyline meant it could be taken for granted and explanatory passages could be kept to a minimum, leaving plenty of scope for comedy. The comic routines were formulated to develop naturally out of the storyline and to be of the kind familiar to Wisdom's fans.

But it was the thought given to Wisdom's character in the film which paid long-term dividends. *Trouble in Store* finds the character fully realised and would remain largely unchanged throughout the Rank films. The team knew that they had to take the Gump, perfected in short sketches in Variety and Pantomime, and stretch and develop it so that it could work in extended narratives. The foundation of the screen persona was to combine the chief characteristics of the Gump with those of the traditional little man against the world. This was clearly not a groundbreaking idea, but it worked perfectly and, importantly, the extension to the persona never undermined the original creation – Wisdom retained his individuality as a clown in the new medium. What's more, the character in the film and his comic persona were essentially one and the same, there is never the feeling that Wisdom is veering towards becoming a character actor – the Variety stage creation, the Gump, remained supreme.

Each of the Gump's traits, familiar to his legion of fans, was given a narrative function. And, in sharp contrast to the Field experience, routines were virtually never incorporated simply as stand-alone attractions. The Rank team took on wholesale the need for the Gump to entertain – often having him do it in situations that were totally inappropriate or doomed to being ill-received, not least because the Gump fails to recognise the signifiers of class. This accorded the easy incorporation of violent slapstick which was already a Wisdom trademark. Nevertheless, Wisdom's character was not just a perennially put-upon eager-to-please innocent, forever taking the knock-backs, but also one who would only take so much injustice before fighting back with a steely determination at whatever physical cost to himself. The need to entertain and to please made it simple to include Wisdom's singing without disrupting the narrative, though his proficiency on musical instruments was seldom displayed due to fears that audiences would not believe it was actually him playing. The Gump's simple-mindedness had often found expression in sketches in which he misunderstands commands or takes them too literally and these were easily incorporated wholesale, as was his love of long intricate routines where one absurdity leads to another in logical sequence.

Wisdom was used to working with a straight-man or 'feed' on stage, generally his writing partner Eddie Leslie. Leslie played his stooge as a stern, sometimes ruthless character, irritated by the Gump's activities and forever belittling him. It was Wisdom's favoured style of straight-man on stage, and while Leslie played his with a working-class stubbornness, his stage partner from 1968 onwards, Tony Fayne, adapted it to a middle-class schoolmasterly haughtiness. Leslie is one of several expert stooges in *Trouble in Store* – he and Wisdom get a good sequence together with Leslie's gangster trying to force a doped pill down Norman's throat – and Leslie worked with Wisdom on developing some of the routines for the film. But Rank also wanted a publicly known straight-man, and went with one of the most experienced in the business, Jerry Desmonde. Desmonde was considered the pre-eminent straight-man of his time, not least for his work with Sid Field, and would prove the perfect foil. His class disdain for the Gump added another layer of comic possibility, and he would work regularly with

Wisdom both on stage and on film from this point on. With a cameo from Margaret Rutherford added as insurance, the project was ready. Once completed, extracts were shown to critics who enthused and a sneak preview proved a triumph, but Rank's abiding lack of confidence meant that the film was nevertheless released with little fanfare. Despite this, the film was a phenomenal success breaking house records in 51 out of the 67 London cinemas in which it opened in 1953 – and Wisdom's future in film was assured.

Trouble in Store provided Rank with a basic format which would sustain Wisdom's film career throughout his Rank contract and beyond. He would go on to complete 12 films for the Organisation in a run which lasted until 1966. At the heart of these was the Gump, and as long as this character remained largely unchanged, Rank were satisfied. What's more, there was an institutional acceptance that no one knew the Gump better than Wisdom himself – it was basically his creation, he was not playing a character created by others. When occasional disputes arose between Wisdom and his collaborators about what the Gump would or would not do, it was Wisdom who would have the last word. This was with the full support of producer Hugh Stewart, who took over that role from 1955, and could cause minor friction with his directors and writers.

One thing which Wisdom always insisted on was that everything which happens in his films, however improbable, could happen in real life. His character might end up – as he does in *Press for Time* (1966) – swinging from the Lady Mayor's living-room light-fitting clutching the Lady Mayor's daughter, but how he got there is worked out with logical precision so that it is believable. It was a characteristic which separated him from the American slapstick clown with whom he was often compared, Jerry Lewis. Lewis was happy to incorporate surreal flights of fancy into his work which was anathema to Wisdom for whom the requirement for believability and empiricism permeated all aspects of the fictional film world. Once, when confronted with a script that would have placed him in a family where all seven children had ended up doing the same highly specialised job, he demanded the writer come up with a genuine example of such a family before he would consider it.[3] A consequence of this insistence on the believability of the fiction is that Wisdom never steps out of character in the way that his film predecessors such as George Formby and Will Hay had done – his character stays solidly within the world of the film. This was a change from his stage persona, which, as a natural consequence of being in front of a live audience, frequently stepped out of character to comment on what was happening.

This insistence on believability also impacted on Wisdom's use of pathos, perhaps the most controversial element in Wisdom's comic makeup and one which he, himself, saw as fundamental. When asked after *Trouble in Store* whether he thought that the pathos in the film had been overworked, he responded forthrightly: 'I'd like to get more in. But this is the sort of thing we hammer out in our conferences. To continue the purely personal viewpoint, though, I'd like to have more situational pathos' (*Picturegoer*, 6 February 1954). For him, it was a crucial part of his work, its sincerity being formed by memories of his horrendous upbringing and it also places him firmly in a long tradition of London comics going back through Charlie Chaplin to the Victorian coster comics such as Gus Elen and Albert Chevalier and beyond. However, on stage he tended to undermine the pathos. After indulging himself with a sob story to pull the heartstrings, he would look at the audience and berate them for being taken in – 'you should see your faces' – but on film such leavening was not allowed. While the pathos could be alleviated within the context of the storyline, it was generally left unapologetically unalloyed. Some critics then and now have found this unpalatable, but Wisdom had a sure sense of his own audience which was fully respected by his production team. When he had an entire film largely structured around the Gump's desire to make a recently-orphaned girl smile in *A Stitch in Time* (1963) it would prove to be his biggest commercial success, out-grossing that year's James Bond film in the UK.

By the time of the release of *Trouble in Store*, John Davis was firmly in control of the Rank Organisation, and *Trouble in Store* represented his ideal film production – cheap, clean and phenomenally popular. Wisdom was under contract, a profitable formula had been struck, and Davis wanted that formula to be endlessly repeated. The income from the Wisdom films played a key role both in the financial well-being of Rank's production arm and in the continuance of Pinewood Studios under the Rank umbrella. In 1954, aided by the success of *Trouble in Store*, cinema attendances were up, Rank was taking a third share of the national box office and more than half of their overall receipts were coming from foreign markets. Wisdom himself was attracting huge audiences in South America, Holland, Denmark, Iran, India, Singapore, Hong Kong and behind the Iron Curtain – Russia, Czechoslovakia and Albania.

While it is not surprising that Rank did not want to tamper with such a successful box office formula, Wisdom was soon feeling constrained by his creation. His cabaret act had been perfected and on stage he was able to present the full range of his talents – singing, musical performance and dancing as well as comedy. His success, now enhanced by his film roles, was such that Val Parnell persisted in his determination to have him play Britain's premiere showcase, The London Palladium, despite the fact that Wisdom was still signed to his huge business rival Bernard Delfont. Delfont was equally determined to get his acts on at the Palladium and so a deal was struck resulting in Delfont presenting international Variety at the Palladium for around 20 years. The quality of Wisdom's stage act at this time has thankfully been preserved for posterity with his television solo appearance on *Sunday Night at the London Palladium* (tx 3 December 1961), which has survived the decimation of so much early British television Variety. But Wisdom was also allowed to stretch himself in the theatre, not just through his annual London Palladium Pantomimes (from 1955) but also on the musical stage, as he proved with his hugely acclaimed run in Frank Loesser's *Where's Charley* through 1958 and 1959.

Wisdom's attempts to persuade Rank to allow him the same freedom on film fell on deaf ears. Projects attempting more sophisticated types of comedy and indeed ideas for dramas – in particular a film on the life of boxer Benny Lynch for which he would have been perfect casting – were firmly rebuffed, leading to some resentment. Wisdom completed his contract in 1959 having made seven films at a rate of one a year: *Trouble in Store*, *One Good Turn* (1954), *Man of the Moment* (1955), *Up in the World* (1956), *Just My Luck* (1957), *The Square Peg* (1958) and *Follow a Star* (1959), the last of which had former assistant director Robert Asher taking over full directorial duties from John Paddy Carstairs for the first time. After *Follow a Star*, Wisdom stayed with Rank on a film-by-film basis and would continue to do so until 1966 and *Press for Time*. But he was now a free agent, and when he was offered the opportunity to expand his outlook beyond the Gump, ironically by John Bryan and Ronald Neame and their Knightsbridge films, he leapt at the chance. The results only proved Rank's financial acumen. The first Knightsbridge film, *There Was a Crooked Man* (1960), is a satire on American overseas influence, scripted by the black-listed Canadian writer Reuben Ship and directed by theatre doyen Stuart Burge. In it, Wisdom plays a war-time safe-cracker drawn into criminal activity before avenging himself on a crooked financier with the unintentional help of the American Army. Despite being among Wisdom's finest films and gaining favourable reviews particularly, and perhaps ominously, from the 'quality' press, it made barely a ripple at the box office. The film disappeared without trace and remains unavailable in any format at the time of writing.[4] The second, and lesser film, was an adaptation from P.G. Wodehouse, *The Girl on the Boat* (1962), with Wisdom largely eschewing slapstick to take on the role of the upper-class romantic in a farce which, indeed, dispenses with almost all of Wisdom's usual strengths, and likewise suffered at the box office.

Somewhat chastened, Wisdom returned to Rank and unparalleled success with two further films with Robert Asher, *On the Beat* (1962) and *A Stitch in Time*. It is not that Rank was completely closed to allowing Wisdom to expand his comic reach. Producer Hugh Stewart was acutely aware of the need to keep his star happy and Rank could ill-afford to lose him, but Stewart certainly couldn't contemplate the kind of figures

Figure 10.2 Wisdom in the rarely seen *There was a Crooked Man* (1960). Image author's own

that the Knightsbridge films achieved. Wisdom was allowed greater leeway as long as the basic figure of the Gump, already less of a simpleton as time went by, remained in place. Getting the Gump out of costume was simple enough – give him a job which required a uniform – in the army, navy or police. More significant were the narrative strategies used to allow Wisdom to display talents beyond the abilities of the Gump including multiple roles, dream sequences and behaving under hypnosis.

The first time that Wisdom took on a dual role was in *The Square Peg*, where the wartime Gump comes face to face with his double, a German General. Interestingly, John Paddy Carstairs, the man so crucial in Wisdom's cinematic development, was against the star taking both roles and mixing comic styles, but Wisdom had the support not only of his fellow writers but also, crucially, that of Hugh Stewart. It would be the last time Carstairs and Wisdom worked together. Another dual role in *On the Beat* enabled Wisdom to become the effete, elegant hairdresser who behind the scenes is actually a ruthless gangster. Hypnosis allowed him to show off his boxing skills in *One Good Turn* and his dancing skills in *Follow a Star*. The song and dance routine, 'You Deserve a Medal for That', in *Follow a Star* is of particular interest as it is one of the few examples of Wisdom allowing his believability rule to be over-ridden – probably because Eleanor Fazan's choreography made the routine irresistible to perform. While the Gump's temporary sophistication is explained through his being under hypnosis, no excuse is offered for the chorus-line to materialise from his fellow diners.

Another innovation in *The Square Peg* was the introduction of Edward Chapman as Mr. Grimsdale, the first of three appearances for the fictional character. Mr. Grimsdale was the Gump's generally sympathetic but slightly pompous boss in whom the Gump imbues with much mistaken confidence, and provides a neat contrast to Wisdom's usual straight-men.

The high-flying financial return of *A Stitch in Time* emboldened Wisdom once more to present Rank with a script for a non-Gump comedy, and once more they refused to produce it. This led to an interesting stand-off. Wisdom went away to do Anthony Newley's Brechtian stage musical *The Roar of the Greasepaint – The Smell of the Crowd* in 1964 while Rank signed up television sensations Morecambe and Wise to take Wisdom's place. Morecambe and Wise's shot at screen stardom is instructive. The duo had lifelong ambitions to make it in the cinema, they were assigned Wisdom's core team – Robert Asher and Hugh Stewart – and they retained their chief scriptwriters from television – Sid Green and Dick Hills – but the whole thing was a disaster. Whereas Wisdom's film career had started out with careful attention being paid to how the transfer was to be made, Morecambe and Wise were shoehorned into over-plotted and unsuitable vehicles which failed to replicate many of the elements which had brought them such success on television. Their three Rank films are a depressing reminder of the difficulties of transferring Variety comedians to feature-length narratives, especially noticeable in their case since a subsequent writer, Eddie Braben, would tamper with their comic personas in order for them to incorporate lengthy sketches into their television programmes with total success. It is a shame that someone of his sensitivity to Morecambe and Wise's appeal was not on hand at Rank to oversee their films.

Unfortunately for Wisdom, while *The Roar of the Greasepaint – The Smell of the Crowd* would provide him with songs which would remain in his repertoire until the end, the show itself was not deemed good enough to bring into the West End. Wisdom's enduring popularity was confirmed, however, with a Christmas Pantomime for the BBC, *Robinson Crusoe* (tx 25 December 1964), one of the BBC's costliest productions to that date with a budget of over £50,000. An estimated audience of 18.5 million showed their confidence in Wisdom was well placed. The following year, Wisdom signed up for another film with Rank, *The Early Bird* (1965). It is a testament to Rank's parsimony that this was the first Wisdom starring vehicle to be made in colour.[5]

The opening of *The Early Bird,* with its multiple falling down stairs sequence, is almost a parody of Wisdom's earlier complaint about Rank: 'They don't seem to realise that I have grown up and can get laughs without falling down stairs' (*Evening News*, 8 May 1964). And it would prove to be his last great British film. He completed two inter-mittently amusing films in 1966 for Titan, in productions bankrolled by Rank – a cameo in *The Sandwich Man* and a starring vehicle, *Press for Time*. The latter is interesting, for there was much talk of the film being a change of style, but it was not to be and with the exception of one great routine (the bike and chandelier sequence in the Lady Mayor's living room, mentioned earlier) it displayed a paucity of new ideas. For the first time, there was a feeling that Wisdom's frustration with Rank was affecting his work. At the end of the decade, he returned to the British studios to make *What's Good for the Goose* (1969) for Tigon, a brave, some might say reckless, break with his Gump image. *What's Good for the Goose* is a rather sour 1960s sex comedy which, while ironically gaining something of a cult following in recent years, alienated his fans at the time, its initial 'A' certificate discouraging family audiences. Wisdom's film career was effectively over.

Ironically, Wisdom's career as a top flight film comedian ended at the very moment when he looked to be at the very peak of his achievements. The disappointment of *The Roar of the Greasepaint – The Smell of the Crowd* was forgotten when from 1966 to 1967 he took the lead in the Broadway musical *Walking Happy*, with a score by James Van Heusen and Sammy Cahn based on Harold Brighouse's *Hobson's Choice*. It was a tri-umphant Broadway debut and Wisdom was nominated for a Tony for his role as a Manchester boot-maker. America was offering him everything he had craved in England. Richard Rodgers cast him as Androcles in his television musical from George Bernard Shaw's *Androcles and the Lion* (tx NBC, 15 November 1967), with a clever screenplay by Peter Stone and majestic support from Noël Coward as Caesar. Wisdom had been wooed by Hollywood before (Albert R. Broccoli had tried to sign him up in 1956 with a contract to run in parallel with Rank's), but now it was a reality. He starred in William Friedkin's *The Night They Raided Minsky's* (1968), perfectly cast as a sensitive up-and-coming 'top banana' in a burlesque show, to critical and popular acclaim.

But a looming divorce brought him back to England and he elected to stay here and bring up his young children. The moment was lost. There would be no revival of his film career. In general, the 1970s were a lost decade for British film-making with American money being withdrawn from the industry as London stopped swinging. After *What's Good for the Goose*, Wisdom, like most of the film industry at the time, was forced into television. He completed several seasons of situation comedy, which largely dispensed with the Gump, for ATV including *Norman* (1970), *Nobody is Norman Wisdom* (1973, 1974) and *A Little Bit of Wisdom* (1974, 1975, 1976). They were competent, reasonably successful but largely unmemorable, especially from a man who had been on the verge of breaking into the American mainstream. And while Wisdom would continue to earn a fortune on the Variety circuits around the world there is an over-riding feeling of stasis in his career from this point on. The one exception was his first straight role as a man dying from cancer in the Stephen Frears's directed *Going Gently* (tx BBC, 5 June 1981). His fellow patient was played by Fulton Mackay and the day nurse was Judi Dench. But his hugely acclaimed performance led to no other significant offers beyond cameos in several long-running television series.

The subsequent career – regional Variety, occasional minor film and television appearances – merely confirm that, in purely professional terms, Wisdom's decision to leave America had had a devastating effect on his career from which it never recovered. And while the public never forgot him, as witnessed by persistent high-flying box office returns for his Variety tours, official appreciation of his film achievements was not forthcoming. Wisdom's critical standing had never been high once the triumphant welcome accorded to *Trouble in Store* had been forgotten. Since then Wisdom had been scorned, patronised or ignored by most film critics (his stage performances were almost always uniformly praised), a neglect which malignly crept into most early histories of British cinema. The skills of the slapstick low-brow comic in cinema have always been undervalued. By the 1990s, a more considered appreciation of popular British cinema had taken hold, and Wisdom's critical reputation was partially restored. A *South Bank Show* tribute (tx ITV, 22 August 1993), retrospectives, life-time achievement awards and a knighthood all stood testament to this.

And so it should. Britain has produced many great comics but only a handful have had the ambition and the skills to go into film and make a series of successful features built around their comic personas in the home industry. It is actually difficult to stretch the list much beyond Gracie Fields, George Formby, Will Hay, Arthur Lucan, Jack Hulbert, Arthur Askey and Frank Randle, and of those, only Formby comes close to challenging Wisdom's status in terms of popularity, longevity of film career and consistency of work.

This piece has centred on the process of the transfer of a live comic to the cinema – a challenging process which few have succeeded in mastering. This transfer is still notoriously difficult, but it is now a very different process with the intermediate platforms of radio and television sketch shows in which to experiment. And these days, comics have to face the fact that there is scarcely a British film industry robust enough to maintain a comic in a film series. Historically speaking, Wisdom's success in this transfer alone places him in the top echelons of British film comedy. Wisdom might ultimately have felt constrained by the Gump, but that was because it prevented him from doing non-Gump film work, not because he was disillusioned with the character itself. Once committed to a Gump film, the only limitations were those imposed by Wisdom himself. And while Wisdom always saw his films as wholesome family fare, this does not mean they were safe and predictable. What other family comic would incorporate a five-minute riff on failing to commit suicide as Wisdom does in *The Bulldog Breed* (1960)? What other comic would begin a film with a ten-and-a-half minute non-dialogue sequence as Wisdom does with the falling-down-stairs routine which opens *The Early Bird*, or incorporate a five-minute routine of putting a stretcher patient into an ambulance as featured in *A Stitch in Time*? While the Gump's need to entertain was an integral part of his character, it could lead to very different situations

Figure 10.3 Wisdom attempts to commit suicide in *The Bulldog Breed* (1960). Image courtesy of ITV Studios Global Entertainment

from the chaotic window-dressing scene in *Trouble in Store* to the misguided attempt to emulate the conjuror in *Up in the World*. Misunderstanding instructions could lead to Lionel Jeffries being covered in ink in *Up in the World*, to Norman collapsing at his medical in *The Square Peg*. These were not mechanically formulaic sequences but routines which grew out of a specific knowledge of the character. Even while being constrained by the Gump, Wisdom was able to display a huge array of talent in these films, particularly gymnastic knock-about, mime and singing. It all justifies his status as Britain's finest film clown.

Notes

1 Peggy Cummins, conversation with author 2009.
2 Jill Craigie, letter to author 1983.
3 Chris Wicking, conversation with author 1999.
4 A copy is preserved in the National Film & Television Archive.
5 Norman had put in a guest appearance at the finale of the colour *As Long as They're Happy* (1955), singing his theme song, 'Don't Laugh At Me'.

Bibliography

Dacre, R. (1991) *Trouble in Store: Norman Wisdom – A Career In Comedy*, Dundee: T.C. Farries.

Macnab, G. (1993) *J. Arthur Rank and the British Film Industry*, London and New York: Routledge.

Sutton, D. (2000) *A Chorus of Raspberries: British Film Comedy 1929–1939*, Exeter: University of Exeter Press.

Wisdom, N. with W. Hall (2002) *My Turn*, London: Century.

11 'From telly laughs to belly laughs'

The rise and fall of the sitcom spin-off

Peter Waymark

When television first emerged as a serious rival to the cinema in the 1950s, the film industry's response was ambiguous. On the one hand, television was something to be feared, mocked and, if possible, resisted. It was largely boycotted by cinema stars, who regarded it as slumming. In the 1953 Ealing comedy, *Meet Mr. Lucifer*, television is 'an instrument of the Devil, a mechanical device to make the human race utterly miserable'. A Film Industry Defence Organisation (Fido) was set up in an attempt to keep feature films off television, ideally for ten years. At the same time, and from a very early stage, television was seen as a source of cinema material. Terence Rattigan's play, *The Final Test*, moved from television in 1953 and Nigel Kneale's *Quatermass* serials (1953, 1955, 1958–9) spawned not one but three feature films (1955, 1957, 1967). In contrast to what happened later, there were few attempts to spin off comedy, the exception being *I Only Arsked!* (1958) which was based on Granada's *The Army Game* (1957–61). Then, for a decade or so, spin-offs were forgotten and only resurfaced at the end of the 1960s.

This time, although dramas such as *Doomwatch* (1972), *Callan* (1974) and *The Sweeney* (twice, 1976, 1978) made it on to the big screen, most of the adaptations were of situation comedies. The reason was obvious: sitcoms were hugely popular. *Steptoe and Son* drew up to 22 million viewers and *Till Death Us Do Part*, 20 million. Against that, total weekly cinema admissions had been falling steadily and by 1970 were fewer than four million a week. The film industry was once more in crisis. American money, which had helped to keep it afloat, had dried up. Television sitcoms, adapted for the big screen, had a clear appeal to an industry desperately looking for new ways to bring people back into the cinema. The spin-offs could be, and were, made cheaply and because the material was already tried and tested they did not need extensive development costs or marketing. The sitcom spin-off became one of the film industry's staples and by the time the cycle had spluttered to a halt in 1980, it had been responsible for almost 30 titles.

The first was *Till Death Us Do Part,* featuring Johnny Speight's working-class bigot Alf Garnett, which appeared early in 1969. According to Ned Sherrin, who was about to enter the film industry as a producer after a successful career in television, 'British Lion [the distributor] made a fortune out of it' (Sherrin 2005: 194). Curiously, perhaps, there was no immediate rush to cash in and it was another two years before the next entrant, Frankie Howerd in *Up Pompeii*.[1] But between 1971 and 1973, spin-offs were appearing every few months. Many were successful, not least *On the Buses* (1971), based on a vulgar but much watched ITV comedy by Ronald Wolfe and Ronald Chesney which ran for seven series between 1969 and 1973. *The Daily Express* reported that the film, launched on the slogan 'From telly laughs to belly laughs', had broken 88 box office records in its first week on general release. In five days it had grossed more than £400,000 and already covered its production costs. The paper noted that 'the makers of the film had so little faith in it that they did not show it to the critics or find it a West End home'.[2] But aware that the TV series had been derided by the critics, the makers may have decided that a press show was unnecessary and best avoided. Although *On the Buses* was only released in August 1971, to coincide with the school holidays, it became the most popular British film of the year and second overall to Disney's *The Aristocats*.[3] Costing £98,000, it eventually made more than £1 million (Walker 1985: 114).

While *On the Buses* was exceptional, it was not the only spin-off money-spinner. In the same year *Up Pompeii* was the eighth most popular film shown in Britain and *Dad's Army* the joint tenth. In 1972, the box-office top 20 included *Steptoe and Son* at five, the most popular British film of the year after Ken Russell's *The Devils*. Made for £100,000 it eventually made a profit six times that much (Walker 1985: 114). Also in 1972, the second *Buses* film, *Mutiny on the Buses*, came in at 17th, *Please Sir!* 19th and *Up the Chastity Belt*, sequel to *Up Pompeii*, 20th. *Love Thy Neighbour* made the top 20 in 1973.[4] The most successful of the later spin-offs was *Porridge*, which made the top 20 in 1979.[5] But some of the franchises outstayed their welcome. The Steptoe sequel, *Steptoe and Son Ride Again* (1973), failed to cover its costs, and both *Holiday on the Buses* (1973) and *Up the Front* (1972), the third Frankie Howerd vehicle, were by far the least successful of their respective trilogies.

The production company most involved in TV spin-offs was Hammer, looking for fresh ideas as its horror cycle was coming to an end. In a way it was only returning to its earlier spin-off history. From the late 1940s, well before *The Curse of Frankenstein* (1957) and *Dracula* (1958), it produced cinema versions of radio hits such as *Dick Barton* (1948, 1949, 1950), *PC49* (1950, 1951) and *Life With the Lyons* (1954) (which, in a reversal of the usual process, subsequently transferred to television) and went on to make the *Quatermass* films and *I Only Arsked!*. In the 1970s, it was responsible for more comedy spin-offs than any other company, starting with *On the Buses*. Hammer hit on the idea after noting that '*On the Buses* has toppled *Coronation Street* from the top of the TV ratings more than once'.[6] *On the Buses* had two sequels and Hammer also made *That's Your Funeral*, *Nearest and Dearest* and *Love Thy Neighbour* (all 1973) and *Man About the House* (1974). There would have been even more but the box-office failure of *Nearest and Dearest* and *Love Thy Neighbour* put paid to planned sequels and other abortive projects included *My Wife Next Door* and *The Rag Trade*, another creation of the writers of *On the Buses*, Ronald Wolfe and Ronald Chesney (Heard and Barnes 2007:151).

Hammer's closest rival in spin-off output was Associated London Films (ALF), responsible for *Till Death Us Do Part*, *Up Pompeii* and its two sequels and the Steptoe films. ALF was the cinema offshoot of Associated London Scripts, a writers' co-operative set up in the mid-1950s by Eric Sykes, Spike Milligan, Frankie Howerd, Alan Galton and Ray Simpson and later joined by Johnny Speight. A key figure was Beryl Vertue, who had started with Associated London Scripts as its secretary, became Howerd's agent and by the 1970s was ALF's managing director. She sold the idea of *Up Pompeii* to Nat Cohen, head of Anglo-Amalgamated and later EMI (Sherrin 2005:202) and also set up the Steptoe films with Cohen, taking the screen credit of executive producer. Cohen's EMI was another big spin-off player, being also the distributor of *On the Buses* and its sequels.

A perhaps unlikely participant in the cycle was the National Film Finance Corporation (NFFC), set up in 1949 as a state-financed bank to advance loans to independent producers. It may have been intended for more ambitious projects than TV spin-offs but it backed *Till Death Us Do Part* and *Up Pompeii*. Both were successful and the NFFC continued to receive profits from *Up Pompeii* for several years. During the 1970s, the Conservative Government decided on a change of policy, bringing in private finance to supplement money from the state and deciding that the NFFC would now back 'only projects which have a particularly good chance of achieving profitability'.[7] During the first year of the new dispensation, 1972–3, the NFFC approved loans for only four films, of which two were spin-offs: *Steptoe and Son Ride Again* and a Dick Emery vehicle, *Ooh ... You Are Awful* (1972). The Steptoe film proved to be a particularly bad choice.

Hammer was probably right not to give *On the Buses* a general press launch. The publications which did review it were scathing. The trade paper critic Marjorie Bilbow called it 'crude, spiteful and misogynistic',[8] while James D. White in the British Film Institute's *Monthly Film Bulletin* said that the 'attitudes informing the script – of idiot sexuality and rabid anti-feminism – are unpleasant in the extreme'.[9] The reactions of the national press, had they been shown *On the Buses*, might have depended on where the papers stood in the market. *Up Pompeii*, which did get a press show, suggests how. For David Robinson in the *Financial Times*, 'the script could have been conceived by a smutty minded schoolchild – practically every joke seems to be concerned with the male sex organs'.[10] Alexander Walker in the *Evening Standard* took a middle ground, conceding, reluctantly, that *Up Pompeii* was probably what the public wanted: 'Groan as we may ... most people who go for such fun will find it right up their street.'[11] Critics on popular papers were more generous, perhaps reflecting what they saw as the tastes of their readers. For Ernest Betts in *The People* 'laugh of the week is *Up Pompeii*, with the great rubber-faced clown Frankie Howerd'.[12] Overwhelmingly, however, the more considered critical response to the spin-offs was negative with even the better examples deemed to be inferior to the TV originals. Two specific complaints recurred. The first was that in stretching a half-hour sitcom to 90 minutes or so for the cinema, much of the impact of the TV version had been lost. The other was that in making the transition to the big screen the material had become coarser.

Stretch marks

The challenge of 'opening out' was at its most extreme with *Till Death Us Do Part*. On television, the four main characters were normally confined to one set, representing the Garnett family's parlour, which was only 12ft square. This claustrophobic setting allowed no escape from Alf's rants, which were at the heart of the show, though there were important checks and balances. Alf tries to drown opposition by shouting it down but does not go unchallenged. The other three characters function, to a greater or lesser extent, as a counterweight. Mike, the son-in-law, is the left-wing antithesis to Alf and usually holds his ground. Rita, the daughter, is less vocal but usually backs Mike. Else, the wife, has less to say but her interventions are often deflating, throwing Alf off his stride by taking the conversation in another direction. There was little in the way of plot but the quality of Speight's writing was usually enough to sustain the half hour. When the show moved out of the house it was less successful. For an Easter Monday special (tx 27 March 1967), running for 40 minutes instead of the usual 30, the Garnetts relocated to a pub for a sing-song round the piano. Many viewers found the episode disappointing. In particular they felt that Alf had been swamped by the guest stars, who included Jimmy Tarbuck, Arthur Mullard and, as a foil for Alf's racist jibes, the black actor Kenny Lynch.[13] Here were lessons for the cinema spin-off, which would be hard pushed to spend 90 minutes in one room.

The answer was to go back more than 25 years and start an elaborate back story on the eve of the Second World War. This gave it a structure which the TV episodes rarely had or needed, tracing Alf's personal history and allowing him to vent his prejudices against a meticulous recreation of the period, with Bisto advertisements, Anderson shelters and the deprivations of rationing. The critic Raymond Durgnat called this solution 'elegant and appropriate', and suggested that the film was a lower-class parallel to Noël Coward's *This Happy Breed* (1944).[14] But once the war is over, the narrative skips 20 years, more or less to the present, and becomes scrappy. The characters of Rita and Mike, so important to the TV version, do not appear until halfway through and, largely removed from the cramped family setting, Alf's diatribes do not have the same resonance.

On television, *Dad's Army* also traced a narrative through the Second World War, starting with the formation of the Local Defence Volunteers, later the Home Guard. The film picks up on this, drawing on material from the early TV episodes as it introduces the characters and setting with dialogue often up to TV standard. Having done this, however, the narrative starts to sag with a series of incidents, any of which on its own would have been sufficient to sustain a television half-hour but are here strung together haphazardly. In an attempt to pull things together and provide a strong climax the script has three Germans baling out of their plane and holding a parish meeting to ransom. The introduction of the enemy was widely regarded as a mistake, not least by cast members such as Ian Lavender. David Robinson wrote: 'The very essence of *Dad's Army* comedy is that all the distracted White Rabbit rushing about is engaged against an enemy that is never seen but remains a monstrous looming presence in the unit's communal imagination.'[15]

Giving a 90-minute film sufficient plot to carry the narrative, without losing the subtlety of characterisation which marked out the best TV sitcoms, was a basic spin-off dilemma. Even such experienced and accomplished writers as Ray Galton and Alan Simpson never quite solved it. Simpson said the problem of writing for films was not having to fill out but reducing three hours of material to 100 minutes, leaving the plot but cutting some of the best comedy material, ending up with a very tight screenplay and nobody having any room to move (Simpson and Galton 2002: 183). He may have been thinking of *Up the Chastity Belt*, the second of the Frankie Howerd vehicles, on which he and Galton worked. According to Howerd, the writers were told that the film was too short, though the script had enough material for three hours. 'So Galton and Simpson went away and wrote more, all of which had to be filmed on a very tight budget, and the result was as long as *War and Peace*. So out came the scissors and the people in the cutting room ended up knee deep in discarded film … editing three miles of film down to just an hour and a half inevitably resulted in a bit of a hotchpotch' (Howerd 1976: 264). As well as the hazards of opening out and cutting back, the *Up* films suffered from not having an audience for Howerd, a stand-up comedian, to play off. Ned Sherrin, who produced the films, admitted that Howerd's 'unique comic quality has never been captured on screen' and 'nor did we manage to pin it down'. Howerd 'thrived on the tightrope of live performance' and in the cinema 'he was robbed of his most powerful ally, laughter' (Sherrin 2005: 202–3).

Galton and Simpson were better known for their own creation, *Steptoe and Son*. Like *Till Death Us Do Part*, on television it was largely confined to one set and similarly claustrophobic. It was essentially a two-hander, charting the relationship of two people who are stuck with each other. If Harold did manage to make the break from his possessive father then the series would be over. In the interests of plot, the film of *Steptoe and Son* comes close to making that happen as Harold first of all gets married and then wonders whether he has become a father. The film is strongly plotted but not

Figure 11.1 Frankie Howerd and Eartha Kitt in *Up the Chastity Belt* (1971), the second of the *Up Pompeii* spin-offs. Image courtesy of Hammer Productions.

only is the tightness of the TV series dissipated as the action moves out and away from the Steptoes' shabby living room but wordplay is too often sacrificed for horseplay and the central relationship is diluted. Much of the film is less about Harold and his father than Harold and Zita, the stripper he marries who may have given birth to his child, even if we know that the screenplay will contrive to have father and son back on their own by the end, ready to resume their antagonism. In the sequel, *Steptoe and Son Ride Again*, there is even more plot as Harold is conned into buying a racing greyhound which fails to perform, finds himself in debt to a local villain and gets his father to feign death so that they can collect the insurance money. Once more the Harold–Albert relationship is sacrificed and knockabout prevails over subtle writing.

The film version of *Porridge* (1979) is generally regarded as one of the better spin-offs, perhaps partly because the writers, Dick Clement and Ian La Frenais, managed to keep a high degree of creative control. It was made by Witzend, the production company set up by Clement, La Frenais and Allan McKeown, and directed by Clement. Even so, they had to face up to the problem of putting in more plot than in the average TV episode while trying not to sacrifice the interplay of character. Like *Steptoe and Son*, *Porridge* is about people who are stuck in one place, in this case prison. Should Ronnie Barker's Fletcher escape, or be released, the rationale for the series would be gone. Indeed Clement and La Frenais wrote a follow-up series, *Going Straight* (1978), in which Fletcher is out on parole and trying to adapt to life outside. The first half of the film stays true to the TV series, with many of its echoes. The main characters are introduced from scratch almost as if to assume (which seems unlikely) that many in the audience would not have seen *Porridge* on television. There are good jokes but more incident than plot. Bitty and slow moving, it is like a TV episode which has over-run. The film changes gear as plot takes over, with a football match between the inmates and visiting celebrities and an escape plan by Fletcher and his young cellmate. The match is broad knockabout, far from the subtlety of the TV *Porridge*, while in order to restore the equilibrium on which sitcom depends the writers contrive to have the two escapees return themselves to prison. Once more the opening out of a claustrophobic TV situation helps to dilute the original.

A sitcom which managed the move to the cinema better than most in formal terms was *On the Buses*. Although the humour of the TV series was basic, the show's structure astutely combined two favourite sitcom sites, the workplace and the family, linked by Reg Varney's Stan Butler. He shared home with his interfering mother, his sister Olive and her workshy husband, while at work at the bus depot he and his conductor friend Jack were a couple of middle-aged jack the lads, lusting after clippies and feuding with their boss, the perpetually harassed Inspector Blake. For the film, each strand was given a new plot. There is domestic upheaval as Olive becomes pregnant, while at work the male chauvinist staff are appalled when the company takes on women drivers. Little opening out is needed as the TV series already has scenes in the depot and on the bus routes. The first sequel, *Mutiny on the Buses* (1972), is by contrast more loosely plotted and little more than a series of unconnected incidents. The third film, *Holiday on the Buses* (1973), takes the cast away from home and work and relocates them to a holiday camp. 'Going on holiday' was a favourite ploy for TV spin-offs, and it appears in various

ANGLO-EMI FILM DISTRIBUTORS LIMITED PRESENT A HAMMER FILM PRODUCTION "MUTINY ON THE BUSES" A starring REG VARNEY
DORIS HARE   BOB GRANT   ANNA KAREN   MICHAEL ROBBINS also starring STEPHEN LEWIS as the Inspector
TECHNICOLOR ®   RELEASED BY MGM ● EMI
This copyright advertising material is licensed and not sold and is the property of National Screen Service Ltd. and upon completion of the exhibition for which it has been licensed it should be returned to National Screen Service Ltd.   Printed in Great Britain

Figure 11.2 Bob Grant, Stephen Lewis (as the Inspector) and Reg Varney in *Mutiny on the Buses* (1972).
Image courtesy of Hammer Productions.

forms in *Please Sir!* (1971) (school trip), *Steptoe and Son* (Spanish honeymoon), *The Likely Lads* (1976) (caravan holiday), *Are You Being Served?* (1977) (trip to the 'Costa Plonka') and *George and Mildred* (1980) (weekend package holiday). Taking characters out of their familiar surroundings and setting them down in a new location may have been an easy plot device but much was lost in the process.

Holiday on the Buses also used a common spin-off device, of bolstering the regular cast with guest stars. Wilfrid Brambell was joined by Arthur Mullard and Queenie Watts, reprising their characters from two other Wolfe and Chesney sitcoms, *Romany Jones* (1972–5) and *Yus My Dear* (1976). In the *Dad's Army* film, Liz Fraser was Mrs. Pike, taking over from Janet Davies. Veteran of countless film comedies, Fraser was reckoned to be the bigger name. For *Up the Front*, Zsa Zsa Gabor was brought in to play the spy Mata Hari. In *The Alf Garnett Saga* (1972), sequel to *Till Death Us Do Part*, the regulars were joined by Kenny Lynch and British comedy stalwarts including Roy Kinnear, John Le Mesurier and Joan Sims. If that was not enough, Arthur Askey, Eric Sykes and Max Bygraves played themselves, as did the footballers George Best and Bobby Moore. While spin-offs basically traded on audience familiarity with characters and situations they had seen on television, it was felt that the cinema should offer something extra. Guest stars were part of this. Whether they enhanced films or simply got in the way, is a good question.

Par for the coarse

The impetus to offer more than the television version may also help to explain why the films seemed coarser. The different approaches to censorship are revealing in this context. Television had its own internal censorship, based on the notion of a watershed at around 9pm. Before this, programmes were assumed to be suitable for viewers of all ages. After it, more adult material was permissible. Most sitcoms went out before the watershed, which did not mean they were free from controversy. One show transmitted after 9pm was *Up Pompeii!*, with language being the problem. Before the series was aired, the star, Frankie Howerd, was worried that it would be too bawdy for a television audience, uneasy that vulgarity would become filth and anxious the show would damage his reputation as a family entertainer. He agreed to do a pilot and see how it went before committing himself to a series. In the event he was reassured, especially after hearing that the wife of Charles Hill (the BBC Chairman) liked it (Howerd 1976: 253–4).

Cinema films wanting clearance for general release had to be submitted to the British Board of Film Censors (BBFC), which was gradually responding to a more liberal climate. Several of the TV spin-offs tried to take advantage of this, with screenplays which went further than television would have allowed. The BBFC awarded certificates according to what it judged to be the suitability of the material for different age groups. Up until July 1970, there were three certificates: U, denoting passed for general release; A, which advised parents and guardians that the film contained material they might prefer children under 14 not to watch; and X for films deemed suitable only for persons of 16 and over. From July 1970, the system was modified. The U and A certificates were unchanged but there was a new AA rating for films considered suitable only for people aged 14 and over, while the X certificate now restricted films to people of 18 and over. Most comedy spin-offs ended up in the A category, though in some cases only after cuts. The A was more restrictive, at least in theory, than pre-watershed television.

The comedy series which caused most trouble for the BBC was *Till Death Us Do Part*. This was mainly on account of its language, which had always offended viewers more than anything else (and still does). The frequent use of 'bloody' was a particular cause of complaint, Michael Mills, the BBC Head of Comedy counting 43 'bloodys' in a 36-page script and insisted it was too many.[16] The use of 'crap' also caused ructions within the BBC, even involving the Chairman, Lord Normanbrook. The matter was first raised by the critic Peter Black, who was a supporter of the show but dismayed by a word which he could not even bring himself to write, saying it had been 'used in a sense in which it does not mean an American dice game'.[17] Normanbrook picked this up and asked Kenneth Adam, the Director of Television, for an explanation. Adam replied that the producer, Dennis Main Wilson, had decided that the word was justified in its context despite an instruction from Frank Muir, Mills's predecessor, that it should be avoided. Adam said the decision was 'clearly wrong' and Main Wilson had been 'admonished accordingly'. Normanbrook scribbled a note on the bottom of Adam's memo: 'I have shown this to the DG [Hugh Greene, the Director-General]. The disregard of instructions from a superior … is disquieting.'[18] In the script for the final programme of the third series (tx 16 February 1968), Alf and Mike, his son-in-law, argue over whether man was created by God (Alf) or evolved from monkeys (Mike). When Alf says God is everywhere, 'in Wapping, in this house', Mike finishes his drink, turns up his glass and says: 'Got him!' Michael Mills insisted on this being removed, along with Mike's remark that 'God sounds worse than bloody Hitler'. Johnny Speight contended that taking out the 'God in the glass' passage (which he borrowed from Aldous Huxley) would be a structural alteration which entitled him under his contract to withdraw the script. He relented when it was pointed out to him that this, and the reference to God and Hitler, could lead the BBC being sued for blasphemy.[19] *Till Death Us Do Part* posed a continual dilemma for the BBC management. They accepted that Speight was a talented writer they were reluctant to lose (he was given a large pay rise, from £600 an episode to £1,000) and who was entitled to mirror society as he saw it. But there was anxiety about scheduling the show early in the evening when many children would be watching. On the other hand, transmitting it after the watershed might mean losing part of the huge audience, which by the second series was averaging 17 million people.

When the screenplay for the film of *Till Death Us Do Part* was submitted to the BBFC, two cuts were requested from the distributor British Lion, removing the expressions 'bugger 'im up' and 'bloody arse crawling'. An A certificate was issued. This did not please a Mr C.W. Rodwell, who wrote to John Trevelyan, the BBFC Secretary, saying it should have an X. He thought it unsuitable for small children, of whom he saw several unaccompanied in the audience, and took specific exception to Warren Mitchell appearing nude (he stood up naked in a bath, his hands covering his private parts) and the frequent use of 'bloody'. Trevelyan pointed out that the programme went out quite early in the evening and 'the film does not go substantially further than anything that was shown on television'. He added: 'I am told that audiences generally find the film funny and the scene [of Mitchell naked] acceptable.'[20] Even so, the nude scene would almost certainly not have been allowed on television, nor the two deleted expressions. Moreover, the word 'crap' was allowed, when Alf was complaining about having spam for tea yet again, and so was the 'God in the glass' exchange (although not 'God is worse than bloody Hitler'). These may be small things but still evidence that, in transferring the show from television to the cinema, Speight was trying to push out the boundaries of the permissible.

The screenplay for *Up Pompeii* was clearly doing the same and, unusually for a sitcom spin-off, the BBFC awarded it an AA certificate. This brought a letter from Nat Cohen, chairman of the distributors, Anglo-EMI, to Trevelyan, saying that families had complained to cinema managers that they had been unable, because of the classification, to take children with them. They found it hard to understand why their children could not see the film after seeing the television series. Trevelyan replied that 'many of the jokes in *Up Pompeii* are dirtier than those in the *Carry Ons* [to which the BBFC was giving an A certificate] and the film has a great deal more nudity than we would want to accept in the new A category'. To get an A they would have had to cut the film 'quite a lot'.[21] The resultant coarsening was picked up by John Russell Taylor: 'The limitations of what may be shown on television at a family viewing hour [albeit after the watershed] mean that this modern evocation of the world of Plautus and Terence has to pick its words and visuals with some ingenuity to get its points over. On the big screen this no longer applies; but with permissiveness the whole joke of the convention vanishes.' [22]

Negotiations between Hammer and the BFFC over *On the Buses* began with the submission of a draft screenplay in September 1970. The BBFC's examiner, Audrey Field, called it, rather patronisingly, 'simple, good-hearted dirt for the workin' chap' and noted 'scenes of advanced snogging and visual humour like symbolic drawing down of a radio aerial when one of our heroes is foiled again in his attempts at sexual conquest'. She added: 'It looks to me like an "A with cuts" but it may well be that they intend a riot of yet unscripted obscenity and are aiming at AA'. In giving the BBFC's response to Sir James Carreras, Hammer's managing director, John Trevelyan was clear that the draft went further than the television episodes: 'The TV show goes in for humour based on lavatories and knickers rather than sex jokes; this treatment follows the TV pattern but adds sex jokes and possibly some sexy visuals.' If the film was to get an A certificate dialogue with sexual innuendo and jokes about a family planning clinic should be removed, 'the attempted seduction of Stan by Betty should not be allowed to progress too far' and 'we should not see Jack's bare bottom as he gets into bed with Sally'. In May 1971, Michael Carreras (son of Sir James) wrote to Trevelyan, noting that the BBFC were about to see the film and saying 'it is imperative to us that we do not get anything more harsh than an A certificate'. Hammer were trying to have it both ways, pushing as far they could go on the sexual content while insisting on the most generous certification. Trevelyan was having none of it, setting out further cuts if the film was to make the A category. These involved removing the shots of Stan peeling a banana as Jack is making love to a girl and of Stan pushing down a TV aerial after his unsuccessful attempt to make love. Trevelyan was also anxious that there should be no emphasis on the first syllable of 'countryside' in the phrase 'a bit of Irish countryside'. Hammer complied and got its A certificate. The screenplay of *Mutiny on the Buses* had less sexual content and was passed with an A as it stood, but for the third film, *Holiday on the Buses*, the examiner suggested a list of cuts. Stephen Murphy, Trevelyan's successor, was prepared to be lenient and insisted on only two: a shot of a woman's breasts as a halter neck falls down and reaction shots of Jack's head as he makes love.[23] The woman exposing her breasts was coarsening at it most blatant. The character had no role in the narrative and did not appear again.

In submitting the script of *Steptoe and Son* to the BBFC, Beryl Vertue, managing director of Associated London Films, wrote that 'for obvious reasons that we do not want to alienate the affections of the public we have followed very much the same lines as the television series … we are expecting at worst an A certificate from you'. Stephen Murphy was quick to disabuse her. For an A, he wrote, 'you cannot have the regular bad language, e.g. "piss off", "bugger" (more than once) and some other words, nor can you have nudity in the strip scenes. And please, please real caution with the stag [night] comic'. The film eventually got its A but only after removing several lines of dialogue and toning down the striptease act so that there were no shots of the woman's breasts, of her removing her panties or of her naked as she left the stage.[24] The sequel, *Steptoe and Son Ride Again*, got its A without cuts but the screenplay was still noticeably cruder than the TV episodes. Early on Harold calls on a 'woman in flat', as the character is billed, to collect some old clothes. As she bends over a drinks cabinet, showing her knickers, she asks Harold: 'Can you see anything you like?' The scene has no connection with the rest of the film and seems to be there only because 'woman in flat' is played by Diana Dors, another instance of the need to introduce an instantly recognisable guest star.

Unusually for a spin-off, *Dad's Army* got a U certificate, and without cuts, but there were still signs of coarsening. The film was made by Columbia Pictures, who seemed to have little sympathy with the TV original and were determined to do it their way. The screenplay by David Croft and Jimmy Perry was rewritten and rewritten again, because Columbia wanted a stronger plot and faster pace. Perry admitted that the decision-making power had been taken out of their hands (McCann 2001). The suggestion that Sergeant Wilson is sleeping with Mrs. Pike and is Frank Pike's father was hinted at on television but left largely to the viewer's imagination. In the film it is made more explicit. Similarly it is hard to imagine the television episodes, which were notably free from smutty innuendo, containing the line by Arthur Lowe's Captain Mainwaring to Warden Hodges, 'I must ask you to keep your hands off my privates'. Lowe seems to say the words as if he is ashamed of them. Again, when the vicar says 'I don't know how I'll manage without my [church] bells', the answer comes back: 'Don't worry, we'll leave you with one – that's all you need.'

Death and afterlife

By the late 1970s, the spin-offs were becoming increasingly rarer and the cycle was almost exhausted when it came to a doubly sad end. The early death of Richard Beckinsale had robbed *Rising Damp* (1980) of one of its main characters but the film still went ahead without him. Shooting on *George and Mildred*, itself a spin-off from *Man About the House* which also made it into the cinema, was completed with the original cast but before the film was released the female lead, Yootha Joyce, died. Despite the extraordinary success of *On the Buses* and good returns from half a dozen others, spin-offs failed to arrest the inexorable decline in cinema attendances. In due course the spin-offs went back to where they had started and became a popular item in the TV schedules, particularly at holiday time. Ironically, many more people saw these films on television than they had in the cinema. When the film of *Dad's Army* was first shown on TV in 1979 it was watched by more than 13 million people.

Notes

1 Unlike the TV series, the film of *Up Pompeii* does not have an exclamation mark.
2 *The Daily Express*, 13 August 1971.
3 *CinemaTV Today*, 1 January 1972, based on information supplied by distributors.
4 *CinemaTV Today*, 1 January 1972; 30 December 1972; 22 December 1973.
5 *Screen International*, 22 December 1979.
6 *ABC Film Review*, June 1971: 23.
7 National Film Finance Corporation, annual report for the year ended 31 March 1973.
8 *Today's Cinema*, 9 July 1971.
9 *Monthly Film Bulletin*, August 1971: 168.

10 *Financial Times*, 19 March 1971.
11 *Evening Standard*, 17 March 1971.
12 *The People*, 21 March 1971.
13 BBC Written Archives T12/1255/1, Audience Research Report *Till Death Us Do Part*, 2 May 1967.
14 *Films and Filming*, March 1969: 54–5.
15 *Financial Times*, 19 March 1971.
16 BBC Written Archives T12/1321/1: Mills to Dennis Main-Wilson, 24 November 1967.
17 *Daily Mail*, 22 June 1966.
18 BBC Written Archives R87/2811/1: Normanbrook to Adam, 22 June 1966; Adam to Normanbrook, 24 June 1966.
19 BBC Written Archives RCont 18: Mills to Head of Copyright and Legal Adviser, 9 February 1968.
20 BBFC file, *Till Death Us Do Part*.
21 BBFC file, *Up Pompeii*.
22 *The Times*, 19 March 1971.
23 BBFC files, *On the Buses, Holiday on the Buses*.
24 BBFC file, *Steptoe and Son*, 1971.

Bibliography

Heard, M. and Barnes, A. (2007) *The Hammer Story: The Authorised History of Hammer Films*, rev. edn, London: Titan Books.

Howerd, F. (1976) *On the Way I Lost It*, London: W.H. Allen.

McCann, G. (2001) *Dad's Army*, London: Fourth Estate.

Sherrin, N. (2005) *The Autobiography*, London: Little, Brown.

Simpson, A. and Galton, R. (with Ross, R.) (2002) *Steptoe and Son*, London: BBC.

Walker, A. (1985) *National Heroes: British Cinema in the Seventies and Eighties*, London: Harrap.

Filmography of TV programmes cited in text

(where no director is credited the producer usually took on this role as well)

Are You Being Served? (BBC, 1973–85) main producer: David Croft; main directors: Ray Butt, Bob Spiers; main writers: Jeremy Lloyd and David Croft; main cast: Mollie Sugden, Frank Thornton, John Inman, Trevor Bannister, Wendy Richard, Nicholas Smith.

The Army Game (ITV Granada, 1957–61) main producers/directors: Milo Lewis, Max Morgan-Witts, Eric Fawcett; main writers: Larry Stephens, Sid Colin, Lew Schwartz, Maurice Wiltshire; main cast: Geoffrey Sumner, William Hartnell, Michael Medwin, Alfie Bass, Norman Rossington, Charles Hawtrey, Bernard Bresslaw, Bill Fraser.

Callan (ITV Thames, 1967–73) main producer: Reginald Collin; main directors: Peter Duguid, Jim Goddard, Mike Vardy; main writer: James Mitchell; main cast: Edward Woodward, Russell Hunter, Lisa Langdon, Anthony Valentine.

Dad's Army (BBC, 1968–77) producer: David Croft; directors: Harold Snoad, Bob Spiers; writers: Jimmy Perry and David Croft; main cast: Arthur Lowe, John Le Mesurier, Clive Dunn, John Laurie, Arnold Ridley, James Beck, Ian Lavender.

Doomwatch (BBC, 1970–1) producer: Terence Dudley; main directors: Darrol Blake, Jonathan Alwyn, Lennie Mayne; main writers: Gerry Davis and Kit Pedler; main cast: John Paul, Joby Blanshard, Simon Oates.

George and Mildred (ITV Thames, 1976–9) producer/director: Peter Frazer-Jones; writers: Johnnie Mortimer and Brian Cooke; main cast: Brian Murphy, Yootha Joyce.

Going Straight (BBC, 1978) producer/director: Sydney Lotterby; writers: Dick Clement and Ian La Frenais; main cast: Ronnie Barker, Richard Beckinsale, Patricia Brake, Nicholas Lyndhurst.

The Likely Lads (BBC, 1964–6) producer/director: Dick Clement; writers: Dick Clement and Ian La Frenais; main cast: James Bolam, Rodney Bewes, Sheila Fearn.

Love Thy Neighbour (ITV Thames, 1972–6) main producers/directors: Stuart Allen, Ronnie Baxter, Anthony Parker, William G. Stewart; main writers: Vince Powell and Harry Driver; main cast: Jack Smethurst, Kate Williams, Rudolph Walker, Nina Baden-Semper.

Man About the House (ITV Thames, 1973–6) producer: Peter Frazer-Jones; writers: Johnnie Mortimer and Brian Cooke; main cast: Richard O'Sullivan, Paula Wilcox, Sally Thomsett, Yootha Joyce, Brian Murphy.

My Wife Next Door (BBC, 1972) producer: Graeme Muir; writer: Richard Waring; main cast: John Alderton, Hannah Gordon.

Nearest and Dearest (ITV Granada, 1968–73) producers: Peter Eckersley, Bill Podmore; directors: June Howson, Bill Podmore; main writers: Tom Brennand and Roy Bottomley, John Stevenson, Vince Powell and Harry Driver; main cast: Hylda Baker, Jimmy Jewel.

On the Buses (ITV London Weekend, 1969–73) producers/directors: Stuart Allen, Derrick Goodwin, Bryan Izzard; main writers: Ronald Wolfe and Ronald Chesney, Bob Grant and Stephen Lewis; main cast: Reg Varney, Cicely Courtneidge/Doris Hare, Michael Robbins, Anna Karen, Stephen Lewis, Bob Grant.

Please Sir! (ITV London Weekend, 1968–72) main producers: Mark Stuart, Philip Casson; main directors: Mark Stuart, Howard Ross; main writers: John Esmonde and Bob Larbey; main cast: John Alderton, Deryck Guyler, Noel Howlett, Joan Sanderson.

Porridge (BBC, 1974–7) producer/director: Sydney Lotterby; writers: Dick Clement and Ian La Frenais; main cast: Ronnie Barker, Richard Beckinsale, Fulton Mackay, Brian Wilde.

The Quatermass Experiment (BBC, 1953) producer/director: Rudolph Cartier; writer: Nigel Kneale; main cast: Reginald Tate, Isabel Dean, Duncan Lamont.

Quatermass II (BBC, 1955) producer/director: Rudolph Cartier; writer: Nigel Kneale; main cast: John Robinson, Monica Grey, Hugh Griffith.

Quatermass and the Pit (BBC, 1958–9) producer/director: Rudolph Cartier; writer: Nigel Kneale; main cast: André Morell, Cec Linder, Anthony Bushell.

The Rag Trade (BBC, 1961–3) producer/director: Dennis Main-Wilson; writers: Ronald Wolfe and Ronald Chesney; main cast: Peter Jones, Miriam Karlin, Reg Varney, Esma Cannon, Sheila Hancock.

Rising Damp (ITV Yorkshire, 1974–8) main producers/directors: Ronnie Baxter, Vernon Lawrence; writer: Eric Chappell; main cast: Leonard Rossiter, Frances de la Tour, Richard Beckinsale, Don Warrington.

Romany Jones (ITV Thames, 1972–5) producer/director: Stuart Allen; main writers: Ronald Wolfe and Ronald Chesney; main cast: James Beck, Jo Rowbottom, Arthur Mullard, Queenie Watts.

Steptoe and Son (BBC, 1962–74) main producers/directors: Duncan Wood, John Howard Davies, Douglas Argent; writers: Ray Galton and Alan Simpson; main cast: Wilfrid Brambell, Harry H. Corbett.

The Sweeney (ITV Thames, 1975–8) producer: Ted Childs; main directors: Tom Clegg, Douglas Camfield, David Wickes; main writers: Ian Kennedy Martin, Trevor Preston, Roger Marshall; main cast: John Thaw, Dennis Waterman, Garfield Morgan.

That's Your Funeral (BBC, 1971) producer/director: Douglas Argent; writer: Peter Lewis; main cast: Bill Fraser, Raymond Huntley.

Till Death Us Do Part (BBC, 1966–75) producer: Dennis Main-Wilson; main director: Douglas Argent; writer: Johnny Speight; main cast: Warren Mitchell, Dandy Nichols, Una Stubbs, Anthony Booth.

Up Pompeii! (BBC, 1970) producers: David Croft, Sydney Lotterby; writers: Talbot Rothwell and Sid Colin; main cast: Frankie Howerd, Elizabeth Larner, Kerry Gardner.

Yus My Dear (ITV London Weekend, 1976) producer/director: Stuart Allen; writers: Ronald Wolfe and Ronald Chesney; main cast: Arthur Mullard, Queenie Watts.

12 From window cleaner to potato man

Confessions of a working-class stereotype

I.Q. Hunter

What is the worst British film ever made? Snobs – and Andrew Marr[1] – might plump for *Sing As We Go* (1934) and the deranging cheeriness of Gracie Fields. Connoisseurs of trash would certainly advance the case for *Fire Maidens from Outer Space* (1956), *Gonks Go Beat* (1965) and Hammer's prehistoric farrago, *Slave Girls* (1966); while highbrows may prefer the claims of late period Michael Winner – *Dirty Weekend* (1993), *Parting Shots* (1999) – or, if churlishly averse to sentimental kitsch, the triumphant populism of *Love Actually* (2003) or *Mamma Mia! The Movie* (2008). But surely everyone would agree that, when it comes to recent British cinema, the very worst films fall reliably into three categories. First, there are cheap horror movies such as *Zombie Undead* (2010); second, Mockney gangster films such as *Honest* (2000) and *Revolver* (2005), as well as anything starring Danny Dyer (*Outlaw* (2007), *Straightheads* (2007), *Pimp* (2010)); and, third, comprising the most debased category of all, 'low comedies' like *Ali G Indahouse* (2002), *Sex Lives of the Potato Men* (2004), and *Fat Slags* (2004). In fact, *Fat Slags* is currently the lowest rated British movie on IMDb, with a score of 1.7 out of 10. Ranking number 19 in the bottom 100 films 'as voted by our users', this is the film to beat for the absolutely worst of British.[2]

These sex comedies and TV spin-offs, which Ricky Gervais denounced as 'terrible, Lottery-funded, tacky shit' (Logan 2009), are the quintessence of bad British cinema. Their shame is compounded by their affinity with what is generally considered the industry's unsurpassable nadir – the sexploitation boom of the 1970s, when *Confessions of a Window Cleaner* (1974) could somehow become the biggest British film of the year.

This chapter reconsiders these crude embarrassments to British comic history from the 1970s to the present day. Rather than harmless farces and knockabout comedies like *Bean* (1997), my emphasis will be on the unrespectable comedy of bawdy, toilet humour and the gross-out. This is a branch of British cinema in which there are no masterpieces, very few cult items, and not much that is even watchable – an uninterrupted series of aesthetic botches and (mostly) commercial failures. Having watched these films so you don't have to, I shall focus not, as might be expected, on gender but instead on class and especially the working-class body.

Body horrors

Low comedy, which can be traced back to Ancient Greek comedies about slaves and servants, is generally about the antics of the lower orders. It implies not only slapstick and physical comedy, as opposed to wit and verbal sparring (the province of the middle and upper classes), but also the comedy of sex, grossness and bad taste, and hinges on the tension between social order and bodily desire, and the social repression of both low life and the unruly lower parts of the body. Low comedy suggests carnival and subversion; it is what Linda Williams called a 'body genre' (Williams 1991), and works on the senses to the detriment of intellectual distance. As George Orwell, writing on the saucy postcard artist Donald McGill, put it, low comedy is 'the voice of the belly protesting against the soul' (Orwell 1970: 192); it is quite inextricable from issues of class.

Low comedy in British cinema emerges from (Northern) working-class humour, Music Hall and Pantomime, and finds its apotheosis in the *Carry On* films, with 'their focus on a specific social institution (or film genre) whose workings are disrupted by individuals with no respect for the rules' (Leach 2004: 153). As Laraine Porter writes:

> The bawdy sexual innuendo of picture postcards and *Carry On* films represents the anarchic spirit associated with a release from the everyday tedium of work and a 'regression' into the carnivalesque underbelly of heterosexual monogamy where base desires are given a voice and men have licence to pursue the objects of their lust ...
>
> (Porter 1998: 84)

That is not to say that crudity and gross-out in British cinema are explicable wholly in terms of working-class populism. Since the 1960s, comedies in the middle-class art movie tradition have frequently pushed against the limits of taste. Lindsay Anderson's under-rated *Britannia Hospital* (1982) offered a grotesque Surreal allegory of the end of consensus in which Brechtian satire collided with horror, slapstick and explicit references to both the *Carry Ons* and sexploitation (Robin Askwith of the *Confessions* series plays a prominent role) (Hedling 2009: 43). Equally Bahktinian was *Monty Python's The Meaning of Life* (1983), an uneven Buñuelian exercise in baiting the middle classes, and an unusually satirical use of gross-out body comedy. Notable – and influential – was the film's Mr. Creosote (Terry Jones), the vast bourgeois diner whose consumption of a '*waffer* [sic] thin mint' to round off his *grande bouffe* ends explosively. This typifies the tension between unyielding bodily desire and social etiquette at the heart of low comedy. Mr. Creosote's unfortunate demise does not, however, enact the revenge of the socially inferior, and as with most satire boom films, the Pythons' use of gross-out is quite distinct from the tradition of working-class bawdy (it is closer, in fact, to the elite black comedy of Peter Greenaway's *The Cook, the Thief, His Wife, and Her Lover* (1989)).

Low can imply a certain rough authenticity, reflecting an intrinsic and irredeemable aspect of the national character. Leon Hunt used the wider term 'low culture' to refer to the unrespectable populist culture of the 1970s – commercial rather than folk – which was directed mostly at working-class men and hitherto beneath the radar of academic attention – notably sleazy horror films, pulp paperbacks and sexploitation movies: 'The "low" can be distinguished both as a doubly marginalised district within the popular and as an ostensibly irrecuperable textual community' (Hunt 1998: 8). 'Low' in this sense might be said to mean 'badness' as well as 'politically incorrect', and any notion that these texts were an unmediated expression of the repressed desires of 'ordinary' Britons is compromised by their mass-produced tawdriness. Certainly low comedies from the 1970s onwards are 'bad objects' in most histories of British cinema, insofar as their crudity, populism and values, especially in matters of race and gender, are offensive to middle-class liberal opinion. The *Carry On* films have crept into the canon, but most low comedies are still among the abject of British cinema and the sex comedies of the 1970s often regarded as the worst offenders of all. But the low comedies are not as a rule 'outsider' films or 'Badfilms'. Even the most delinquent, from *Come Play with Me* (1977) to *Fat Slags* and *Lesbian Vampire Killers* (2009), boast casts of TV stalwarts and few are as genuinely outlaw as, say, Roy 'Chubby' Brown's videos of his stand-up shows at Blackpool. On the one hand, the films seem very British indeed in their concern with vulgarity, class and bad taste; on the other, for a nation so convinced that it is defined by its sense of humour, these supposedly populist laugh-fests are typically and bewilderingly neither popular nor funny.

Pulling it off in the 1970s

In the early 1970s there were two major kinds of comic successes, sitcom films, spun off from TV shows, and sex comedies. Between 1968 and 1980, 30 sitcoms were adapted for the big screen and met with great commercial success. The first film version of *On the Buses* was – a fact often repeated in surprise and shame – the highest grossing British film of 1971, beating even the Bond film, *Diamonds Are Forever*. The sitcom film's content was replicated by the sex comedies. Titles such as the four *Confessions* films (*Window Cleaner, Pop Performer* (1975), *Driving Instructor* (1976) and *from a Holiday Camp* (1977)), *Percy* (1971), *Confessions of a Sex Maniac* (1974), *Can You Keep It Up for a Week?* (1974), *Penelope Pulls It Off* (1975), *Eskimo Nell* (1974), *I'm Not Feeling Myself Tonight* (1975), and *Adventures of a Taxi Driver* (1976) have come to define the limp British contribution to erotic cinema. They and the sitcom films shared a common world of working-class families (Barber 2010: 5) and indeed both might be said to be in the social realist tradition of British cinema, insofar as 'social realism within Britain has been associated with the making visible of the working class' (Hill 1999: 135). The sex comedies were exploitation films, compromise solutions to the illegality of hardcore porn. Sexploitation had been successful in the UK from the late 1950s, but with few exceptions, such as Pete Walker's *School for Sex* (1969), the sex comedy did not really take off till the 1970s, helped by the rise in the age of admission into 'X' certificated films to 18 in 1970. They quickly became an important component of the British film industry in a period of radical decline, providing work and taking advantage of the Eady Levy.

Sex comedies peaked in 1975. Six were made in 1971, seven in 1972, eight in 1973, ten in 1974, 12 in 1975, eight in 1977, five in 1978 and two in 1979 (Hunter 2008: 3–5). They proved a remarkable commercial success, some of them breaking out of dedicated sex cinemas, such as the Jacey chain, and reaching mainstream and 'couples' audiences. *Confessions of a Window Cleaner*, backed by Columbia, was one of the biggest hits; by 1979 its profits were more than £800,000 (Barber 2010: 2).

These films were in the Music Hall, naughty postcard tradition of farce – 'a harder, cinematic version of Brian Rix losing his trousers at the Whitehall Theatre', as one of sexploitation's key producers, Stanley Long, put it (*Screen International*, 23 October

1976). They combined simulated sex scenes with saucy humour in the tradition of the *Carry On* films, which themselves petered out with *England* (1976) and *Emmannuelle* (1978); weak imitations of the sex comedies, they earned the series its first 'AA' ratings. The sex comedies were full of familiar stereotypes, from nymphomaniac foreign women, to cuckolded husbands, and uptight establishment figures. Although there were *Carry On* staples such as randy doctors and naughty nurses (*What's Up Nurse!*, *What's Up Superdoc! Rosie Dixon – Night Nurse* (all 1978)), more often the protagonists were handymen, taxi drivers, and milkmen – individuals in transient professions rather than unionised or factory jobs or some welfare state institution, who were stumbling enthusiastically through the new sexual opportunities of the Permissive Society. These freelance sexual adventurers were more often hapless and bewildered than empowered and predatory; but for all the films' leering crassness there was at least an enthusiasm for sex comparatively new in British cinema, and an attempt to reclaim sex as part of Britain's unrespectable heritage. A few period sex comedies like *Keep It Up Downstairs* (1976) mocked the hypocrisies of the Victorian period or, as in *Games that Lovers Play* (aka *Lady Chatterley versus Fanny Hill*) (1970), incorporated an element of historical bawdy. Tony Richardson's film of *Tom Jones* (1963) was a key reference point and, as well as his semi-sequel *Joseph Andrews* (1977), a number of sexy literary adaptations, such as *Mistress Pamela* (1974), *The Bawdy Adventures of Tom Jones* (1976) and *Fanny Hill* (1983), discovered a precursor of contemporary licence in the 18th century.

Most of the film industry was drawn into sex comedy, taking advantage of both loosening censorship and the currency of sexual freedom. Veteran directors such as Val Guest (*Au Pair Girls* (1972), *Confessions of a Window Cleaner*) and Jack Arnold (*Sex Play* (1974)) essayed the genre. Norman Wisdom found himself in bed with Sally Geeson in *What's Good for the Goose* (1969), while the Boultings and Peter Sellers scraped barrels in *Soft Beds, Hard Battles* (1974). Ralph Thomas and producer Betty Box followed *Doctor in Trouble* (1970) with a less innocuous medical comedy, *Percy*, starring Hywel Bennett and Denholm Elliott, which was about a penis transplant. As with *Confessions of a Sex Maniac* (1974) – an ultra-low-budgeter, unrelated to the Askwith films, about an architect whose work is inspired by the shape of breasts – the abiding theme is men helpless to control their bodies, desires and libidos. Sex is a source equally of nervous laughter and outright fear.

There were also, unsurprisingly, close links between the sexploitation films and the burgeoning pornography business and its 'porn barons', 'the sleazy sensibility of Soho film clubs having recently seeped into the mainstream' (Willetts 2010: 313). David Sullivan, who published *Whitehouse* and *Ladybirds* magazines, bankrolled a number of films to showcase his girlfriend, Mary Millington, including *Come Play with Me* (1977) and *Confessions from the David Galaxy Affair* (1979). Paul Raymond, the publisher of *Men Only* and *Mayfair*, did the same for Fiona Richmond (*Hardcore* (1977) and *Let's Get Laid* (1978)). *Come Play with Me* was directed by George Harrison Marks, who made one of the very first British sexploitation films, the chaste nudist epic, *Naked – as Nature Intended* (1961). *Come Play with Me*, 'Britain's longest running movie ever' (Sheridan 2011: 175), is a remarkably bizarre film, verging on the inadvertent surrealism of paracinema, in which Music Hall routines and songs are interspersed with softcore sex scenes. Sullivan's magazines promoted it as hardcore but, like all the sex comedies, it was actually pretty mild. The films are pornographic only in the sense that their characters inhabit a world ruled by sexual desire and the plots are organised around moments of nudity and brief bouts of simulated hanky-panky.

Consensus has emerged about the sex comedies' place in cultural history. Leon Hunt argues that they map the expansion of permissiveness to the working classes ('a sense of trickling *down* – to working – and lower-middle-class consumers – and *out*, to suburbia' (Hunt 1998: 25)) as well as documenting a new individualism and a breakdown of deference. This 'permissive populism' was not really progressive, and its impatience with authority for getting in the way of the private pursuit of hedonism was embodied in the proto-Thatcherite ideology of *The Sun*: 'Sex was part of the discursive notion of "fun" … snatched from the jaws of do-gooders and moralistic spoilsports who wanted to deny the consuming working classes their momentary pleasures … the compensatory "fun" for performing undervalued labour' (Hunt 1998: 26). The films nevertheless show discourses of sexuality in transition. There is a nervous embrace of sexual freedom by the young (and upper class and foreign), a vague anti-Establishment sentiment, and an inchoate hostility to the persistence of Victorian values – 'the grotesquely elongated shadow … of that monstrous dwarf Queen Victoria', as John Fowles famously said in *The Magus* (1977: 15). Although anti-Victorianism is more strident in sexploitation documentaries such as *Naughty!* (1971) and *The Pornbrokers* (1973) (Hunter 2008: 9), it is vigorously present too in the best of the sex comedies, *Eskimo Nell*. A *film à clef* about the sexploitation industry, *Eskimo Nell* is also a trenchant satire of Mary Whitehouse and the Festival of Light, burlesqued in the absurdly named Lady Longhorn and her Society for Moral Reform. The pleasure-grasping individualism of the sex comedies, like that of *On the Buses*, represents the working-class counterpart of the apolitical 'extension of the counter culture of the mid-1960s' of *Monty Python's* satire – 'an oblique demand for sexual and personal liberation by emotionally stunted, if highly educated, young middle-class males, symbolically wrenching their own umbilical cords and exhorting others to do the same' (Wagg 1992: 271). The sex comedies were remarkably prescient in highlighting the impact of permissive consumerism. The working class represented and spoken to in *Confessions of a Window Cleaner* is one for which sex and consumerism are complementary ways of escape. As Sian Barber suggests, while the film is highly conventional in emphasising marriage as an ideal, it also celebrates 'sex as a means to overcome class distinctions' (Barber 2010: 7).

From bawdy to gross-out

Sex comedies died off at the start of the 1980s along with the rest of the British sexploitation boom and indeed the sitcom film (by then sitcoms were more likely to have Christmas specials than spin-offs). The abolition of the Eady Levy and the arrival of video are usually cited as the main causes. At the very end of this period there was one uniquely dreadful hold-over from a previous era of comedy, in which were gathered, as in a black museum of comic horrors, attitudes and low comic tropes soon absent from British cinema. *The Boys in Blue* (1983) was a vehicle for the popular TV double act from Oldham, Tommy Cannon (the straight man) and Bobby Ball (the farceur, harmlessly randy 'like a Jack Russell'). The 'boys' play policemen in the village of Little Botham (pronounced 'Bottom'), whose station, which doubles as a supermarket, is threatened with merger. The boys resort to inventing crimes to solve but soon find themselves grappling with a ring of art thieves. Like Norman Wisdom, Cannon and Ball are 'little men' at odds with a snooty Establishment, which they are eager to join rather than disrupt. Indeed the film is perturbed by the unsettling of class boundaries – the chief villain (Roy Kinnear) is a vulgar self-made millionaire who has taken over a stately home – and you can easily read the film as an allegory of the Britain of traditional conservative fantasy (rural, orderly, with a servile lower class) encountering the new amoral energies of entrepreneurial Thatcherism. With its nostalgically cosy view of the police, *The Boys in Blue* was a very old-fashioned farce – not surprisingly, since the screenplay by director Val Guest was cannibalised from his script for Will Hay's *Ask a Policeman* (1939). Ideologically, the film retreats from the sexual individualism of the sex comedies. For all the boys' talk of 'birds' and 'tarts' and the excitement caused by glimpses of Suzanne Danielle's legs (she is the only significant woman in the cast), nervousness about women triumphs in the end. Ball declares that you can't trust them and the boys return to sexless homosociality. This astonishingly unfunny film, produced by Greg Smith, for whom Guest had made *Confessions of a Window Cleaner*, would have benefitted from some gratuitous bad taste (as when the material – sleepy town, big crimes – was later drastically reworked in *Hot Fuzz* (2007)). As it is, *The Boys in Blue* is a film stranded in time, valuable only as a cheerless anthology of elements of 1930s farce, Wisdom-ish slapstick, *Carry On*, and very mild sexploitation, toned down to suit its main audience of children.

Cannon and Ball were out of fashion by the time of their last ITV show in 1991. By then the populist, essentially working-class, comedy they personified was sidelined by a new wave of comedians, most of them middle class, whose use of low comedy tropes would be very different. The 1980s saw the arrival of 'alternative comedy' from the Comedy Store and the Edinburgh Fringe as well as the Cambridge Footlights production line. As Stephen Fry puts it: 'What punk had done for music the alternative comedians were doing for comedy' (Fry 2011: 207). This wave of comedians, self-consciously progressive in matters of race and gender, started to oust the likes of Benny Hill from TV and exile working-class comics such as Bernard Manning and, eventually, Jim Davidson to stand-up and video.

This new generation, especially those associated with Channel 4's *The Comic Strip* (Dacre 2009: 114), quickly made their mark in cinema with a wide range of comedies, such as *Morons from Outer Space* (1985), *Eat the Rich* (1987), *The Pope Must Die* (1991) and *Peter's Friends* (1992), as well as linking up with the key comic influence of the period, Monty Python, in *Nuns on the Run* (1990). Occasionally tasteless (especially *Eat the Rich*) these films were scatological rather than sex-minded, and their low comedy had more in common with the anti-bourgeois satire of the Pythons (or Greenaway) than working-class populism (the most memorable representative of the lower classes that generation came up with, on film or TV, was the dim and repulsive Baldrick in the *Blackadder* series). As with the subsequent wave of comedians, typified by Chris Morris, Steve Coogan, Armando Iannucci and *Little Britain*, the comedy was frequently low in the sense of crude and deliberately offensive, but it neither emerged from, nor took much interest in, what remained of the working class (though it might take pot shots at the so-called 'underclass', as with *Little Britain*'s dim and feckless teenage single mother, Vicky Pollard). The enemy for almost all post-Python comedians is more usually, however, the *Daily Mail*-reading lower middle class. Significantly the most grotesquely offensive single piece of comedy in recent years was Morris's 2001 *Brass Eye* special, 'Paedogeddon', which outraged *Mail* readers by satirising media coverage of child abuse, and in which the working class was a baying crowd of Morlocks; the programme's chief defenders were middle-class liberals. By then the 'politically incorrect' low populism of working-class bawdy was, though not entirely vanquished, mostly a stranger to cinema screens.

Notable as a lone reaction against and comment on the class base and ideology of 'alternative comedy' was 1993's *UFO*, starring Roy 'Chubby' Brown. Brown is an immensely popular Northern stand up comedian, technically brilliant and staggeringly obscene, whose shows, in which the 'fat bastard' connects superbly with his audience, are like white working-class revivalist meetings – 'carnival spaces where the policed speech of the official world outside the theatre gives way to a linguistic economy where unfettered crudeness rules' (Medhurst 2007: 193). In his comedy as the 'bluest comedian in Britain', Brown comes across as not only an heir to Max Miller – and his own hero, Ken Dodd, 'the best comedian of all' (Brown 2007: 241) – but as an outsider and genuine 'alternative' whose comedy had 'an anti-PC under-the-counter word-of-mouth cachet', an authentic voice of solidarity that belonged, like Bernard Manning, to an increasingly marginalised class despised for its racism and reactionary gender politics: 'The more my bawdy, vulgar end-of-the-pier humour was outlawed or denigrated as offensive or unfashionable, the more the public wanted to see it, simply because we all like what's naughty' (Brown 2007: 332–3).

Brown has had considerable success with his video and DVD releases such as *Clitoris Allsorts* (1995), *Saturday Night Beaver* (1996) and *Too Fat to Be Gay* (2009). His first video, *From Inside the Helmet* (1990), sold 250,000 copies (Medhurst 2007: 188). *UFO* ('You Fuck Off' rather than 'Unidentified Flying Object') is his one film vehicle, a sex comedy in which Chubby is kidnapped onto Starship Eve by female aliens from planet Clitoris (next to Uranus), and put on trial under the Female Supremacy Act 2390 for being 'the most foul-mouthed sexist little shit in the universe'. Brown, kitted out as his stage persona in flying helmet and goggles and multi-coloured jacket and trousers, is the traditional downtrodden and hassled working-class husband – 'Is this a happy face?', he asks – and his comedy is a way of snatching moments of fun from a joyless working and domestic life. It is appropriate that with one exception (Solo (Roger Lloyd Pack), a hermaphrodite) all the ETs are women, since Brown represents an outmoded traditional working-class masculinity entering a wholly alien world of humourlessness, sexlessness and social control. The world he comes from, depicted with cartoonish nostalgia, is that of the sitcom film, the sex comedy and *Fiesta* magazine – on a 'rough estate' in Middlesbrough, he lives in an end of terrace with ducks on the wall; his wife (an 'old fucking slag' with 'turnstiles on her flaps') is shagging the milkman. Brown carries over from his stage act his sense of complicity with his audience, talking to and winking at us as he communicates his dirty shared knowledge – 'Never trust a woman. How can you trust something that bleeds for five days and doesn't die?'[3] Much of the humour is based on the association of working-class sexuality with fatness and excess. Like the heroes of 1970s sex comedies, Chubby is sex-mad (he 'was born to fuck') but his fatness makes him the object of ridicule, which counteracts to some extent his relentless objectification of women. He is both sex machine and loser – 'the last person I had sex with was my wrist' – and the punishment for his unapologetic sexism is the 'Genesis' treatment. Having got all the aliens pregnant, he must now give birth himself – a new spin on working-class men 'learning to labour'. The film differs from earlier sex comedies in its reliance on verbal humour rather than nudity (though there is a brief shower scene); it is not, in any sense, a softcore porn film. Brown is dismissive of *UFO* because 'It's just not common enough. It's not about ordinary people: I'd rather it was consigned to the vaults' (Brown 2007: 334–5). But it is striking that, while the 1970s sex comedies centred on young working-class masculinity, this film, for all its misogyny and homosexual panic, is about middle-aged working-class masculinity dealing with its obsolescence and the threat of feminisation.

UFO was something of a one-off in the cinema in attempting to reinvigorate traditional low comedy with contemporary blue working-class humour. There were a handful of other sex comedies in the 1980s and 1990s. *Car Trouble* (1986), in which Julie Walters commits adultery with a Jaguar salesman, exploits lower-middle-class social embarrassment. *Rita, Sue and Bob Too* (1986), directed by Alan Clarke from plays by Andrea Dunbar, celebrates working-class 'immorality', sexual licence and entrepreneurialism in Bradford. A key film of the Thatcher-era, it anticipated the discursive re-categorisation of the working class ongoing since the 1980s – the replacement of the division between the 'respectable' and 'unrespectable' working class by that between 'the underclass' and pretty much everyone else. Other sex-focused comedies looked to the past, as would later films such as *Kinky Boots* (2005) and *Made in Dagenham* (2010), in order to represent the working class positively. *Wish You Were Here* (1987), set in the late 1940s, and *Personal Services* (1987), both inspired by the life of the sex party hostess, Cynthia Payne, were cosily accepting of sex and its 'perversions' as variations on standard British eccentricity.

These were not sexploitation films but rather in the social realist tradition, which, with the exception of Mike Leigh, increasingly focused on the underclass rather than the working class. *Preaching to the Perverted* (1997) was more in the tradition of the 1970s sex comedy, especially in its attack on the repressiveness and hypocrisy of the Establishment, here embodied in a Tory MP engaged in a moral crusade against the BDSM community and its (actually very British) enthusiasm for a 'bit of fladge' – that is, consensual bondage, discipline and sado-masochism. The film is strikingly sympathetic to (and quite knowing about) the BDSM scene, and close to a 'rom-com' in depicting its innocent Christian protagonist, hired to infiltrate and expose the House of Thwax club, falling in love with the dominatrix who runs it, Tanya Cheex. The film works rather like earlier sexploitation documentaries such as *The Wife Swappers* (1969) and *Commuter Husbands* (1972); but, unlike them and the wife-swapping drama, *The Big Swap* (1998), it details a subculture rather than exposes novel sexual practices behind suburban net curtains. A handful of subsequent sex comedies also investigated the sexual underground. *I Want Candy* (2007), about a bunch of students making a porn movie, is more or less a retread of *Eskimo Nell*; *Dogging: A Love Story* (2009), a rom-com about sex in Newcastle car parks; and *Swinging with the Finkels* (2011), a half-hearted exploration of wife-swapping in middle-class Jewish suburbia.

More obviously 'low' were what might be called British 'gross-out' films, whose transgression derives from extreme bad taste. William Paul traces gross-out back to American comedy and horror films of the 1970s, such as *National Lampoon's Animal House* (1978), which 'assaulted us with images of outrageously violent or sexual behaviour, or violently sexual, or sexually violent' (Paul 1994: 5). A later cycle dates from American films such as *Dumb and Dumber* (1994), *There's Something about Mary* (1998), *American Pie* (1999), and, often considered the lowest of its many low points, Tom Green's *Freddy Got Fingered* (2001). These gross-out films owed more to the filthy emeticism of John Waters' *Pink Flamingos* (1972) than to sex comedy, and were aimed squarely at young audiences. From the late 1990s, a number of British gross-out films were spun-off from TV – more often from sketch shows than sitcoms – as vehicles for performers such as Rik Mayall and Ade Edmondson (*Guest House Paradiso* (1999)), Harry Enfield and Kathy Burke (*Kevin & Perry Go Large* (2000)) and Sacha Baron Cohen (*Ali G Indahouse*).

Guest House Paradiso, derived from the sitcom *Bottom* and as bad as any of these films, is a revealing case-study of intermingling strands of British comedy cinema. It updates the format of the 1970s sitcom movie – 'opening out' the material and coarsening it even further – but the result is apocalyptic postmodern abstraction rather than any sort of heightened social realism, and punctuated with cartoonishly extreme Three Stooges-style violence. The guesthouse itself is, as one might expect, a microcosm of British snobbery, class terror and sexual frustration, but the effect is closer to the Surrealism of *The Bed Sitting Room* (1969) – or, later, *The League of Gentlemen's Apocalypse* (2005) – than to *Fawlty Towers*. The protagonists are not working class but rather insane grotesques who, for all their aspirations, have fallen, Withnail-like, off the social scale. The film is, however, clearly in the tradition of the British situation comedy and its abiding rule that:

> [S]uccessful sitcom in Britain has always hinged on ideas of authenticity and pretension in class identities: one central character may be pompous/aspiring/ convinced s/he is better than all this, only to be trumped, time and time again, by a doggedly unreconstructed companion.
>
> (Wagg 1998: 2)

The classic 'bedsitcom' (though it is usually about flat or house-sharing), from *Hancock* to *Steptoe and Son* and *The Likely Lads*, through *Rising Damp*, *Bottom*, *Men Behaving Badly*, *Spaced*, *Gimme Gimme Gimme* and *Peep Show*, is bleakly Pinteresque, even Beckettian, in centring on socially stranded and inadequate men (and, very occasionally, women).

If American gross-out was one source of inspiration, another was the vulgar taboo-breaking comic *Viz*. First appearing in Newcastle upon Tyne in 1979, *Viz* achieved its greatest influence in the 1990s, the decade in which the 'New Lad' phenomenon, often dated from the launch of *Loaded* magazine in 1994, 'ironically' celebrated the unreconstructed masculinity of the 1970s. *Viz* repackaged working-class Northern humour, but (unlike Roy 'Chubby' Brown) put quotation marks around its use of comic stereotypes in the approved postmodern style. The magazine walked a hazardous line between celebrating and disapproving of obnoxious recurring characters like Sid the Sexist and the culture that nourished them. Some of *Viz*'s characters, such as the Fat Slags, Roger Mellie and Billy the Fish, were spun off into TV series, but the first film adaptation was *Fat Slags*.

The film's heroines, San and Tray, are two enormous sex-obsessed Northern women. The objects of grotesque comedy, they are nevertheless, as in the magazine, triumphant in getting food and sex, and as a caricature of a contemporary social type may well have, as the magazine's readers seem to feel, more than a 'hint of truth' (Huxley 1998: 285–6). The film's cartoon version of the North is less nostalgic than *UFO*'s. It is a 'North' of obesity, stereotyped jobs (in a post-*Full Monty* twist, the girls work as welders in a smelting plant; the men are uniformly useless) and grotesque squalor (they live at 69 Shit Street in 'Fulchester'). By contrast there is an equally clichéd 'Cool Britannia' London of high end shops (Naomi Campbell works in one) and globalised finance, as well as tourist postcard clichés like Pearly Kings, punks and businessmen in bowler hats. The plot contrives an encounter between social extremes of greed and excess when a concussed American billionaire falls for the two girls on a talk show about 'Why are Northern tarts so fat?' and determines to make them media superstars. Littered with cameos from TV comics, the film is a grosser version of *Spice World: The Movie* (1997); in fact, one of the stars is Geri Halliwell of the Spice Girls and the film's mocking celebration of unapologetic female excess owes something to the group's popularisation of 'Girl Power' and its ideology of empowerment through conspicuous consumption. At the same time, like Waynetta Slob (*Harry Enfield and Chums*), Vicky Pollard and Nessa Jenkins (*Gavin & Stacey*), the Fat Slags' obesity reinforces the identification of the working class, and especially working-class women, with *really* 'fat bastards' (the girls' diet is mostly kebabs and their wildest dream is to work at Little Chef). This 'Othering' of the working class is underlined by the film's parody of London's ignorant contempt for the North; the girls' heavily accented Geordie boyfriends are suspected of being illegal immigrants, and the North is effectively a foreign country (this reworks a joke made in *Monty Python's The Meaning of Life*, which captions establishing shots of the North as 'The Third World'). *Fat Slags*, appalling as it is, retains interest as a haphazard cognitive mapping of the media-saturated excesses of British culture before the crash of 2008. More significant, it shows how grossness was becoming not only a mode of comedy, but also a key signifier of the working class, whose return of the repressed was as a monster of promiscuity, stupidity and mountainously wobbling flesh.

At the fearsome extreme of gross-out comedy are the American *Jackass* TV series and films (2002 onwards) and their British, more accurately Welsh, equivalent, *Dirty Sanchez*, a Channel 4 TV series spun off into a film in 2006. *Dirty Sanchez: The Movie* is a staged documentary about young men engaged in dangerous stunts, mostly involving gag-inducing bodily abuse. The format is part-freak show and part-performance art. As in some contemporary hardcore porn and shock sites, as well as TV reality shows like *I'm a Celebrity – Get Me Out of Here!*, there is a genuinely realist impulse, a disturbing fetish in fact, for demonstrating the unlikely capacity of the body for endurance and for capturing unmediated emotional and physical responses.

Dirty Sanchez: The Movie stars, as *The Daily Mail* put it, saying it should have been banned, 'three sado-masochistic Welsh chavs plus one equally talentless Londoner'.[4] Like the comedy rap group Goldie Lookin Chain (also from Newport, South Wales), the boys conjure a culture of pubs, tattoos, and skater culture, confirming an association between Wales and grotty masculinity forged, thanks to Rhys Ifans, in *Twin Town* (1997) and *Notting Hill* (1999). A vestigial plot links scenes of beer enemas, penises shot with airguns, and the like (a scene of their sucking excrement from rabbits' anuses did not, however, pass the BBFC, though, on the grounds of animal cruelty rather than psychotic bad taste). In a cameo as Satan, Howard Marks – another Welsh reprobate – instructs the boys to 'wreak havoc, inflict panic and commit the seven deadly sins' (which is how working-class lifestyles are often represented anyway these days). Very obviously homoerotic and, from its title on, anally fixated, the film is obsessed with male bodies queered by arousal and torment. Pritchard, in the 'Envy' section, has 'I ♥ Dainton' tattooed on his cock; there is a competition to see who can masturbate to produce the most semen; and in a triumphant face-off with Japanese rivals, the Tokyo Shock Boys, one of the Sanchez troupe imbibes the liquid from a beer enema (an act that, if replicated in what the BBFC primly calls a 'sex work', would undoubtedly get it banned). At the same time, there is a fascinated terror of crossed gender boundaries and feminisation. For example when Pancho, the smallest of the troupe and the habitual object of their bullying, is in pain during liposuction, one of the others tells him to 'push hard', as if Pancho were giving birth, and holds his hand like an expectant father. This sequence ends with a queasily transgressive scene in which Pancho's drained 'man fat' is consumed, a sort of mock-cannibalism that implies other ways of exchanging bodily fluids. In a scene where the boys kiss a series of Thai women to guess which one is the 'ladyboy', Dainton discovers he has kissed a man and promptly vomits. 'I've got a missus and kids back home,' he moans, though such scruples are forgotten when a Thai girl later gives him a handjob. Actual – rather than symbolic, deniable or displaced – homosexual activity turns out to be the most stomach-churning gross-out of all. Towards the end the boys are instructed in some desert survival by Captain Mike Hawke, a growly American hard man, who gives them mindless tasks to toughen them up – something previous generations of working-class men might accomplish by physical labour and perhaps also the experience of war. Underlying the film's comic machismo and all this male bonding through intimate violence and group sex tourism, there is a sense of nostalgia and compensation for a lost, respectable world of masculine agency and socially sanctioned toughness. Although not much is made of the boys' 'chavviness' (though there is one scene in which, dressed as rabbits, they are shot at by chortling 'toffs'), the film celebrates them as anarchic subcultural outsiders, whose unusual, media-friendly skills keep them from falling back into the underclass. There is a useful link here to what Claire Monk calls the 'underclass cycle' of the 1990s:

> The youth underclass films present joblessness and social exclusion as an accepted state. The young male underclass of *Trainspotting* [1996] and *Twin Town* is emphatically not framed as a 'social problem' requiring a 'solution' but, with a certain knowing detachment, as a subculture. Rather than seeking to provoke social anger, the films encourage an empathetic complicity between their audience and the two films' jobless young male inhabitants. ... The lives led by the protagonists are thus framed as a lifestyle with certain attractions for a young, post-political male audience.
>
> (Monk 2000: 278)

Rather like the male strippers in *The Full Monty*, the *Dirty Sanchez* team redeploy, and commodify, their obsolete male bodies by displaying them in parodies of erotic performance. The violent comedy of the gross-out is essential to their act, for it is what enables them to deny both the homoerotic and the feminised aspects of their hysterical exhibitionism.

Other TV-related gross-out films of the 2000s include *Gladiatress* (2004), a parody of Roman epics by the *Smack the Pony* team; the film's humour, based on anachronism and *Airplane!* (1980)-like references, was much less accomplished than *Monty Python's Life of Brian* (1979) or indeed *Carry On Cleo* (1964). By far the most successful TV spin-offs were Sacha Baron Cohen's excruciating exercise in cultural misunderstanding *Borat: Cultural Learnings of America for Make Benefit Glorious Nation of Kazakhstan* (2006), and the gory 'zom-com' *Shaun of the Dead* (2004); both films explored, once again, themes of male inadequacy, delusion and embarrassment. *Lesbian Vampire Killers* (2009), a vehicle for James Corden from *Gavin & Stacey*, was a poor attempt to repeat the genre parody of *Shaun of the Dead*. The film's appalling reviews prompted Chris Tookey of *The Daily Mail* to note that 'it appears to have been made for binge-drinking teenagers – and by them'. He went on to remark: 'The history of British cinema is strewn with disastrous misadventures by TV comics, from Morecambe and Wise through to Ant and Dec [*Alien Autopsy* (2006)]' (Tookey 2009). Now, it is certainly not the case that TV spin-offs are always commercial and critical disasters (though, of all the sitcom films of the 1970s, only *The Likely Lads* (1976) has gained much of a reputation). *Borat* and *Bean* were international hits and *The Inbetweeners Movie* (2011) achieved a record opening weekend for a British comedy in the UK of £13.22 million. But it is received wisdom nevertheless that British comedy cinema is dogged by the persistent failure to translate successful TV comedians and formats to film (Logan 2009).

'A sump of untreated dung': *Sex Lives of the Potato Men*

The most interesting, albeit most comprehensively reviled, of these gross-out comedies is *Sex Lives of the Potato Men*. Although Simon Sheridan, heroically against the current, declared it the 'funniest British comedy for over 20 years' (2011: 234), it continues to be overlooked and comprehensively misunderstood.[5]

Sex Lives has been called the worst British film ever made (though with an average IMDb score of 4.3, it currently fares much better than *Fat Slags*; many of the user comments are also very positive about it and praise its fearlessness and unfortunate accuracy). *Sex Lives* achieved a remarkably high profile on its release largely because, much to press disgust, it was backed with Lottery money from the UK Film Council's development fund (£939,000, half of the £1.8 million budget; the rest came from Entertainment Film Distributors (EFD)). Some critics, such as Mark Lawson, drew the moral that 'state cash ... has no place in an overwhelmingly commercial art form' (Lawson 2004).

Sex Lives of the Potato Men is a sex comedy of sorts with a strong cast of TV actors – Johnny Vegas, Mackenzie Crook, Lucy Davis (*The Office*), Mark Gatiss (*The League of Gentlemen*), and Julia Davis (*Nighty Night*). The plot is about a couple of Brummies ('white van men', albeit in a green van) whose wives and girlfriends have left them and who are out to enjoy the *Loaded* lifestyle. As one of them, Dave (Vegas), says: 'From now on it's going to be fanny, blow jobs, big tits and beer – that's the kind of lifestyle I want.' They are Potato Men because their work is humping potatoes to chip shops (though it may also imply unflattering points in common with the shapeless lumpy vegetable). They cling to a very low rung of the social ladder and exist in a state of permanent desperation. Ferris (Crook) still lives with his mother-in-law, who insists on giving him blow jobs; Tolly (Dominic Coleman) is obsessed with jam and fish-paste sandwiches; and Jeremy (Gatiss), who has been dumped by his girlfriend Ruth (Lucy Davis), spends his days stalking her and finally stealing her dog. Although their adventures involve numerous sexual opportunities – orgies, threesomes, masturbation and voyeurism – all of which permutations prove tiring and unfulfilling. Their lives mostly centre on the pub (as in *Shaun of the Dead*); this is yet another post-*Full Monty* film about bewildered men adrift in a feminised world of consumerism and service industries.

To be honest, though not a 'sump of untreated dung' (Christopher 2004), the film doesn't really come off. As well as many flat lines, it is often poorly paced and flabbily edited. Overall the tone is melancholy and despite the title there are none of the expected staples of the sex comedy – no nudity, for example, or unmotivated toplessness (except for Vegas). Despite numerous sexually active working-class bodies, no one seems to be having much fun. Politics is notably absent too; there is none of the antagonism between larky pleasure-loving workers and their joyless bosses that energised *I'm All Right Jack* (1959), *Saturday Night and Sunday Morning* (1960), *Carry On at Your Convenience* (1971) and *On the Buses*. Unlike the kitchen sink films or the sex comedies of the 1970s, there is little sense in *Sex Lives* of the centrality of family and none of working-class solidarity; indeed the social location of the characters is difficult to judge in traditional terms. There are certainly echoes of *Saturday Night and Sunday Morning*, for example, in the film's allusions to abiding working-class themes such as male escape, the boredom and necessity of work, the threat of women and domesticity, and the draining of masculine culture by consumerism and television. But *Sex Lives* is set at a time when consumerism has triumphed, the working class and its unions are marginalised, and social mobility, if it exists at all, is personified by independent and aspirational women, who have left their men far behind.

The sexual permissiveness that Timmy Lea pursued in the *Confessions* films has become compulsory in *Sex Lives of the Potato Men*, so much so that it now defines the men's identity and status: 'My sex life is all I've got,' Ferris whines. Women are happy to initiate and participate in sex – even old ladies want to give blow jobs – but now they are demanding and in control. Sex is 'a game' so banal and mechanical that it is no better than a chore, like DIY – 'Twenty-four hours a day it's either blow jobs or crazy paving', complains Dave. The proletarianisation of sexual plenty means that sex is much like fast food – easily available but not very nourishing. Indeed, sex is wittily connected with food throughout the film – tomato ketchup ejaculates from bottles; sex is had on potato bags and in a chip shop called 'Fishy Fingers'; men are defined by the foods they deliver (as well as Potato Men, there is the self-explanatory Gherkin Man); and Tolly's unspeakable sandwiches are sub-Proustian attempts to recall the taste of 'fanny-juice and strawberries' when his wife spread jam on herself. Philip French remarked, in a hostile but insightful review, that 'The characters live in a condition of physical, moral and spiritual squalor … Intentionally or not, *Potato Men* takes a more unflinching look at the brutalised Britain of today than any movie I've seen' (French 2004). This, indeed, was the point of the film. It evokes with nauseating relish, as well as pathos and empathy, the 'long spiritual decline of the working class' and what, in 1989, Tony Parsons famously anathematised as 'the tattooed jungle' (Parsons 1995: 227) – the pornografied tabloid Britain of dogging, spit-roasts, contact mags and Fred West.[6] In the end, however, Dave slouches away from his new lifestyle and returns to home and family. 'I don't want to sound like a complete poof,' he explains, 'but I used to like talking with my wife.'

The director of *Sex Lives*, Andy Humphries, defended his film in *The Guardian*. He maintained that it was an analysis rather than a symptom of the world it luridly depicted, and that it satirised both the modern working-class male and New Lad culture: 'I took the stupidity of men and made a stupid cartoon version of it.' But his main argument was class-based:

> I think the real reason my film has had so much attention is that it shows the kind of bodies and the class of people that are almost never shown having sex in the movies … My movie is based on my real experiences, unlike some idealised vision of the noble working class.
>
> (Humphries 2004)[7]

In that sense the film, like *Rita, Sue and Bob Too*, *Shameless* and even *Fat Slags*, offers working-class excess as a form of resistance to middle-class conformity. But all those examples point up the difficulty nowadays in representing the working-class positively. Unlike the nostalgic evocations of the traditional working class in *Kinky Boots* and *Made in Dagenham*, which belong to the 'literary tradition' of British 'social comedy', as Dacre calls it (2009: 114, 115), films (and indeed TV programmes) about the contemporary working class usually depict it in terms of criminality or youth subcultures, or as grossly pathological. *Sex Lives* takes pleasure in showcasing Johnny Vegas's fat body as a deliberately carnivalesque subversion (like the sexed-up but comically normal bodies in a 'readers' wives' porn magazine). The fat body in comedy can be celebrated as luxuriously expansive and cheerfully Falstaffian, as with Hattie Jacques, Roy 'Chubby' Brown and to some extent Matt Lucas, Dawn French and Jo Brand. But the fat working-class body is more often defined as sprawling and undisciplined, both symptom and symbol of consumerism itself. In TV make-over and body-shock shows such as *Wife Swap*, *How Clean is Your House*, *You Are What You Eat*, and *Life of Grime*, which became popular in the 2000s, the obese working-class body is contrasted with the middle-class ideal of a slim body, closely policed and self-disciplined. The working-class body needs to be remodelled, augmented, and, preferably, replaced (rather as there is a common fantasy of exchanging the British working class itself for its hard-working and cheery Polish equivalent). Like the class itself, these bodies lack distinct edges. Tattooed, shell-suited, hooded, they and their owners are toxic, dysfunctional, sexually incontinent; and, a term used frequently after the riots of 2011, 'feral', beyond control and understanding. Ideally they would not be visible at all.

The representation of the working class as an underclass of repulsive chavs is reiterated, with admittedly differing levels of sympathy and analysis, in *Twin Town*, *The Martins* (2001), *A Way of Life* (2004), *The Great Ecstasy of Robert Carmichael* (2005), *Harry Brown* (2009) and 'hoodie horror' films such as *Eden Lake* (2008), *F* (2010) and *Cherry Tree Lane* (2010) (Walker 2011) (the SF film, *Attack the Block* (2011), is a rare instance of inner-city youth portrayed with a degree of nuance and understanding). The perception has changed of the working class, and specifically the white English working class – *viz* the salt of the earth has become its scum. Once it carried the burden of history – now it is an irrelevance and embarrassment.[8] *Sex Lives*, the lowest of the low comedies, is also the most revealing in showing the decline of working-class men from liberated beneficiaries of the sexual revolution to sad losers incapable of change.

Low comedy remains key to British comedy, in the sense that bad taste, naughtiness and irresponsibility are felt to be intrinsic to the British 'character'. But few low comedy films, except for some outright slapstick films like *Borat*, *Bean* and *Mr. Bean's Holiday* (2007), are successful at the box office. Some aspects of low comedy identified with the pre-PC era of the 1970s have been revived, and older generations of comedians, from Dick Emery to Bruce Forsyth and Bob Monkhouse, have been re-appreciated for their skill. To some extent, this is merely a selective and ironic rehashing of certain aspects of low comedy, stripped of their dangerous contradictions, and as served up as camp or queer or harmlessly 'subversive' – think of the hopeless revival of *Carry On* in *Carry On Columbus* (1992) or, more recently, the ineffectual reboots of *St. Trinian's* (2007, 2009). These are heritage films, of a sort, reclaiming bawdiness through pastiche. Low comedy has been retooled for a new generation of TV comics, usually middle class and given to aggressive smuttiness and cruelty (and often class snobbery), and it is now designed to attack lower-middle-class sensitivities rather than to make working-class humour visible. In other words, low comedy has been severed, on film at any rate, from links to (white) working-class culture and all that now implies – not solidarity or authenticity but racism, sexism and homophobia. Working-class men are the butt of low comedy and not, as in the 1970s, its rampantly priapic heroes.

Notes

1 See Lawrence Napper's Chapter 3 in this volume.

2 www.imdb.com/chart/bottom (accessed 12 September 2011).

3 I have no idea whether this joke originated with Brown; it later turned up in *South Park: Bigger, Longer & Uncut* (1999).

4 www.dailymail.co.uk/tvshowbiz/reviews/article-425329/Movie-review-2006-censor-banned.html (accessed 12 September 2011).

5 I did attempt to salvage the reputation of *Sex Lives of the Potato Men* in a conference paper soon after it came out (Hunter 2005).

6 Parsons's article, 'The tattooed jungle', was originally published in the men's style magazine *Arena*, September/October 1989 (and its thesis repeated in a 1992 Channel 4 documentary, *Without Walls: The Tattooed Jungle*). It is republished in Parsons 1995: 227–32.

7 It is important to understand, too, that the UK Film Council backed the film to promote not only commercial film-making but also, strange as it may seem, social inclusion. Precisely because of its low populism, the film had a good chance of attracting young working-class men into cinemas. In reply to *The Daily Mail's* front-page headline, 'Fury as lottery money funds vile sex film' (21 February 2004), the UKFC explained:

We also have a remit from the Government to deliver a wide range of films to a wide audience across the country. The money is not there to serve a few film auteurs and a small community of cineastes. Our aim is to reach a demographic that does not necessarily think of going to the cinema. This film is targeted at mainly teenage men who may not even read the reviews.

(Demetriou 2004)

As John Hill points out, social groups ABC1 account for double the cinema admissions of groups C2DE, and thus 'if cinema-going was ever a working-class leisure pursuit, it could hardly be said to be so now' (Hill 2004: 36). *Sex Lives* 'was not only likely to make money but also to appeal to audiences who, unlike many middle-class critics, actually purchased lottery tickets' (Hill 2004: 34). However patronising it may have been to assume that only the film equivalent of *Nuts* or *Zoo* could reach out to young working-class men, Humphries is probably correct that *Sex Lives* alienated middle-class critics because its representation of the working class was, for once, neither *by* nor *for* people like them.

8 Contempt for the white working class was the topic of a number of books around the time *Sex Lives* came out, such as Michael Collins's *The Likes of Us* (2004) and Ferdinand Mount's *Mind the Gap* (2004). Andy Medhurst (2007: 195–202) offers an astute and trenchant analysis of this in relation to Roy 'Chubby' Brown, 'whose comedy yearns for ... an order where white working-class identities are valid and valuable, where "classlessness" is revealed as a pernicious lie' (197). In 2011, after the election of a Conservative-led coalition headed by products of Eton and Oxbridge, the theme was powerfully taken up again in Owen Jones's *Chavs: The Demonization of the Working Class*.

Bibliography

Barber, S. (2010) 'The pinnacle of popular taste?: The importance of *Confessions of a Window Cleaner*', *Scope: An Online Journal of Film & TV Studies*, 18 (October), www.scope.nottingham.ac.uk/article. php?issue=18& id=1246 (accessed 2 September 2011).

Brown, R.'C'. (2007) *Common as Muck!: My Autobiography*, London: Sphere.

Christopher, J. (2004) review of *Sex Lives of the Potato Men*, *Times*, 19 February, http://entertainment. timesonline.co.uk/tol/arts_and_entertainment/film/article1023200.ece (accessed 15 September 2011).

Collins, M. (2004) *The Likes of Us: A Biography of the White Working Class*, London: Granta Books.

Dacre, R. (2009) 'Traditions of British comedy', in R. Murphy (ed.), *The British Cinema Book*, 3rd edn, London: British Film Institute/Palgrave Macmillan.

Demetriou, D. (2004) 'The critics agree: Johnny's "Sex Life" is a disaster. So how did it ever get made?', *The Independent*, 21 February.

Fowles, J. (1977) *The Magus: A Revised Version*, London: Triad Grafton.

French, P. (2004) review of *Sex Lives of the Potato Men*, *The Observer*, 22 February.

Fry, S. (2011) *The Fry Chronicles*, London: Penguin.

Hedling, E. (2009) 'Lindsay Anderson and the development of British art cinema', in R. Murphy (ed.), *The British Cinema Book*, 3rd edn, London: British Film Institute/Palgrave Macmillan.

Hill, J. (1999) *British Cinema in the 1980s*, Oxford: Oxford University Press.

——(2004) 'UK film policy, cultural capital and social exclusion', *Cultural Trends*, 13.2 (June): 29–40.

Humphries, A. (2004) 'If it's too smutty, you're too snooty', *The Guardian*, 27 February, www.guardian. co.uk/film/2004/feb/27/2 (accessed 8 September 2011).

Hunt, L. (1998) *British Low Culture: From Safari Suits to Sexploitation*, London: Routledge.

Hunter, I.Q. (2005) '*Sex Lives of the Potato Men* and the decline of the British working class', paper at MeCCSA and AMPE Joint Annual Conference, University of Lincoln, 7 January.

——(2008) 'Take an easy ride: Sexploitation in the 1970s', in R. Shail (ed.), *Seventies British Cinema*, London: British Film Institute.

Huxley, D. (1998) '*Viz*: Gender, class and taboo', in S. Wagg (ed.), *Because I Tell a Joke or Two: Comedy, Politics and Social Difference*, London and New York: Routledge.

Jones, O. (2011) *Chavs: The Demonization of the Working Class*, London: Verso.

Lawson, M. (2004) 'A load of Slotpm', *The Guardian*, 21 February, www.guardian.co.uk/film/2004/feb/21/news.comment (accessed 8 September 2011).

Leach, J. (2004) *British Film*, Cambridge: Cambridge University Press.

Logan, B. (2009) 'British comedy films: Make 'em laugh! Well, that's the theory', *The Guardian*, 12 November, www.guardian.co.uk/film/2009/nov/12/british-comedy-movies (accessed 8 September 2011)

McGillivray, D. (1992) *Doing Rude Things: A History of the British Sex Film*, London: Sun Tavern Fields.

Medhurst, A. (2007) *A National Joke: Popular Comedy and English Cultural Identities*, London and New York: Routledge.

Monk, C. (2000) 'Underbelly UK: The 1990s underclass film, masculinity and the ideologies of "new" Britain', in J. Ashby and A. Higson (eds), *British Cinema, Past and Present*, London and New York: Routledge.

Mount, F. (2004) *Mind the Gap: The New Class Divide in Britain*, London: Short Books.

Orwell, G. (1970) 'The art of Donald McGill', in S. Orwell and I. Angus (eds), *The Collected Essays, Journalism and Letters of George Orwell: Volume II My Country Right or Left 1940–1943*, Harmondsworth: Penguin Books.

Parsons, T. (1995) *Dispatches from the Front Line of Popular Culture*, London: Virgin Books.

Paul, W. (1994) *Laughing Screaming: Modern Hollywood Horror and Comedy*, New York: Columbia University Press.

Porter, L. (1998) 'Tarts, tampons and tyrants: Women and representation in British comedy', in S. Wagg (ed.), *Because I Tell a Joke or Two: Comedy, Politics and Social Difference*, London and New York: Routledge.

Sheridan, S. (2011) *Keeping the British End Up: Four Decades of Saucy Cinema*, 3rd edn, London: Titan.

Tookey, C. (2009) 'Consistently abominable: *Lesbian Vampire Killers*', *Mail Online*, 20 March, www.dailymail.co.uk/tvshowbiz/reviews/article-1163268/Consistently-abominable-Lesbian-Vampire-Killers.html (accessed 8 September 2011).

Wagg, S. (1992) 'You've never had it so silly: The politics of British satirical comedy from *Beyond the Fringe* to *Spitting Image*', in D. Strinati and S. Wagg (eds), *Come On Down? Popular Media Culture in Post-War Britain*, London and New York: Routledge.

——(1998) 'At ease, Corporal: Social class and the situation comedy in British television, from the 1950s to the 1990s', in S. Wagg (ed.), *Because I Tell a Joke or Two: Comedy, Politics and Social Difference*, London and New York: Routledge.

Walker, J. (2011) 'F for "frightening"?: Johannes Roberts takes on Hoodie Horrors', *Diabolique*, 3: 24–32.

Willetts, P. (2010) *Members Only: The Life and Times of Paul Raymond*, London: Serpent's Tail.

Williams, L. (1991) 'Film bodies: Gender, genre and excess', *Film Quarterly*, 44.4: 2–13.

13 Making *Ben-Hur* look like an epic

Monty Python at the movies

Justin Smith

Between 1971 and 1983 the British comedy team Monty Python made four feature-length films for the cinema: *And Now for Something Completely Different* (1971), *Monty Python and the Holy Grail* (1974), *Monty Python's Life of Brian* (1979) and *Monty Python's The Meaning of Life* (1983). The first and last of these exploited the sketch format on which their original BBC television show, *Monty Python's Flying Circus*, was based (four series, 1969–74). But from the early 1970s, the cult appeal of their distinctive brand of surreal British humour was also marketed through audio recordings, books and live shows, gaining international recognition over 40 years culminating in the recent success of the stage musical *Spamalot*. It is the purpose of this chapter to examine the role of the Monty Python films in transforming the innovative work of a group of comedy writers and performers into worldwide popular comic currency. This affords an opportunity to reassess the unique contribution of Monty Python to British comedy cinema.

And Now for Something Completely Different (1971)

The idea for their first feature came from London Playboy impresario Victor Lownes who had originally wanted to buy the television series to sell in the United States. But reticence from the American networks about an untried, unconventional and distinctively British television comedy, prompted Lownes to suggest a feature-length packaging of a selection from the first BBC series, to market to the campus college circuit (Cleese in Chapman et al. 2003: 192–3). Lownes invested around 40 per cent of the £80,000 budget, while American interest in the form of Patricia Casey's Kettledrum Productions put up the rest. Ian MacNaughton assumed the role of director.

Enthusiasm for working in film was shared amongst the team. During the six-week shoot at a disused dairy in North London, Michael Palin wrote: 'Morale in the unit is very high ... From the performance point of view, I enjoy the security of being able to do a performance several times' (Palin 2007: 49). Terry Jones recalls, 'It had always been in the back of my mind to do movies so I was very keen' (Chapman et al. 2003: 195). However, tensions also became apparent during the production: 'When it came to the film Ian [MacNaughton] made it quite clear that he didn't want any opinion from me ... Ian was very hyped up for the film' (Jones in Chapman et al. 2003: 195). But the director was also drinking heavily. Eric Idle attests: 'I think the pressure on Ian having the two Terrys over his shoulder was also one of the reasons he drank like crazy' (Chapman et al. 2003: 197).

This experience marked an intensification of the creative struggles which were already emerging from the experience of the first television series, where the Pythons had quickly adapted to the working practices of the medium and had gained a grasp of how they wanted their original material presented. Terry Jones recalls that 'in the TV shows I would say, "Ian, I think we've got to move the camera a little bit that way, or I think this is the better angle for this"' (Chapman et al. 2003: 195). The visual sense of how their humour worked was foremost in the minds of Terrys Jones and Gilliam, even at this early stage in their film careers.

The post-production assemblage of the film was itself a learning curve for the Pythons in judging how well their sketch material worked over 90 minutes. Cleese recalls: 'However we edited the film, people got bored half way through because there was no story' (in Chapman et al. 2003: 195). For Gilliam this also was a question of comic stamina: 'It's somewhere about an hour in that you start running out of steam' (Chapman et al. 2003: 195). Terry Jones insists that the ordering of the sketch material rather than its overall length was the vital matter: 'It's not a question of how funny they are, but it's where they are and where they come' (Chapman et al. 2003: 195).

Sterner lessons still were in store in terms of the film's marketing and distribution. While it achieved considerable box-office success in the UK, on the back of the first television series and as part of what had recently become established as a trend of British TV comedy show spin-offs, the US market (which had been its *raison d'être*) remained largely impenetrable. Gilliam attributed this to uninspired marketing on the part of the film's Hollywood distributor, Columbia:

> They sold it in some stupid way where it bombed. And in England where we didn't want it shown particularly because it was old material, it was a huge success. So this was us learning about the film business. But it was frustrating because Terry Jones and I were always in there wanting to be directing and it became more and more frustrating.
>
> (in Chapman et al. 2003: 196–7)

With hindsight, *And Now for Something Completely Different* can be seen to have had two broad effects. First, it developed the team's experience of, and enthusiasm for, working in feature film, and galvanised their resolve to achieve creative mastery of their own original material in this medium. Second, it arguably cemented in the British national consciousness the peculiar phenomenon that was *Monty Python's Flying Circus*; the film's UK release in September 1971 coincided with a repeat showing of the second BBC television series. The Pythons' own choice of series one material to include in the film doubtless did much to reinforce the now iconic status of sketches such as 'Dead Parrot', 'Nudge, Nudge', 'Self-Defence', 'Lumberjack Song', 'Blackmail' and 'Upper-Class Twit of the Year', and made a catchphrase of the title itself. That the Pythons themselves found the process of recycling their early material tedious, the creative struggles of film production frustrating, and the mishandling of the film's marketing disheartening, served to strengthen their determination to take control of their own product.

Monty Python and the Holy Grail (1974)

Having begun working on ideas for a feature film in spring 1973, by the autumn of that year, and with the summer's *First Farewell Tour* behind them, the script for what would become *Monty Python and the Holy Grail* began to take shape (Palin 2007: 166). Terry Jones approached Mark Forstater to produce the film, but his inexperience coupled with the Pythons' own decision to direct the project themselves, was greeted with indifference by potential investors (Jones in Chapman et al. 2003: 239). In their search to find backers, the team's manager John Gledhill, having been turned down by EMI, Rank and the National Film Finance Consortium, talked to a number of business associates including Tony Stratton-Smith, head of their record company Charisma, and West End theatrical impresario Michael White, who had produced Cleese and Chapman in their *Cambridge Circus* review in 1963.

Stratton-Smith persuaded some of his clients, including members of Pink Floyd and Led Zeppelin, to contribute to a fighting fund. Palin reflects: 'I think they thought it was somehow quite cool, it was a cult thing' (Chapman et al. 2003: 234). But, the financial commitment of these star-fan investors was also strategic. As White's business partner, producer John Goldstone reports:

> Initially [White] was actually prepared to put up all the money himself, but the terms that we were negotiating with the Pythons didn't give them the kind of control they were really looking for ... So effectively the Tony Stratton-Smith group put up half the money and Michael put up the other half. And the conditions under which we were going to do this were that I would be responsible for selling the film.
>
> (John Goldstone, personal communication, 15 April 2011)

Although novices in the film business who had struggled to attract finance, the Pythons (with Mark Forstater as chief negotiator) thus managed to arrange a deal which allowed them creative autonomy. However, their freedom was restricted by a working budget which amounted to a meagre £150,000 (John Goldstone, personal communication, 15 April 2011). Although their initial creative challenge had been to extend Python's successful comedy formula to a 90-minute narrative, the practicalities of shooting the script proved an even sterner test.

While Cleese had provided the impetus and the steer for *And Now for Something Completely Different*, the disparate sketch ideas which formed the nucleus of *Monty Python and the Holy Grail* were driven and shaped by the writing team of Michael Palin and Terry Jones. Jones and Gilliam, it had already been agreed, would co-direct, with Jones's emphasis on script and performance, and Gilliam's on visual style. Originally the play on Arthurian legend, which kicked off with Palin's idea for Arthur (Chapman) and Patsy (Gilliam) with coconuts, had a modern setting, with the quest ending in the Grail Department at Harrods – a very *Flying Circus* conceit. But Jones's and Gilliam's enthusiasm for the medieval period, perhaps inspired by seeing Pasolini's *Canterbury Tales* (1971), imposed a tighter structure on the early sketch material only about ten per cent of which, according to Cleese, made the shooting script (in Chapman et al. 2003: 236). Palin reflected, 'I think what really worked was that the events in the story could be broken down into an old university revue format – ten sketches and three songs – and we also managed to join them together rather well' (Chapman et al. 2003: 236). As with the television shows, a vital element here in providing what Palin calls 'little bits of sealant that kept the narrative watertight', was Gilliam's animation, which cleverly combines Arthurian legend's literary heritage with visual elements from illuminated manuscripts.[1] But arguably Gilliam's equally important contribution was in achieving a grimly realistic period setting, as a way 'of doing an antidote to the Hollywood vision of the Middle Ages … really dirty' (Jones in Chapman et al. 2003: 239).

This visual quality was achieved by a combination of factors. First, Gilliam and Jones set off together on an extensive location scout in Scotland and Wales. Despite being forbidden to use their first choice Highland castles by the Scottish Department of the Environment for fear Monty Python should be 'doing things which were not consistent with the dignity of the fabric of the buildings', they eventually secured the use of Doune Castle in Perthshire and Castle Stalker on Loch Linnhe near Oban, and identified suitably wild tracts of rugged landscape in and around Glencoe (Jones in Chapman et al. 2003: 239). Second, the physical difficulties of filming on a tight budget in such remote locations made the construction of scaffolds and rostrum platforms, or the laying of extensive dolly-tracks virtually impossible, so the scale of the set-ups was restricted. There are few panoramic views of this strikingly dramatic landscape; it is a grimly naturalistic world of base dimensions. Third, most of the comic visual effects were achieved by simple blue-screen, while the atmospheric mood was created by using smoke, filters and old film stock. The film is uniformly under lit, for which Terry Bedford, the cinematographer, was responsible. Indeed, Mark Forstater credits Bedford with the entire look: 'What comedy films came out of Britain before this, that have anything like this look? The answer is zero. And the reason is not Terry Jones or Terry Gilliam but Terry Bedford' (Mark Forstater, personal communication, 14 April 2011). But credit must also be given to the special effects photography of Julian Doyle and to production designer Roy Smith, especially for the ingenious set-dressing of the incredibly flexible space which the ruined Doune Castle proved to be. And visual continuity and period authenticity are also achieved to a remarkably high standard through Hazel Pethig's thrifty but effective costume designs.[2] The knights' 'string-vest' chainmail in particular took on a convincingly weighty appearance when wet. Indeed, the vagaries of the Scottish climate in the month of May were just one of the challenges which faced the crew.

The visual coherence of the film is remarkable given the conditions under which the shoot proceeded, with two novice directors presiding over an under-resourced unit and a cast of fellow Pythons who became increasingly disgruntled (in the case of Cleese) and drunk (in the case of Chapman). Cleese lost his temper with Gilliam over numerous re-takes, Chapman bottled out of crossing the Bridge of Death, and even Michael Palin's normally mild-mannered temperament was tested by the mud-eating scene. Finally, he contemplated: 'The long and wordy Constitutional Peasants scene. Feel heavy, dull and uninspired – wanting above all else for it to be the end of the day' (Palin 2007: 200).

Nonetheless, the demands of the shooting environment arguably added immeasurably to the realism of the performances. Palin's Dennis does indeed sound like a world-weary

Marxist shop-steward the source of whose condition of alienated labour is precisely in being transplanted into a mythical medieval narrative. Thus, the success of the *Holy Grail* is not simply in the silliness of some of the best individual sketch ideas, such as Jones' and Palin's 'Knights Who Say "Ni"', Chapman's and Cleese's 'Witch-Ducking', and Idle's and Innes' 'Brave Sir Robin'. Rather it lies in the systematic disruption of the coherent imaginative world. The fact that this is a mythical world (based on Arthurian legend) which is realised with a plausible degree of historical verisimilitude, establishes a post-modern playground of surreal disjunctions and comic *bricolage*. For example, the 'accidental' killing of the 'Famous Historian' is more than just a Milliganesque caricature of A.J.P. Taylor; it represents the death of history's grand narrative, our rational inability to explain the relationship of history to national mythology. It is perhaps no accident that Monty Python's mid-1970s revival of Arthurian myth chimed with a number of other filmic examples on both sides of the Channel.[3] Nowhere is this sustained repertoire of self-reflexive devices more effective than in the anti-cinema references. The veracity of this imaginative world is challenged by the equally ana-chronistic incursions of modern-day historians and French knights, which build towards the closing-down of the shoot itself by the police, thus denying the medieval narrative, its conventional Hollywood epic battle finale and reducing the screen image to a trail of leader-strip. But the Intermission card, the fake Scandinavian Moose sub-titles, and the struggle at Swamp Castle to prevent the whole ensemble descending into musical self-parody, are all features of a running joke about cinema itself. Just as much of the power of *Flying Circus* had arisen from its subversion of the conventions of television, so the *Holy Grail* trades self-consciously on not being a Hollywood version of the Middle Ages. Arguably this aspect of the film's impact was not fully realised until well into post-production, and was profoundly dependent upon a crucial alteration to the soundtrack.

An investors' preview showing in October 1974 was, according to Michael Palin, a gloomy affair. It revealed that the period authenticity, particularly at the level of sound-effects, undermined the comedy drastically. 'The film was 20% too strong on authenticity and 20% too weak on jokes' (Palin 2007: 212). Before the UK premiere on 3 April 1975, a substantial re-edit and the addition of pre-recorded music (which 'lifted it into the area of swashbuckling parody') were required, jettisoning a good deal of material and reducing Neil Innes' score to a couple of songs (Idle in Chapman et al. 2003: 264). The addition of library music from DeWolfes, which is all they could afford, proved to be the vital element which successfully underscored the epic parody.

Monty Python and the Holy Grail was an instant commercial success in the UK, grossing £19,000 in its first week in London, and earning plaudits from Alexander Walker in the *Evening Standard* and *Time Out* in the capital (Palin 2007: 251) and from the popular national press (Palin 2007: 253). Among the tabloids, Michael Palin was particularly pleased with the *News of the World* who 'said that the credits on their own were funnier than most comedy films' (Palin 2007: 252). But interestingly, the broad-sheets were more muted and, surprisingly, shared their rather snooty reservations with the youth-oriented music papers *Sounds* and *New Musical Express*. And the dedicated film press was equally divided, between Geoff Brown's condemnation of Python as merely 'mechanical purveyors of the Absurd' (Brown 1975) and Gordon Gow's insistence that 'this is decidedly a work of genuine filmic interest: a handy piece of plumage for the British cinema's somewhat tattered cap' (Gow 1975).

But from the point of view of Monty Python's continued ascendency, it was the film's breakthrough in the American market which really signalled a sea-change, because this was by no means assured. The ground had been prepared by the success of the team's Canadian and US tour two years before, and the sale of the first *Flying Circus* series to PBS in October 1974. And by the eve of the film's release in February 1975, Python led the PBS Channel 13 ratings (Palin 2007: 229). Executive producer John Goldstone had gained a UK distribution with EMI. But in the United States, where he had no obvious entrée, Goldstone tried the FilmEx Festival in Los Angeles in February 1975, where it was accepted for a festival screening. To his amazement, when

> we got to the cinema … there was a whole queue of people which I thought was for some other film, not ours. And it was extraordinary. There was clearly something already going on. I think it was partly the import of the albums that started a groundswell which was grassroots at that point.
>
> (John Goldstone, personal communication, 15 April 2011)

This unexpected reception led to distribution interest from 'Cinema 5 which was in fact, essentially, a cinema owner in New York. They had some of the premium sites, but they did distribution as well' (Goldstone, personal communication, 15 April 2011). Don Rugoff's Cinema 5 agreed to handle the film, and to open it in New York on 27 April. 'And he was the one who had the idea of giving out coconuts to the first 200 people who turned up. And in fact, on the first day, thousands of people turned up. Again, the groundswell had been growing … and it just kind of went from there' (Goldstone, personal communication, 15 April 2011). On the first day the film was screened continuously and broke the house record with a take of $10,500 (Palin 2007: 258). Within five years of its first release, the National Film Trustee Company, which had been appointed to distribute the proceeds amongst the film's multiple investors, recorded world-wide revenues in excess of £2.5 million.[4] A reasonable return on a film made for less than £300,000.

Back in the UK, the popular press seized on this triumphant British success. *The Sun* quoted Terry Jones as claiming, 'It's becoming a bit like Beatlemania'. PBS ratings for the *Flying Circus* had led to cinema sell-outs and, Jones continued, 'the Americans are pressing us to get together for a stage tour'. He added: 'We'll almost certainly be doing another film in Britain next year after the success of the *Holy Grail*' (Spencer 1975). *The Times* celebrated the Python's live show at New York's City Center the following year. Parallels with The Beatles' Shea Stadium performance of the previous decade led Iain Johnstone to chuckle that *New York Daily News* gripes 'might have given more pleasure to the cast (who, like a pop group, have undergone the change from quasi-rebels to cult figures) … As with the Beatles', he continued, 'most of the seats had been sold anyway' (Johnstone 1976).

Not only had American success established that the Python's very British humour could have broad appeal outside Europe, it also proved that the *Holy Grail* represented a genuine graduation to feature-length format. Amidst the euphoria of this success they had already been asked what their next film would be called. In inimitable fashion Eric Idle swiftly announced: 'Jesus Christ – Lust For Glory' (Goldstone, personal communication, 15 April 2011). In another moment worthy of comparison with the Beatles in America, Idle's sensational remark, like John Lennon's, set the Pythons on course for even greater notoriety, and celebrity, both in the United States and back home. And another ex-Beatle, George Harrison, would turn out to have a hand in its making.

Monty Python's *Life of Brian* (1979)

The fact that *Life of Brian* has proved the most controversial and widely known of Monty Python's four feature films is arguably because it is the only one which, quite apart from being funny, is actually *about* something – the hypocrisies of idolatry. And it is a theme which has proved, for all its comic worth, to be remarkably prescient in its social commentary. It also provoked fierce criticism at the time of its release, from those who misread its target.

A key decision in the development of the script, which was completed in Barbados in January 1978, was to abandon the initial idea of grappling with the gospel story. 'I think we realised at that point we couldn't make a film about Jesus Christ', Idle recalls, 'because ... what he's saying isn't mockable, it is very decent stuff' (in Chapman et al. 2003: 279). Instead, Palin writes, they debated 'the idea of there being Messiah fever in Judea at that time. That was really the key to it and gave us the theme' (in Chapman et al. 2003: 279). The story would establish, historically, a parallel universe in which, through a case of mistaken identity, an ordinary man is pursued as a new messiah. There are similarities here to the conception of the *Holy Grail*, in that the success of the humour (and in this case the power of the satire too) depends upon the establishment of a fantasy world which is materially grounded and visually coherent. If there is one common strength which sustains Python's film work it is this quality. *The Life of Brian* has the look of a biblical epic and it reproduces its Tunisian locations, where Zeffirelli shot *Jesus of Nazareth* (1977), with a remarkable degree of verisimilitude.

The scripting process was this time much more controlled. There are a number of explanations for this. By now the six members of the Python team were all working on their own individual projects and reunited only for business meetings and to focus on film work. There was a shared enthusiasm for Python on film, following the experience of the *Holy Grail*, and the promise of a much larger working budget. John Goldstone was appointed as sole producer and provided the kind of support which allowed them creative freedom and editorial control. Graham Chapman had got off alcohol, was functioning better as a creative team-member, and had committed to playing the lead, Brian Cohen. Finally, once they had agreed on the theme and conducted some research they arrived, for the first time, at a single story (with an ending) which guided their group writing and script development. Michael Palin remembers:

> *Brian* was our last really good group experience in writing terms ... [I]ndividuals or writing groups would take a certain section and move it on or write a stoning scene which obviously fitted in next to something. And then the various characters that one had written, like the Centurion who goes all the way through played by

John, would be the result of group discussion ... The way we worked in Barbados was unheard of since the very earliest Python shows.

(Palin in Chapman et al. 2003: 284)

Upon their return to London in late January 1978, John Goldstone presented them with the terms of a deal he'd negotiated with EMI's Barry Spikings and Michael Deeley, and production plans were made for location shooting to begin in April. However, Bernard Delfont, head of EMI's entertainments division, summarily intervened by telegram to Deeley:

> Have looked rather quickly through the script of the new Monty Python film and am amazed to find that it is not the zany comedy usually associated with his films. But is obscene and sacrilegious, and would certainly not be in the interest of EMI's image to make this sort of film.
>
> (Deeley and Field 2008: 140)

Deeley immediately tried to reason with his boss, insisting that the film was not sacrilegious,

> but Delfont wouldn't listen to my case. He was not used to being corrected and his final furious expostulation was, 'I'm not going to be accused of making fun of fucking *Jesus Christ!*' I warned him that we would have to pay off the producer, and his response was, "Do what you have to do to get out of this".
>
> (Deeley and Field 2008: 139)

Idle and Goldstone went off to the United States to try, unsuccessfully, to find alternative backers. But if anything they found the religious theme was more sensitive to the major studios there than in the UK:

> Then Eric said, 'George Harrison has always been a big fan, we should try him'. I was a bit sceptical. The budget was $4m ... and I thought, 'this is an awful lot of money for one person to put up'. But it turned out not to be. He was very keen to do this.
>
> (John Goldstone, personal communication, 15 April 2011)

According to Idle (in Chapman et al. 2003: 285), Harrison mortgaged his own home in order to realise the capital and put Goldstone in touch with his business manager, Denis O'Brien: 'And they just went with it, and created a financial structure that would work for George, and in doing so created a new vehicle company ... so it became HandMade Films' (Goldstone, personal communication, 15 April 2011).

The eight-week shoot in September and October 1978 went smoothly. A tight script, a healthy production budget, conducive locations and good team morale all helped. Terry Jones worked wonders with the team of locals and British tourists recruited as extras for the crowd scenes. Terry Gilliam, despite ceding directorial control to Jones, enjoyed exercising his creative freedom in production design, extracting the full potential of local colour to achieve a fine degree of authenticity. In this way the film's best sequences may be considered to be those where the comic performances are fully integrated with a vivid and richly-textured *mise-en-scène*. Although Palin's Pilate and Cleese's gruff Centurion may provide the most laughter, the Roman scenes are arguably less original and more stagey than the cameos: Palin's ex-leper, and Ben the ancient prisoner, Cleese's Reg and Idle's Stan, the Revolutionaries, and the Prophets. The opening (nativity) and closing (crucifixion) scenes are *tours de force*, as is the Sermon on the Mount, with its sublime juxtaposition of the comic world of the fractious crowd and the distant, biblical story (faithfully rendered in Kenneth Colley's convincing Messiah). The sympathetic story of Brian (consummately rendered by Chapman) gains in pathos as the eponymous but reluctant hero escapes his mother Mandy (Terry Jones) and finds romance with Judith (Sue Jones-Davies). Judith herself is noteworthy as perhaps the only progressive female character in all of Python's output. Moreover, the plausibility of this 'straight' narrative of Brian's life is crucial; it provides the structural backbone which hold the 'sketches' together.

John Goldstone secured a US distribution deal with John Calley at Warner Bros., and the film opened in New York and Los Angeles on 17 August to strong business. Denis O'Brien had moved swiftly earlier in the summer to recommend that his company EuroAtlantic should work with the Pythons to 'structure' the earnings from *Life of Brian*, and he formally became their manager, which caused some disquiet with Anne Henshaw who had represented the team since John Gledhill's departure in 1974. At Cinema 1 in New York it took $13,000 on the first day (Palin 2007: 633). When the film finally opened in London, following its UK censorship *débâcle*, it took £40,000 in its first week at the Plaza – outstripping the previous record-holder, *Jaws*, by £8,000 (Palin 2007: 661).

Meanwhile, John Goldstone, in anticipating potential difficulties in selling the film, had invited James Ferman, Secretary of the BBFC, to a preview screening at the beginning of April, and was keen to involve him in deliberations over the issue of blasphemy. Goldstone and the Pythons were wary of the Festival of Light's successful recent prosecution of *Gay News* using the Blasphemy Laws at the hands of Lord Justice Scarman. Therefore, prior to submitting the film for classification, Goldstone sent Ferman the opinion of two QCs, John Mortimer and Michael Grieve, who had been shown the film on 14 June. They found that the Python's film 'would seem to lack the element of vilification which was the keynote of the *Gay News* case'.[5] On 24 July, the BBFC examining team reported. Tony Kerpel adjudged that 'on dialogue alone the film is clearly "AA"'. But on the more serious matter of the subject he suggested: 'It will certainly cause offence to many people', and 'were this a film about somebody mistaken for Mohammed we would be more careful about the causing of offence to religious and ethnic feeling. I don't see why staunch Christians should get any less consideration from us'.[6] Fellow examiner Rosemary Stark agreed: 'Dialogue and some nudity ... make the AA appropriate. However,' she warned, 'there are other problems, if not of law then certainly of taste, and some early alarm raised by pressure groups led to a hefty file of condemnatory letters before the film was even completed'.[7]

Certainly the files on *Life of Brian* held at the BBFC (one of press cuttings and another entirely of correspondence) bear out the level of reaction the film provoked (both from the public and from local authorities) before and after its UK release. This controversy had the immediate effect of making what was instantly a popular and critical success even more widely known. So much so that Ferman drafted a standard letter of response setting out the board's position. Remarkably, given the censorship controversies of the early 1970s, *Life of Brian* was viewed by more local authorities than any other film during the decade. More than 50 councils had licensed the film for exhibition without preview. Of the 101 councils who had seen the film, 62 adopted the BBFC's recommended 'AA' certificate, 28 had upgraded it to 'X', and 11 had banned it altogether. 'It is unusual,' Ferman remarked, 'for a film with a "AA" certificate to be tested so extensively, and it was probably only the allegations of blasphemy provoked by the film's Biblical theme that induced so many councils to exercise their discretionary powers in this case.'[8] But in assuring local authorities and concerned Christians alike regarding the legal matter of blasphemy, he concluded:

> a faith which could be shaken by such good-humoured ribaldry would be a very precarious faith indeed ... Britain is not a theocratic state led by some unbending ayatollah and true religion would be all the healthier in a world which occasionally indulges an honest and good-natured sense of humour.[9]

Ferman's judgement, perhaps one of the most reasoned pronouncements from a film censor on a comedy entertainment, not only addresses the concerns of those who condemned the film, it also acknowledges *Life of Brian*'s seriousness. John Cleese reflects with pride on the achievement: 'I think it is the most mature thing we did. I'm always surprised the Americans prefer *Holy Grail*, but the English much prefer *Life of Brian* and so do I. I think it's mature and I also think ... we were making some very good jokes about very important things' (in Chapman et al. 2003: 306–7).

Monty Python's The Meaning of Life (1983)

After *Life of Brian*'s success and the video releases of their feature films which followed, Monty Python's show *Live at the Hollywood Bowl* at the end of September 1980 confirmed their accession to international celebrity stardom. Denis O'Brien, their business manager, was all too well aware of this commercial opportunity and told John Cleese, 'Look, you've got *Life of Brian*, if you do another film, you'll never have to work again' (Idle in Chapman et al. 2003: 311). While attracted by this prospect sufficiently to begin writing again almost immediately, the Pythons were also becoming wary of O'Brien's investment plans and the secrecy and complexity of his business operation. In May 1981 they parted company. John Goldstone remembers:

> I had one of those wonderful dream months in Hollywood fending off the offers to do the next Python film ... And we decided on Universal because they were just so flexible in terms of what we could do. They fully understood the need for final cut and creative control.
>
> (Goldstone, personal communication, 15 April 2011)

But the ease with which they were able to access an $8 million budget from a major Hollywood studio didn't make the task of following the success of *Life of Brian* any less challenging. Although the team produced an incredible amount of material, they struggled with their endemic problem of finding an overarching narrative framework. Michael Palin recalls, 'We tried so many different ways of trying to get the story together ... it was much more of an uphill struggle' (in Chapman et al. 2003: 311). Terry Jones eventually succeeded in persuading the others to pursue the idea of an original sketch-format film: 'I wanted to see if you could make a film and it could have a shape to it, but still be just a sketch film' (in Chapman et al. 2003: 312). What resulted, following the Pythons' now obligatory writing sojourn to the Caribbean (this time Jamaica), was derived from a sort of 'seven ages of man' idea. Despite producing some wonderful sketches that made it into the final film, all the Pythons share a sense of frustration and disappointment that the chemistry wasn't quite there and the whole turned out to be rather less than the sum of its parts. Eric Idle believed that the script needed one more re-write, but John Cleese wouldn't comply (Idle in Chapman et al. 2003: 315). Michael Palin recalled Cleese's and Chapman's frustration that they weren't producing the goods as a writing partnership (in Chapman et al. 2003: 315). Gilliam concluded: 'The rhythms weren't right', which is astute commentary from an irregular Python writer about the orchestration which successful comedy requires, and shows a shrewd awareness of its internal dynamic (Gilliam in Chapman et al. 2003: 315).

Gilliam himself contributed *The Crimson Permanent Assurance* which had been planned as an animation sequence to be inserted at the difficult 60-minute point in the narrative. But he decided to make it live action and overspent his budget on something much longer than intended, which ended up fronting the film. And arguably, as his intervening film career attests, this contribution was pure Gilliam, rather than Python. The musical numbers are actually among the best things in the film. 'Every Sperm is Sacred' and 'The Galaxy Song' rank alongside 'Always Look on the Bright Side of Life' and 'The Lumberjack Song'. And notwithstanding their writing difficulties, Chapman and Cleese's opening hospital sequence in the 'Birth' section is beautifully timed comedy. Cleese's schoolmaster, delivering a sex education class, also ranks as one of his best Python performances. And Terry Jones' monstrous Mr. Creosote has become a wonderfully repulsive legacy of the film's charming offensiveness. But the finale 'Death' is disappointing, and there are longueurs in between. It is almost as if Python had run out of steam. In their end was their beginning.

Despite the partial dissatisfaction of the team, and some lukewarm responses from British critics, *The Meaning of Life* was a commercial success on both sides of the Atlantic, and even won the Grand Prize of the Jury at Cannes in May 1983. It is a measure of the vagaries of the creative industries that accolades are often bestowed not on the best work produced, but when brand reputations are at their peak. It is only then that the once subversive becomes accepted, by that indiscernible process of cultural recuperation.

Conclusion

Cinema retains an unrivalled potential to elevate a creative form to the status of near-mythic immanence, and to disseminate that product globally, in a way that no other medium can. It is that unique process that transformed Monty Python from British cult phenomenon to international notoriety. But it is a transitive phenomenon that is not only about reach, but about ownership. Python proved that comedy travels, across time as well as territories, but that above all it communicates as a shared and learned discourse – an alternative explanatory system. Film was the primary medium by which Python's particular language entered the vernacular. In assessing that transformation it is important to keep in mind that the Pythons' greatest filmic achievements were rooted in an acute awareness of the mythic potential of the medium of cinema. This extended far beyond the genre parodies of other comedy: the *Carry On*s, Frankie Howerd, Mel Brooks. Python's success was in making tremendous comic mileage out of a studied preoccupation with myth (whether it be Arthurian legend or Biblical scripture), and playing fast and loose with its epic proportions, its rituals and taboos. The best comedy is anthropological; those films have much to teach us about the power and endurance of our primary cultural myths. And cults like Monty Python offer us, their followers, wonderfully liberating ways to explode them. In such hands comedy can be an incendiary device indeed.

Notes

1 This aspect of the film alone has been the focus of a fascinating article by Martine Meuwese (Meuwese 2004).

2 Doubtless Hazel Pethig's experience of working with the team throughout the television series benefited her contribution to the film, and she subsequently worked on *Jabberwocky* (Gilliam, 1977) and *Life of Brian* (Jones, 1979).

3 These include: *Gawain and the Green Knight* (Stephen Weeks, 1973), *Lancelot du Lac* (Robert Bresson,1974), *Perceval le Gallois* (Eric Rohmer,1978) and *Excalibur* (John Boorman, 1981). One can be sure that when a cultural myth is revived in such a sustained manner there is something more profound that marketing band-waggoning taking place.

4 Revenue figures for *Monty Python and the Holy Grail*. Held in BFI Special Collections.

5 John Mortimer QC and Michael Grieve QC, *Opinion, Re: Monty Python and 'The Life of Brian'*, Wright and Webb, Solicitors: 3. BBFC file on *Monty Python's Life of Brian*.

6 Tony Kerpel, examiner's report dated 24 July 1979. BBFC file on *Monty Python's Life of Brian*.

7 Rosemary Stark, examiner's report dated 24 July 1979. BBFC file on *Monty Python's Life of Brian*.

8 James Ferman, local authority survey on film censorship covering letter, dated 31 July 1980. BBFC file on *Monty Python's Life of Brian*.

9 James Ferman, standard response on *Life of Brian*, published in BBFC *Monthly Bulletin* to local authorities, No. 3, 1980. BBFC file on *Monty Python's Life of Brian*.

Bibliography

Unpublished sources

BBC Written Archives. Monty Python files series T12.
BBFC file on *Monty Python and the Holy Grail*.
BBFC file on *Monty Python's Life of Brian*.
BBFC file on *Monty Python's The Meaning of Life*.
BFI Special Collections file on revenues for *Monty Python and the Holy Grail*.
Forstater, Mark, interview with the author, 14 April 2011.
Goldstone, John, interview with the author, 15 April 2011.
Jones, Terry, interview with the author, 7 July 2011.

Published sources

Brown, G. (1975) Review of *Monty Python and the Holy Grail*, *Monthly Film Bulletin*, April: 84–5.

Chapman, G., J. Cleese, T. Gilliam, E. Idle, T. Jones, M. Palin with B. McCabe (2003) *The Pythons' Autobiography by the Pythons*, London: Orion Books.

Deeley, M. and Field, M. (2008) *Blade Runners, Deer Hunters and Blowing the Bloody Doors Off: My Life in Cult Movies*, London: Faber & Faber.

Gow, G. (1975) Review of *Monty Python and the Holy Grail*, *Films and Filming*, May: 40.

Hardcastle, G. L. and G. A. Reisch (eds) (2006) *Monty Python and Philosophy*, Chicago, Illinois: Open Court/Carus Publishing.

Johnstone, I. (1976) 'Python in New York', *The Times*, 25 April 1976.

Landy, M. (2005) *Monty Python's Flying Circus, TV Milestones Series*, Detroit: Wayne State University Press.

Meuwese, M. (2004) 'The animation of marginal decorations in *Monty Python and the Holy Grail*', *Arthuriana*, 14.4 (December 2004): 45–58.

Murrell, E. (1998) 'History revenged: Monty Python translates Chrétien de Troyes' *Perceval, Or the story of the Grail* (again)', *Journal of Film and Video*, 50.1 (Spring 1998): 50–62.

Palin, M. (2007) *Diaries 1969–1979: The Python Years*, London: Orion Books.

Spencer, J. (1975) 'Americans grabbed by Python', *The Sun*, 2 August 1975.

Topping, R. (2007) *Monty Python: From the Flying Circus to Spamalot*, London: Virgin Books Ltd.

Wilmut, R. (1980) *From Fringe to Flying Circus: Celebrating a Unique Generation of Comedy, 1960–1980*, London: Eyre Methuen.

14 Travels in Curtisland

Richard Curtis and British comedy cinema

James Leggott

For good or ill, Richard Curtis has been one of the most influential, profitable, and talked about figures in British comedy. As the scriptwriter of *Four Weddings and a Funeral* (1994), he helped to inaugurate a cycle – some might say a brand – of British romantic comedies with aspiration for an international audience that included his own *Notting Hill* (1999) and the self-directed *Love Actually* (2003). Yet his writing and co-writing credits also include *Bean* (1997), *Bridget Jones's Diary* (2001) and *Bridget Jones: The Edge of Reason* (2004), as well as the enduringly popular television comedies *Blackadder* (1983–9), *Mr. Bean* (1990–95) and *The Vicar of Dibley* (1994–2007). And few overviews of Curtis and his standing within British culture go without reference to his charitable work as founder of the Comic Relief and Make Poverty History campaigns, not least because a campaigning impulse has evidently driven some of his writing, most notably the telefilm *The Girl in the Café* (tx BBC 2005). Curtis's projects are always deemed newsworthy, from the controversy over the violence and alleged poor taste of his short campaigning film *No Pressure* (2010) about climate change, to discussion of whether his script for a 2010 episode of the television series *Doctor Who* had given his career a much needed 'shot in the arm' (Bradshaw, 2010).[1]

That there are enough narrative, thematic and tonal similarities between all of his major films to establish Curtis as *auteur* is usually taken as a given. But even before he began directing his own scripts, he had enjoyed a degree of involvement in the film-making process that was rare (unique, perhaps) among British screenwriters. He has described himself as the 'luckiest man in movies' (Owen 2003: 74) for having the chance to write multiple redrafts – with the assistance of his partner Emma Freud – and the power to influence casting choices, select the director, and to intervene during the shooting and editing process. Curtis has also made no denial that his scripts are largely based on his own career and personal experiences. Prior to writing *The Tall Guy* (1989), he had experienced the stalling of a US-set film project – the story of a father and son simultaneously being cheated on by their partners – apparently because MGM executives queried aspects of the characterisation, dialogue and plot (Owen 2003). Curtis then resolved from that point only to write 'on something [he] was a hundred per cent sure of and no one in the world knew more about than [him]' (Owen 2003: 69). Thus his next script, *The Tall Guy*, was influenced by his experience of the London Borough of Camden (the original title was apparently *Camden Town Boy*) and his work as a comedic straight man with Rowan Atkinson (Curtis 2003), whilst the central concept of *Four*

Weddings took shape after a period of frequent wedding attendance, *Notting Hill* was informed by his familiarity with a particular social and geographical *milieu* (Curtis had famously lived in the same blue-doored house where Hugh Grant's character resides on screen), and *Love Actually* gave full expression to a philosophy about love and human dependency that had simmered throughout the entire Curtis *oeuvre*.

Although all these films invite straightforward *auteur*ist analysis, the boundaries of Curtisland stretch widely to accommodate collaborative work such as the *Bridget Jones* films but also Curtis-inspired romantic comedies, especially those produced by the Working Title production company, with which Curtis has been associated since *The Tall Guy*. The two *Bridget Jones* films – co-scripted by Curtis, the novelist Helen Fielding (a friend of Curtis and an advisor on his earlier scripts) and Andrew Davies – provide a convoluted case-study for authorial complication, as well as an encapsulation of the pleasures (and irritations, for some) of the Curtis-affiliated text. One single moment in *Bridget Jones: The Edge of Reason* sums up well the accumulation of in-jokes and cross-references under which the film almost entirely collapses. A fight between the two lead male characters vying for the heroine's affections, played respectively by Hugh Grant and Colin Firth, results in the latter taking a soaking in a public fountain: the obvious and explicit intertext is Andrew Davies's BBC adaptation of *Pride and Prejudice* (1995), which included a famous scene where Firth's Darcy emerged from a lake to the approval of Elizabeth Bennet (and many fans), but the casting also evokes memories of *Love Actually*, in which Firth's melancholy Darcy-like character similarly takes a dip at a key stage in his blossoming relationship with his Portuguese home-help.

But Curtis's films have also permeated British cultural and political life in odd and unexpected ways. For example, one could cite the then Prime Minister Tony Blair's 2005 Labour Conference speech, in which he acknowledged a popular desire for him to 'do a Hugh Grant in *Love Actually* and tell America where to get off' (Blair 2005). Curtis was even cited in response to Hugh Grant's investigative report of April 2011 for the *New Statesman* on the culture of phone hacking at the News International organisation (Grant 2011). Writing in the *Sunday Mirror* newspaper, Jason Cowley noted, somewhat improbably and inaccurately, that the 'whole thing [had] been like something out of a Richard Curtis movie: famous actor, a bit lost in life, suddenly finds an improbable new role' (Cowley 2011).

Cowley's comment, an admittedly cheap gag, illustrates the way in which Curtis and his films have been hidden in plain sight in popular and academic discussion. Curtis has been given major attention in scholarship on contemporary British cinema, and also in relation to questions of theology, philosophy, genre and national culture. *Four Weddings* and *Notting Hill* have been granted substantial analysis with regard to their representation of class (Dave 2006; Neville 2010), their enunciation of Englishness (Higson 2010), their deployment of fairy-tale tropes (Murphy 2001), their use of comedy (Mather 2006), and the significance of Hugh Grant as romantic lead (Spicer 2004), among other perspectives, almost to the point of exhaustion. However, in prioritising issues of nationality and genre, such analysis has occasionally lost sight of Curtis's experimentation with varying kinds of comic film, the differences as well as similarities between his films, and his relationship with broader developments in British film and television comedy.

Curtis and the temper of the times

It is first necessary to consider why and how Curtis's films have invited so much attention by political and cultural commentators. In his *Observer* review of the 1960s-set *The Boat That Rocked* (2009), Philip French (2009) noted ruefully that Curtis had been the 'dominant figure' in British film comedy for 15 years, a stretch of time that was half as long again as the 'heyday' of Ealing comedies from the mid-1940s to the mid-1950s. French went on to make unfavourable comparisons between the 'infantilised farce' of *The Boat That Rocked* and the best of the Ealing era, which had more effectively reflected the 'temper of the times: the discontent with austerity and bureaucracy in *Passport to Pimlico* [1949] and *Whisky Galore* [1949], the dominance of class and unearned privilege in *Kind Hearts and Coronets* [1949]'.

French's comments, typical of the critical mauling of *The Boat That Rocked*, captured the distaste felt by many broadsheet and cultural commentators at Curtis's supposed stranglehold over British film culture, as did the gleeful reporting of the film's poor performance at the UK box office.[2] The three major Curtis movies since *Four Weddings* had each triggered expansive, and usually sniffy, analysis of Curtisland, deemed by many an unpalatably selective and politically suspect version of Britain, populated by characters in thrall to American culture and to a facile romance of instant attraction. Ironically, given his somewhat heavy-handed efforts to incorporate campaigning messages into his television work (the episode of *The Vicar of Dibley* devoted to Make Poverty History being a case in point), Curtis has frequently been taken to task for failing to represent the ethnic, social and regional varieties of contemporary Britain, with *Notting Hill* in particular finding censure for its narrowly white portrayal of a famously multicultural neighbourhood.[3]

However, by the late 2000s, numerous commentators were taking notice of the coincidence of the Curtis and New Labour eras, and interpreting a consensus that Curtis had finally 'lost his spark' as an unhappy ending of the kind never witnessed in the *auteur*'s own films.[4] With hindsight, *Four Weddings* now seemed more than ever a summary of Blairite philosophy, with its aspirational vision of a Britain no longer defined (supposedly) by class difference or past traditions of labour (the film tells us nothing about what the characters actually do for a living, if at all). At the same time, the film chimed with John Major's 'more concerned, caring Conservatism' (Neville 2010: 3), from which the roots of much new Labour rhetoric and policies can arguably be sourced. As Carl Neville notes, the film's depiction of an 'idealised England in which groups of posh, bright young things, only nominally drawn from a variety of backgrounds, gad about an England filled with Heritage properties and roomy flats' (Neville 2010: 3), happened to resonate well with Major's famous – and occasionally ridiculed – vision of a classless Britain. Furthermore, in a lengthy 2009 article for *The Observer*, Tim Adams noted the eerie timing of the film, in being released the day after the death of the previous Labour leader John Smith, and its early tangling of New Labour geography and Curtisland into 'an apolitical place, full of can-do possibility, obsessed with the educated middle class, perfectly relaxed about the filthy rich, much more in love with sentiment than ideas, and insatiable in its optimism' (Adams 2009).

Writing for *The Guardian* online, Danny Leigh (2008) declared Curtis to be the perfect filmic figurehead for the Blair/Brown pre-credit crunch era, with *Notting Hill*'s apparent paean to the gentrification of inner London emblematic of an *oeuvre* of 'assaultive promos for the just-out-of-reach middle-class values that launched a hundred thousand unpayable mortgages'. The re-evaluation of the 'special relationship' between the UK and America in the Bush–Blair era, in the context of unpopular military campaigns in Iraq and Afghanistan, also suggested a trajectory from the enthralment by Hugh Grant's character in *Notting Hill* to Hollywood glitz and wealth, to the same actor's portrayal in *Love Actually* of a Prime Minister who doggedly stands up to the personal and political bullying of a boorish US President.

From the perspective of the post-2010 Coalition era, the Curtis films of the preceding 20 years were clearly in danger of resembling relics from a different political age, whilst also becoming out of step with developments in British film and television culture. *The Boat That Rocked*'s celebration of the laddish camaraderie generated by a group of (almost entirely) men marooned together as colleagues on a pirate radio made it a belated addition to a cycle of homosocially fixated dramas and comedies encouraged by the likes of *The Full Monty* (1997) and *Lock, Stock and Two Smoking Barrels* (1998) and then ultimately stalled through critique and parody in films such as *This is England* (2006) and *Doghouse* (2009).

From a writer who had hitherto displayed little interest in 'blokeish' scenarios and humour, the one-dimensional treatment of female sexual desire in *The Boat That Rocked* was troubling as well as surprising. Furthermore, the film's commemoration of British youth culture of the mid-1960s, as both unifying and politically radical, evoked memories of how the music and fashion of that era had also been valorised and reworked during the short-lived vogue – at least amongst certain quarters of the media and some opportunistic politicians – for all things 'Cool Britannia' in the mid-1990s. At the same time, the film's prioritisation of comic incident above romantic storylines felt like an acknowledgement of the declining fortunes of the British romantic comedy, a format closely associated with Curtis and the Working Title production company, who had been involved with all of his work since *The Tall Guy*. Given the company's reputation for 'mid-Atlantic' strategies of casting, style and marketing – which had been given no small impetus by the international success of *Four Weddings* – the incorporation of more European personalities and settings than American ones in *Love Actually* suggested an element of market re-orientation, whilst the necessity to re-edit and re-title *The Boat That Rocked* for its American release (as *Pirate Radio*) could be interpreted as either a misjudgement or (more generously) as proof of a relatively modest attempt at reaching a specifically indigenous audience.[5]

Curtis and British comedy

Such reflectionist readings of the Curtis films run the risk of obscuring their place within the development of British comedy. At the very least, his films endure as an archive of contemporaneous trends in television and live comedy, through their deployment of emerging performers (for example, James Dreyfus and Dylan Moran in *Notting Hill*, Julia Davis and Martin Freeman in *Love Actually*, and numerous cast members of *The Boat That Rocked*). But Curtis's efforts to inaugurate a British take on the romantic comedy genre, his attempts to inflect scenarios and characterisation strategies most usually associated with television sketch comedy with a degree of psychological nuance and emotional weight, and his experimentations with narrative form, are often underrated.

Curtis has admitted to the general similarity of the plots of *Four Weddings* and *Notting Hill*, but a broader survey of his films reveals a consistently ambitious approach to storytelling. For example, in its last third, *The Tall Guy* suspends its romance plot to foreground an elaborate theatrical spoof. Even more adventurously, *Four Weddings* uses its title and its focus upon specific formal occasions to generate narrative suspense and surprise (particularly over who actually dies, and the participants in the final wedding), whilst also giving the film an air of self-reflexivity – and thus sophistication – more associated with art cinema (such as the work of Peter Greenaway, known for similar games of numbering). Although *Love Actually* is not the first British film to juggle interweaving story strands in the fashion of Robert Altman, its sheer scale of characters and geography, and its monomaniacal fixation upon the importance of love, goes beyond such feasible influences as Michael Winterbottom's *Wonderland* (1999), David Kane's *This Year's Love* (1999) and *Born Romantic* (2000).

Furthermore, Curtis's films do not quite maintain homogeneity of tone, performance style or even aspiration. *The Girl in the Café* has a striking interiority, due in part to its sparseness of incident, cast and settings, its exclusive focus upon a budding relationship (leaving certain aspects of character history unexplained), the absence of comic scenarios and characters (as befitting the intended political message), and its sequences of conversational awkwardness reminiscent of the films of Mike Leigh and some American independent film-makers.[6] In complete contrast, the loosely plotted *The Boat That Rocked* gives only perfunctory attention to its initially central storyline about a teenager's entry into adulthood, emphasising instead the dynamics of its ensemble of DJ characters, and leaving its comically-skilled cast to interact and (it would seem) improvise through episodic set-pieces.

The extraordinary success of *Four Weddings* inevitably leads to an assessment of Curtis's previous scripts as apprenticeship work, even though his films continued to experiment with form and comic style. From an auteurist point of view, *Dead on Time* (1983), *The Tall Guy* and the television film *Bernard and the Genie* (1991) most certainly do betray the Curtis signature, while also pointing towards how his 'rom-com' mechanics evolved through a process of trial and error. Hindsight makes it difficult to read these films as anything other than signposts towards the 'Curtis era', but this runs the danger of clouding their interesting relationship to British comedy culture of the 1980s, a period that witnessed a new phase of 'alternative comedy' in live venues and on television that was only partially captured by a film industry in considerably ruder health than the decade before.

Co-written with its lead performer Rowan Atkinson, the short film *Dead on Time* is the story of a dull young man who is wrongly told by his doctor that he has only half an hour to live. The unfortunate Bernard – the recurrence of characters with this name would become a running gag in Curtis scripts – hurriedly explores the worlds of art, religion and love in a last-ditch attempt to 'do everything'. The ticking-clock premise is essentially there to knit together a series of gently satirical sketches about British institutions (doctors' surgeries, banks, record shops, art galleries, etc.) showcasing

Atkinson's dual flair for physical and verbal comedy. With its combination of cultural references and slapstick farce (such as Atkinson dashing around Covent Garden in search of the meaning of life), *Dead on Time* is an interesting distillation of Curtis's collaborative work with Atkinson during the period, which included the fondly remembered historical sitcom *Blackadder* as well as sketches for *Not the Nine O'clock News* (1979–82), *Mr. Bean* and Atkinson's live performances. First seen in his GP's waiting room boring fellow patients with a poorly delivered joke, Atkinson's character is a working model for the tweedy, wimpy, angst-driven, romantically-inclined leading men of future Curtis comedies.

When placed in the context of simultaneous developments in television comedy, *Dead on Time* appears quite traditional, lacking, for example, the anarchic spirit of *The Young Ones* (1982–84) (despite the appearance of two of its performers, Nigel Planer and Adrian Edmondson) or the satirical ambitions of *The Comic Strip Presents* (1982–2005), films aired by Channel Four during the decade. However, in combining throwaway gags with an (admittedly limited) degree of psychological plausibility, *Dead on Time* captures in miniature a tension within and across Curtis's films between the broad humour more typical of his television comedy and the dramatic realism of rounded characterisation and attention to social and geographical detail. Even though the film derives its energies and chief pleasures from Atkinson's increasingly agitated performance, the cameo appearances from television actors, and some unlikely moments of cultural incongruity – such as an aggressive-seeming fan of hard rock advising on the music of Albinoni, and a straight-laced gent leering at the front cover of Wilhelm Reich's *The Function of the Orgasm* [1927] – mugging is kept to a minimum, and Bernard's mounting frustration with the stupidity around him has a degree of believability.

Curtis's first major film, *The Tall Guy*, released in 1989, makes a slightly uneasy fit with trends in British cinema comedy of the 1980s and early 1990s. Oddly, the impact of the alternative comedy boom of the 1980s in live comedy and television – which Curtis had strong connections with via his work on *Blackadder* and other television comedies – was not greatly reflected in the cinema production of the time, perhaps because of assumptions about its niche audience, or the already cinematic tendencies of many of the *Comic Strip* television films.[7] Indeed, whereas British comedy cinema of the 1970s consisted almost exclusively of feature-length spin-offs from mainstream television sitcom and sketch shows, sex comedies and the dying throes of franchises from previous decades (such as the *Carry On* and *Doctor* series), the performers, titles and writers that came to prominence in the subsequent decade – one could cite here the likes of Ben Elton, Victoria Wood, Stephen Fry and Hugh Laurie, among others – rarely translated to the big-screen, and certainly not with any critical or popular success.[8]

The 'low-brow' spin-offs and series tail away notably at this time, to be replaced by a more varied run of commercially appealing comic dramas, which ranged from the subtle, gently satirical films of Bill Forsyth, and the well-observed family dramas of Mike Leigh, to performance-led films with strong literary or theatrical pedigree such as *Educating Rita* (1983), *A Private Function* (1984), *Wish You Were Here* (1987) and *Shirley Valentine* (1989), and one-off cult successes such as *Withnail and I* (1987) and *Leon the Pig Farmer* (1992). There is also a major contribution by former members of the Monty Python comedy team, with collective acting/directing credits that include *Brazil*

(1985), *Clockwise* (1986), *A Fish Called Wanda* (1988), *Eric the Viking* (1989), *Nuns on the Run* (1990) and their own ribald sketch film *The Meaning of Life* (1983). Of the 'alternative comedy' set, only Mel Smith and Griff Rhys Jones, who had their own double-act sketch show during the period, made a significant stab at a cinema career, starring in *Morons From Outer Space* (1985) and *Wilt* (1990); Smith would go on to direct *The Tall Guy* and *Bean*.

Within this history, *The Tall Guy's* slightly uneasy mixture of realism, exaggerated humour, sexual frankness and cultural satire can be seen as emblematic of the differing currents in British comedy of the time, yet also as quite anomalous in its fusion of romantic and comic storylines. With hindsight, *The Tall Guy* has many components that would be re-shuffled, and to greater structural effect and popular success, in *Four Weddings* and *Notting Hill*. Although the film describes an Anglo-American romance, the nationality of Jeff Goldblum's character Dexter is a relatively insignificant aspect of his characterisation. More important is the difference between his theatrical world and the 'civilian' profession of Kate, who dismisses acting as the 'easiest job in the world', and a later plot development requiring Dexter to choose between Kate and a fellow actress, but this is hardly the gulf that Anna and William have to negotiate in *Notting Hill*. As with the later film, there is some dissection of the acting process, and in particular a critique of the insecurities of the comic performer (as the closely named Ron Anderson, Rowan Atkinson gamely plays a monstrous version of himself and his character delivers slapstick routines with apparently real violence) as well as recurring script references to real world problems such as African poverty and nuclear war that seem to function, like the various other sequences in Curtis's films set in prisons, hospitals and funeral parlours, to undercut the self-obsession of the characters (and remind the informed viewer too of Curtis's own charitable endeavours). But in contrast to the glamorous Hollywood world of Anna Scott, Dexter's experience of the West End theatre is that of squalid digs, amateurism and professional danger (he is nearly crushed through a stage-hand's carelessness), and the film makes no effort to visually romanticise theatreland – or London generally – in the way that future Curtis projects would do. Nor does it quite convey the cosy, familial communities of the later films; Dexter's acquaintances, such as his sexually voracious landlady and a blind dog-walker, are mostly one-dimensional oddballs.

In terms of tone, line delivery and visual look, *The Tall Guy* is positioned at a crucial intersection between Curtis's broader television work and the attempted naturalism of *Four Weddings*. Far less glossy, but evidently more modestly budgeted than the later films, *The Tall Guy* balances some attempt at nuanced character motivation, in the vein of adult-oriented romance films such as *The Graduate* (1967), or naturalistic British films such as *Gregory's Girl* (1981), with fanciful elements more associated with television sketch comedy. But the way in which psychoanalysis is both the source of broad comedy and important plot developments conveys some ambivalence towards psychological complexity. Building upon the fleeting Wilhelm Reich reference in *Dead on Time*, the film features a hospital sequence where Dexter is interrogated about his anxiety dreams and his needle phobia by a Dr. Freud and her grotesquely unworldly colleague Dr. Karabekian. But it also leads towards Dexter's unwitting revelation of his infidelity to Kate through the Freudian slip of pausing on a particular word, a moment of psychological nuance comparable with the careful way that Hugh Grant's character in *Four Weddings* is allowed to make the 'wrong' decision of abandoning his true love through the bad advice of a friend. Even the more self-consciously fanciful and parodic moments of *The Tall Guy* – Dexter turning cartwheels in front of a massive moon, a music video sequence featuring the song 'It Must Be Love' (performed on screen by Madness), a comically over-the-top sex scene, Dexter's morose realisation that all songs on the radio refer in some way to his own melancholic state, and a full theatre expressing their pleasure at the happy ending – all make some sense as exaggerated projections of Dexter's heightened emotional state.

To claim *Four Weddings* as a work of social realism would admittedly be perverse, but its accumulation of farcical wedding incidents (typically in the form of interruptions, lapses of taste, or social and linguistic *faux pas*) maintain plausibility, there are occasional documentary-like shots of other guests that help to ground the events in some sort of reality, and the ensemble cast is used carefully to shed light on the dilemmas and self-delusion of Hugh Grant's 30-something male character. Cleverly, the film's tension between the pleasures of disruption and anachronistic swearing, and its celebration of formal contrivance – that is, its lingering upon ritual events, its satisfying rhythm of jokes set up and followed through, its ultimate celebration of the basic 'boy meets girl' plot, and its occasional *tableaux* groupings of the ensemble cast – becomes a means to characterise Charles's anxieties about emotional commitment.[9] *Four Weddings* also pulls off the trick of exploiting stereotypes of class and nationality, whilst debunking essentialisms with gags about 'ghastly Americans' and ersatz Scottishness, the surprise revelation of the provincial, lowly roots of the theatrical-seeming Gareth, and the American Carrie's ability to match Charles with deadpan humour.

The impact of *Four Weddings* and Curtis's own repetition of certain aspects of its ensemble casting and characterisation in *Notting Hill* can easily obscure its curious distinctiveness as a romantic drama marrying psychological nuance with appealing comic set-pieces and ensemble interaction. The scarcity of precedent in British cinema – the nearest equivalent of the period being the afterlife 'weepie' *Truly, Madly, Deeply* (1991) – makes this an even more remarkable achievement. Its sense of timelessness is carefully achieved, yet subtly undercut by references to a female-dominated political era, and the illegality of gay marriages. Although the film largely stays away from contemporary cultural references, a mention of the 'funny' comedian Steve Martin, and a café scene where the heroine shocks the hero with her lack of sexual restraint (by counting her various partners) in a way that evokes memories of the infamous 'faked orgasm' sequence in *When Harry Met Sally* (1989), makes the debt to American romantic comedies all the more apparent.

The success of *Four Weddings* undoubtedly gave impetus to a cycle of romantic comedies that were sometimes formally playful – for example, *Sliding Doors* (1997) – but were mostly repetitive and derivative, ultimately bringing about the steady decline of the genre into the 21st century. In fact, for all the claims about Curtis's continuing dominance over British film, his 'transatlantic' approach to culture clash and his fixation with stories of romantic complication quickly became out of step with developments in British comedy cinema. By the time of *Notting Hill*, comedy was increasingly used as a vehicle to tackle questions of class and ethnic identity, in films such as *The Full Monty* and *East is East* (1999), or incorporated within other genres to produce hybridised films such as *Lock, Stock and Two Smoking Barrels* and *Shaun of the Dead* (2004), or pushed to satirical extremes in provocative films such as *Borat* (2006).

Culture clash

Aside from their generic and political significance, Curtis's films are interesting for the way they consistently work through ideas about popular culture, and their fixation on the notion of culture clash on both a generic and narrative level. It could be argued that the films from *Love Actually* onwards become less effective and relevant, precisely because their particular approaches – *Love Actually*'s multiple stories, *The Girl in the Café*'s political agenda and *The Boat That Rocked*'s episodic plotting – offer less scope for the theme of cultural tension to be dramatised as pleasingly.

'It's not bloody Shakespeare!', splurts Colin Firth's writer character in *Love Actually*, when his manuscript is accidentally swept away. From an early stage, a thematic and formal preoccupation with culture clash has been a key characteristic of Curtis's writing; *Dead on Time* introduced the role of incongruity as a generator of plots and characterisation (as well as throwaway gags), subsequently seen in the Anglo-American romances of *Four Weddings* and *Notting Hill*, as well as the initial hostility to the female vicar in *The Vicar of Dibley* by rural parishioners (not to mention their tendency for unexpected references to sexual deviancy and pop culture). *Dead on Time* also conveys the beginnings of an authorial obsession with the boundaries of high and low culture. Aside from jokes about Tolstoy's *War and Peace* ('bloody Ruskies') and the Mona Lisa (stored in a poster shop 'between the Aborigine reading *Playboy* and the tennis player with no knickers'), there is a florid rant from Bernard in which he implores those around him to seize the moment. 'I've spent my years browsing through the *hors d'oeuvres* of life's rich menu without ever choosing a starter', he says. 'Life is a fast-food store, order a Whopper; Death won't wait while you pansy around with the wine list, he'll sling you out on death's dark highway, before you can say Valpolicella'.

Curtis's films frequently offer a celebration of the potency of pop culture, particularly music, as demonstrated by the Prime Minister of *Love Actually* dancing through the corridors of Downing Street to a version of 'Jump' by Girls Aloud, the key plot role of a CD copy of Joni Michell's *Blue* in the same film, the Genie of *Bernard and the Genie* discovering the joys of fast food and Arnold Schwarzenegger movies, and the whole premise of a nation united through pirate radio broadcasts (and the counter-attack by an uncomprehending Establishment) in *The Boat That Rocked*. Even the self-reflexive gag in *Love Actually* about a desperate and opportunistic Christmas version of The Troggs' 'Love Is All Around' by the ageing rocker Billy Mack – a sort of authorial apology for the UK chart success of the Wet Wet Wet cover as heard on the soundtrack of *Four Weddings* – eventually becomes a vindication of the potency of cheap music, when a popular surge of respect for the singer's own indifference pushes it to the top of the charts. In *Four Weddings*, a film that inaugurated a revival of interest in the poetry of W.H. Auden (as a consequence of the inclusion of *Funeral Blues* [1938] at a key moment), the lead characters make emotional speeches referencing the lyrics of David Cassidy and John Lennon; notably, Hugh Grant's bumbling quotation of The Partridge

Family's 'I Think I Love You' occurs outside the National Film Theatre on London's South Bank, an area more associated with high art than populist entertainment. This high/low conflict is given further accentuation in *Notting Hill* through a thematic exploration of 'authenticity' and cultural imperialism; for example, Anna Scott's career choice between genre films and period dramas, her gift to William of a genuine Chagall canvas and an early joke about some suspiciously anachronistic stained-glass ornaments of the US cartoon stars Beavis and Butt-Head on sale on Portobello Road.

Indeed, a recurring obsession in Curtis's writing is the value and commoditisation of art. The lead character of *Bernard and the Genie* is an altruistic art dealer sacked by his boss for honestly distributing profits to his clients. Upon encountering the Genie, one of his wishes is for the Mona Lisa to appear on his living-room wall, but when police arrive to arrest him for the theft it is magically swapped for a poster of the pop star Kylie Minogue. The plot of *Bean* is entirely predicated upon Atkinson's idiotic, barely articulate character being mistaken for an academic presiding over the presentation of Whistler's *Arrangement in Grey and Black: Portrait of the Painter's Mother* (referred to in the film purely as Whistler's Mother) to an American gallery. The film contains some satirical gags about the gallery's exploitation of its purchase through crass souvenirs ('Whistler's Whistle', etc.) and celebrity endorsement, but otherwise seems to take an equivocal position on its own unashamed populism. *Bean* invites the viewer to fluctuate in sympathy between the idiotic Bean, happier at a theme park than in the rarefied art world, and his professorial host whose career and marriage are placed in jeopardy by Bean's antics. Having destroyed the canvas by accident, Bean hoodwinks an expectant audience with a modified version of a reproduction print of the painting and a speech about Whistler filled with vague, gnomic utterances that are assumed to have profound significance. There is more muted (and conceivably non-deliberate) satire in the plot strand of *Love Actually* involving an art-dealer coming to terms with his unrequited love for the wife of his best friend. He barks at visitors giggling at his display of nude figures with cheekily positioned Christmas hats that 'they're not funny, they're art', and the viewer is encouraged to judge their own lack of humour as a neurotic symptom of his unresolved romantic affection: his inability (like some negative reviewers perhaps?) to see the funny side. In Curtis's films, humour and art remain warring bedfellows.

Such themes of cultural tension bubble most satisfactorily through Curtis's first film, *The Tall Guy*, the story of American 'straight man' Dexter King who falls in love with a nurse, Kate Lemon. One of *The Tall Guy's* most memorable achievements is its lampooning of the preceding decade's trend for blockbusting yet pompous British musical shows of the 1980s such as *Phantom of the Opera* and *Les Misérables*, through Dexter's leading role in an appropriately earnest, tasteless (and fictitious) Royal Shakespeare Company adaptation of the Elephant Man story called *Elephant!* Lengthy rehearsal and performance sequences give Curtis scope for deadly accurate lyrical and musical parody of a kind that harks back to his early career, but also crystallises his ambivalent take on popular culture. Placed alongside other more succinct gags about British theatreland – such as a witty Steven Berkoff spoof, and references to Harold Pinter and Alan Ayckbourn – the *Elephant!* parody is simultaneously a gleeful attack on good taste (in the vein of Mel Brooks's *The Producers* (1968)), a source of flattering in-jokes to those with the requisite cultural capital, and a critique of populist entertainment.

A minor work of 1980s British comedy, *The Tall Guy* nevertheless has a satirical edge absent from later Curtis projects. It falls beyond the scope of this chapter to assess whether a continuation along this partly abandoned path would have altered Curtis's reputation among cultural and political commentators today. However, in view of the opprobrium heaped in some quarters on Curtis for his philosophy, politics or brand of comedy, it seems only fair to counter with a robust appreciation of his willingness to experiment with the narrative possibilities of the British comedy film, to address a mainstream rather than merely niche audience, and to plunge headlong into debates about high and low culture that have haunted much scholarship on British visual culture. To paraphrase the po-faced art-dealer in *Love Actually* snapping at the mockers in his gallery for confusing comedy with art, Curtis's work is both funny and artful, and its nuanced relationship to traditions of British comedy must not be underestimated.

Notes

1 For an overview of the *No Pressure* controversy see McVeigh (2010).
2 Some representative examples of the negative press response, or reportage of it, include Deborah Orr (1999) on the inaccuracies of *Notting Hill*, Andrew Gumbel (2003) on the poor critical reception to *Love Actually*, and Kevin Maher (2009) on the 'hackneyed national fantasy' of *The Boat That Rocked*.
3 For a discussion of this issue, see Alibhai-Brown (2001).
4 In 2009, the *Guardian* newspaper ran an online poll on the question of whether Curtis has 'lost his spark', resulting in an agreement by 64.5 per cent of correspondents. See www.guardian.co.uk/culture/poll/2009/apr/08/richard-curtis-poll
5 For discussion of the history and 'transatlantic' tendencies of Working Title, see Wayne (2006), and Hochscherf and Leggott (2010).
6 Indeed, *The Girl in the Café* seems indebted, in terms of its characterisation, use of setting and overall atmosphere, to such films as *Lost as Translation* (2003), whilst Bill Nighy's extremely mannered performance would not be out of place within films of the so-called 'mumblecore' movement of early-21st-century independent American cinema (such as those by Andrew Bujalski and Lynn Shelton).
7 Five series and six 'specials' of *The Comic Strip Presents* were made for Channel Four between 1982 and 1993, then further three 'specials' were aired between 1998 and 2005. The creative team were also responsible for two feature films: *The Supergrass* (1985) and *Eat the Rich* (1987).
8 It is notable that the transference of British television performers and characters skipped a generation, with comic stars such as Sacha Baron Cohen, Simon Pegg and Ricky Gervais achieving international success in the early 21st century.
9 An interesting point of comparison with regard to the formally experimental exploration of male 30-something 'commitment phobia' is the George Furth/Stephen Sondheim musical *Company* (first performed in 1970), which happened to receive a successful London revival in 1995 at the Donmar Warehouse (and was broadcast on BBC2 in 1997).

Bibliography

Adams, T. (2009) 'A shiny happy place, relaxed about the filthy rich, insatiable in its optimism, in love with happy endings, a very New Labour. Welcome to Curtisland ... ', *The Observer*, 22 March 2009, www.guardian.co.uk/film/2009/mar/22/richard-curtis-the-boat-that-rocked (accessed 25 July 2011).

Alibhai-Brown, Y. (2001) *Imagining the New Britain: Who Do We Think We Are?*, London and New York: Routledge.

Blair, T. (2005) 'Tony Blair's Conference Speech 2005', *The Guardian*, 27 September 2005, www.guardian.co.uk/uk/2005/sep/27/labourconference.speeches (accessed 25 July 2011).

Bradshaw, P. (2010) 'How *Doctor Who* gave Richard Curtis a shot in the arm', *The Guardian*, 8 June 2010, www.guardian.co.uk/film/filmblog/2010/jun/08/richard-curtis-doctor-who (accessed 25 July 2011).

Cowley, J. (2011) 'Hugh Grant takes the leading role in Hackgate', *Sunday Mirror*, 17 July 2011, www.mirror.co.uk/news/top-stories/2011/07/17/hugh-grant-takes-the-leading-role-in-hackgate-115875-23275957 (accessed 25 July 2011).

Curtis, R. (2003) 'Behind the lines', *The Observer*, 16 November 2003, www.guardian.co.uk/film/2003/nov/16/features.review (accessed 25 July 2011).

Dave, P. (2006) *Visions of England: Class and Culture in Contemporary Cinema*, Oxford and New York: Berg.

French, P. (2009) '*The Boat That Rocked*', *The Observer*, 5 April 2009, www.guardian.co.uk/film/2009/apr/05/the-boat-that-rocked (accessed 25 July 2011).

Grant, H. (2011) 'The bugger, bugged', *New Statesman*, 12 April 2011, www.newstatesman.com/newspapers/2011/04/phone-yeah-cameron-murdoch (accessed 25 July 2011).

Gumbel, A. (2003) 'Richard Curtis: The critics have fallen out of love with him, actually', *The Independent*, 15 November 2003, www.independent.co.uk/news/people/profiles/richard-curtis-the-critics-have-fallen-out-of-love-with-him-actually-735839.html (accessed 25 July 2011).

Higson, A. (2010) *Film England: Culturally English Filmmaking since the 1990s*, London and New York: I.B. Tauris.

Hochscherf, T. and Leggott, J. (2010) 'Working Title Films: From Mid-Atlantic to the Heart of Europe?', *Film International*, 8.6: 8–20.

Leigh, D. (2008) 'The view: Why Richard Curtis will go down in history', *The Guardian* online, 19 December 2009, www.guardian.co.uk/film/filmblog/2008/dec/19/richard-curtis-credit-crunch?showAllComments=true (accessed 25 July 2011).

McVeigh, T. (2010) 'Backlash over Richard Curtis's 10:10 climate film', *The Guardian*, 2 October 2010, www.guardian.co.uk/environment/2010/oct/02/1010-richard-curtis-climate-change (accessed 25 July 2011).

Maher, K. (2009) 'Clichés, actually: A fake view of England served up for foreigners', *The Times*, 27 March 2009, www.timesonline.co.uk/tol/comment/columnists/guest_contributors/article5982714.ece (accessed 25 July 2011).

Mather, N. (2006) *Tears of Laughter: Comedy-Drama in 1990s British Cinema*, Manchester: Manchester University Press.

Murphy, R. (2001) 'Citylife: Urban fairy tales in late 90s British cinema', in R. Murphy (ed.), *The British Cinema Book*, 2nd edn, London: British Film Institute.

Neville, C. (2010) *Classless: Recent Essays on British Film*, London: Zero.

Orr, D. (1999) 'It's Notting Hill, but not as I know it', *The Independent*, 20 May 1999, www.independent.co.uk/arts-entertainment/its-notting-hill-but-not-as-i-know-it-1094619.html (accessed 25 July 2011).

Owen, A. (2003) *Story and Character: Interviews with British Screenwriters*, London: Bloomsbury.

Spicer, A. (2004) 'The reluctance to commit: Hugh Grant the New British Romantic Comedy', in P. Powrie et al. (eds), *The Trouble with Men: Masculinities in European and Hollywood Cinema*, London: Wallflower.

Wayne, M. (2006) 'Working Title Mark II: A critique of the Atlanticist paradigm for British cinema', *International Journal of Cultural and Media Politics*, 2.1: 59–73.

15 'The sight of 40-year-old genitalia too disgusting, is it?'

Wit, whimsy and wishful thinking in British animation, 1900–present

Paul Wells

As Andy Medhurst has remarked: 'Comedy is never only textual – it is performed, enacted, an event, a transaction, lived out in a shared moment by its producers and consumers' (Medhurst 2007: 4). In the context of this discussion, I will be exploring how this particular and complex nexus of experience is represented throughout the history of British animation. I intend to engage with this, firstly, through an address of its antecedents in other art forms, thereafter, in four core 'periods' of British animated film production. This will chart how it determined its form and function; played out its own tensions between tradition and modernity; engaged with the commercial cinema sector and the political economy; enjoyed its place within the counterculture; confronted deep-rooted anxiety within the British temperament; and ultimately evolved into what might be viewed as an 'anti-social' and subversive form.

Sources: An 'Englandography'

Animation as a form can essentially embrace and deploy all other art forms, and draws extensively upon a range of sources. British animated comedy finds its tone and outlook mainly from three key traditions: the long established visual culture of British political satire in cartoons, and the playfulness in popular comics, created by Hogarth, Cruikshank, Gillray, Low and Baxendale; the literary observations of British manners by social ironists like Dickens, Chesterton and Saki; and the often suggestive, surreal and slapstick performance idioms in Music Hall, Variety and radio, epitomised by Chaplin, Miller and later The Goons. British animation has embraced these influences in its own self-reflexive form, self-consciously foregrounding the illusionism of the medium to comically enact issues of identity and ideology, and frameworks of shared ideas and cultural practices. This concept of 'shared ideas and cultural practices' within a national context is necessarily an assumed one on the part of the producer in relation to an intended consumer, of course, and often based on loosely determined assumptions about supposedly common characteristics, idioms, and points of recognition. As Medhurst has once again pointed out, 'Britain' becomes largely configured as 'England', and as a consequence, 'every Englandologist, it seems, needs an Englandography, a talismanic catalogue of images, individuals, places, sounds, qualities, events, moments and texts that conjure up and exemplify the version of Englishness each writer seeks to advance or endorse' (Medhurst 2007: 40).

Perhaps this is an inevitability of trying to create a shared discourse about a national culture, as an assembly of things to be remembered and recalled, and to prompt nostalgia for. Bob Godfrey's *Know Your Europeans: The United Kingdom* (1994), an animated musical, partially does this in its parodic songs dedicated to 'Famous British Men' who 'wield sword and pen', and who (from Shelley, Byron and Raleigh to Arthur Daley and Roger Moore, Red Rum and Inspector Morse) offer a version of history suggested by their presence and impact.

Godfrey's parodic interventions and incongruities send up this male-centred, heroic notion of Britain and Britishness, and the 'list'-making construction of national identity, while partly celebrating it. This enables Godfrey to use a tried and trusted 'Englandography', but to use animation to undermine its credibility and meaning. Simply, then, British animators try to use the tools of animation *not* to prompt recognition of 'Britain' and 'Britishness', but the ways these has been constructed and the assumptions made accordingly. This, in turn, I wish to argue, reveals something intrinsically 'British' about such an approach. That is to say, the claim that the British almost feel compelled to find the funny side of a situation and to demonstrate what might be termed the 'will-to-humour', offering an alternative point of view even in the most banal of contexts or under the greatest adversity.[1] In some ways, this manifests itself almost as a desire to undermine formality and seriousness in its own right, through particular kinds of mockery, facetiousness, and understatement. At the heart of this is the notion of 'wit', a double-edged notion of comic practice, which simultaneously wishes to amuse but also signal its own self-conscious cleverness.

Carl Hill has identified such English 'wit' as speaking to 'common sense' and an 'egalitarian tendency', and working as an 'instrument of social and moral discipline'. Hill also notes, however, that there is sometimes an 'ideological duplicity' in the nature of English wit because of a tension between its 'critical and conformist' functions, when '[i]t represents the rule of reason and the forces of progress and innovation, [yet] is ready to turn to the irrational intimidation of ridicule should reason overstep its bounds and threaten social anarchy'. Hill further argues, therefore, that 'wit mediates between the ruling elite and the general populace, keeping the elite in check even as it gives it a mandate to govern' (Hill 1993: 20–3). This balance between playing out critique while insisting upon the maintenance of the fundamental infrastructure and outlook becomes fundamental to the core discourses of British animation. It is crucial to recognise the part animation itself plays in this. Its self-conscious artifice legitimises a self-conscious authorial intent, while offering a vocabulary of expression that inherently reconfigures and interrogates accepted norms and orthodoxies. This invariably creates the humour in a situation in its own right, but in determining 'difference' literally, it is often the case that this difference is thereafter demonstrated incongruously and/or metaphorically, simultaneously pointing up the idea and the joke.

'Ha! Ha! Dat is a vunny ting to vight me!': Form and function, 1900–30

David Robinson notes:

> [T]he art of animation did not begin with the cinema proper. Although the cartoon film-makers were using a new medium – in the camera and the celluloid

film – they were employing basic animation techniques that had been practised and developed for upwards of sixty years before the cinema.

(Robinson 1991: 8)

Robinson's claim draws attention to some of the initial sources for the visual gag, especially as they may be traced to renowned caricaturist George Cruikshank, who created 12-phase zoetrope strips for the London Stereoscopic Company in 1870. *A Rude Blast* features a 'little man' figure humiliated by his umbrella blowing inside out; *Roley Poley*, a fat man perpetually rolling down the road; *The Biter Bit*, a fisherman swallowed by a fish. These early gags represent suggestive hints of what follows in British animation thereafter – a preoccupation with 'human' rather than animal-led narratives, which came to characterise the American animated cartoon; vignettes of social observation concentrating on someone's embarrassment, or the ways in which physical or emotional 'difference' can be a vehicle to laugh at someone; and using the animation itself to 'refresh' or 'make strange', exploring the boundaries of ortho-doxy, and the presence of eccentricity or non-conformity in people and situations. Crucially, Cruikshank brought satirical playfulness and caricature to animation; a tra-dition embraced by two key early British animators, Harry Furniss, whose work includes *Peace and War Pencillings* (1914) and Lancelot Speed, who created *Bully Boy* (1914), cartoons which started to change the characteristics and purpose of early animated films.

Harry Furniss, an Irishman, recognised that caricature could essentially create and define figures in the public imagination; his famed pictures of William Gladstone, for example, always featured him in an austere high collar when he never regularly wore one, yet this became one of Gladstone's most noted characteristics. Furniss was an important figure in the development of British animation, not only because he drew in a way that readily anticipates animated cartoons, but because he was one of the first to theorise the relationship between the graphic arts tradition and the role and function of humour in touring lectures like 'The Frightfulness of Humour' and 'Humours of Parliament', and his books, *The Confessions of a Caricaturist* (1901) and *How to Draw in Pen and Ink* (1905). His later *Peace and War Pencillings* includes an amusing incident: 'Ha! Ha! Dat is a vunny ting to vight me!' exclaims a German soldier as an Australian Kangaroo pouches (punches) the Kaiser, and the Kaiser's famed moustache, likened to a barometer, droops to indicate 'stormy'. Inevitably, the animated films of the First World War use caricature and satire to create an exaggerated yet accessible critique of the enemy, and most particularly, Kaiser Wilhelm II. The Kaiser, of course, was essen-tially the symbol of a 'New Germany', committed to high militaristic purpose, yet insecure as an Imperial power, and on a personal level his deafness, withered arm and tendency to imbalance were all-too-human qualities, which could be ridiculed in pop-ular satire. The iconography of popular illustration – the Kaiser's moustache, the German sausage, John Bull and the bulldog – passed into animated films, and became important shorthand by which the public could embrace significant political insights and perspectives.

Though the Kaiser is configured through a range of critical archetypes, the dominant representation is one of the enemy as 'fool'. Consequently, the Kaiser in all his representational tropes is not just seen as a figure who is the subject and object of 'jokes' – for example, in *The U-Tube* (1917), where his intended conquest of Britain is thwarted when his tunnelling 'U-Tube' is accidentally re-directed to the North Pole – but as a vehicle by which a more absurdist vision of the conflict and its consequences is possible. This notion of 'absurdism' is another central aspect of British animation here, and thereafter, in the sense that it operates as a modernist configuration of 'wit' and embraces comic idioms as a key language of modernity. *Bully Boy* (1914), made by Lancelot Speed, demonstrates Speed's extraordinary skill as an artist, as the Kaiser is depicted with seriousness and dignity, his pose implying status and power in the long-held convention of pre-Hogarthian British portraiture, only for his image to be undermined in a quietly chilling way, as his helmeted head metamorphoses into the devil himself. This ridicules at the same time as it properly acknowledges the scale of the threat. The focus of the film is the shelling of Reims Cathedral – 'The world's greatest gothic work' – which has been destroyed – 'The work of the world's greatest Goth'. These visual and linguistic puns playing up the idea of a more superior 'wit' and integrity, which is not merely the provenance of the artist, but also shared by the audience and, by inference, the nation. One of the most compelling and memorable images, with inevitably Freudian overtones, is a British bulldog devouring a German sausage, the jowls of the dog having a visual association with the Kaiser's moustache. These films were not merely showed as part of traditional cinema billings, but became part of some Music Hall entertainments, propelling 'the lightning cartoonist' to a staple role in both live and cinematic contexts and as a self-evident mediator of consensual, populist views.

George Ernest Studdy, also a well-established illustrator as commissioned by Gaumont to create a series of cartoons called *War Studies* which shared Speed's and Furniss' approach to 'lightning cartoons', with visual jokes like the 'Kamerad' German helmet, which, 'popular in the German trenches', featured two hands being held up in surrender. Studdy noted: 'Life is such a serious business, that a sense of humour is a very necessary safety-valve in the human machine. I think it should be included in one's education, for the man who can see humour in a difficult situation is a better man than he who sees difficulty in a humorous situation!'[2] In October 1924, producer Gordon Craig at New Era Films engaged the American producer, director and animator William A. Ward to collaborate with Studdy and ten assistant artists to produce the first of 26 films featuring Bonzo, 'the Studdy dog'. Bonzo immediately became a popular character, his cartoons representing the first real advances in character animation and comic narrative in British animated cartoons, and a development of visual gags that emerged out of situations rather than singular satirical observations that were the primary focus of animated political caricature (see Babb and Owen 1988). Bonzo had an antecedent in 'Pip' from Lancelot Speed's *Pip, Squeak and Wilfred* cartoons from 1921, and a contemporary in Sid Griffiths' *Jerry the Troublesome Tyke* cartoons of the mid-1920s, anticipating other cartoon dogs such as Joe Noble's *'Orace the 'Armonious 'Ound,* the star of the first British sound cartoons, and Sausage from Joe Noble's *Sammy and Sausage* produced in the 1920s for Pathé; Bob Godfrey's *Roobarb* (tx BBC, 1974) and most notably, Nick Park's Gromit (first screened by the BBC in 1989).

'Not the story you were expecting': Tradition and modernity 1930–50

The period between 1930 and 1950 shows a significant shift both in the ways that Britain viewed and deployed animation, and its use of humour. The 1930s saw documentarian John Grierson's GPO Film Unit promote avant-garde approaches and embrace animation as a creative model of social record, simultaneously encouraging the work of indigenous artists like the Scot Norman McLaren, but also New Zealander Len Lye; and Lotte Reiniger, the renowned cut-out silhouette animator from Germany. Grierson enjoyed the work of comedians like Chaplin, Harry Langdon and the Marx Brothers, and recognised that humour could be aligned with social purpose, but his interest in animation as part of his broader enterprise was largely concerned with promoting experimentation in commercial contexts. Grierson clearly saw that an investment in artworks by animators within the public domain added a progressive dimension to his enterprise through material and technological experimentation across communications media. The animated film was the perfect vehicle to let individual visionaries speak to the nation differently, progressively, yet within the boundaries of established fine art traditions in Britain and the re-definition of film as a 'publication'. This was literally the 'freedom of expression' within a democratic infrastructure, and even if it 'amused' through its aesthetic play, it was not dedicated to the overt creation of comic outcomes. Further, with the rise of the Disney Studio in the United States, effectively defining the classical parameters of animation *per se*, and with it consolidating the notion of the American animated cartoon as a medium fundamentally dedicated to making comic narratives, it was clear that British 'funny' cartoons would find it hard to compete, especially as Disney cartoons and their iconic characters immediately became popular worldwide.

This ultimately had the consequence of marginalising the work of British studios in the history of animation, chiefly the work of Anson Dyer, once ironically known as 'the British Disney'. Anson Dyer made successful *Dicky Dee* cartoons in 1915, and worked throughout the First World War on the topical shorts, realising that British audiences were especially responsive to 'traditional' British subject matter and jokes, and that children were a particular audience for animation, who might engage in cartoons made specifically for them. This resulted in Kine Komedy Kartoons' *Uncle Remus* series in 1919, featuring Brer Rabbit; popular fairy tale stories like *Little Red Riding Hood* (1922) and *The Three Little Pigs* (1922); and Anson Dyer's Shakespeare parodies, including *Oh'Phelia* (1919) and *Othello* (1920) made at Cecil Hepworth's Walton-on-Thames studio. Though Dyer had sought to develop his own character, Bobby the Scout, while working at Walton, it was the creation of the colour *Old Sam* series that defined the next phase in British animated comedy. The cartoons were based on the monologues of Stanley Holloway, whose characters of 'Sam Small' and 'The Ramsbottoms' were rooted in local stories with parochial idioms and dialect. Though the quality of the animation was acceptable, the familiarity of the Disney output, and its more 'universal' comic tendencies, mitigated against the witty rubric of intrinsically British material. *Sam and His Musket* (1935) was based on one of Holloway's most famous monologues, and is concerned with Sam's refusal to pick up his musket when the Sergeant accidentally knocks it from his hand. All the senior ranks of the Army arrive to try and persuade

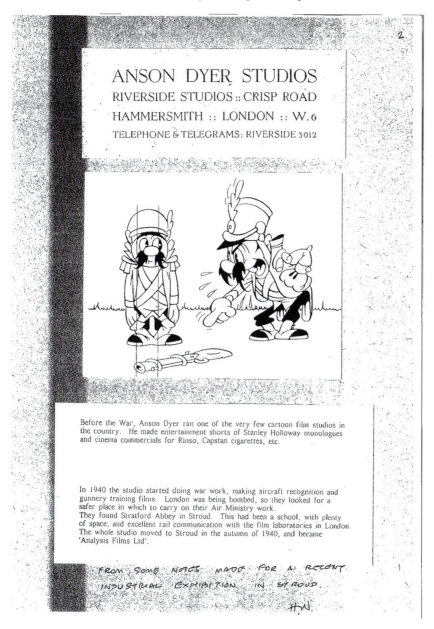

Figure 15.1 Anson Dyer promotional sheet featuring 'Sam'. Image author's own.

him to pick up the musket, but he only ultimately agrees when the Duke of Wellington himself arrives and says 'Gradely, lad ... let battle commence'.

Here is a small incident, a matter of stubbornness and pride, which reveals much about British social hierarchies and class attitudes. It gives the incident an excessive narrative weight, far exceeding its significance, which makes the 'pay off' – the idea that battle had been delayed as a consequence of the conflict – more amusing. Dyer's design and animation, like Speed's, mixes melodramatic villainy in the guise of overstated gestures and large moustaches, with close observation of the military gait and, crucially, the nuances of the parochial rhyme. Here again, then, is the essence of British animation – small narrative vignettes, which resonate with social perspectives, but that wittily engage with the ironies embedded in both everyday and institutionalised practices.

Grierson's seemingly radical strategy of usurping the commercial context for artistic and democratic purposes found direct opposition in the creation of Rank's Gaumont British Animation in 1946, led by ex-Disney supervising director, David Hand, who had supervised *Snow White and the Seven Dwarfs* (1937). Hand led the Cookham-based unit in making Disney-styled short films like the *Animaland* (1948–9) series, featuring Ginger Nutt, Dusty the Mole and Ferdy the Fox, and the *Magical Paintbox* series (1948–50) about regional and national idiosyncrasies. The focus on the indigenous, though sometimes inspired in its visual perspectives (especially in regard to the British land-scape tradition), ultimately played with certain established British stereotypes, which were deployed to the comic ends that could be readily achieved in animation. In *Sketches of Scotland* (1948), for example, the story of Robert the Bruce, and the mythology of his fear of spiders, is rendered in a way that utilises the typology of the whisky-drinking Scotsman to revise the tale. On consuming the whisky, Bruce hallucinates the spider as a set of bagpipes, the animation readily facilitating the visual pun, and he apparently plays these bagpipes in an echoing cave to the terror of the enemy. As the wry narrator concludes, it was 'Not the story you were expecting … '. This 'punchline' could well be the epithet to summarise what British animation had become, and how it continued to consolidate both its approach to the form and its specific use of humour.

'It's a big one, what a big one!': Commerce and counterculture, 1950–80

The post-war period saw the rolling out of the Beveridge Plan, supported by Central Office of Information films advising the British public about new policies and strategic planning. Halas and Batchelor created a series of shorts featuring Charley, a reactionary, sceptical, working-class hero, essentially playing devil's advocate in challenging the new agendas of the proposed welfare state on behalf of ordinary people. This afforded the opportunity for the government to offer explanation and reassurance through the cartoon narrative. These films were largely whimsical as opposed to amusing, inviting viewers to laugh at Charley's ignorance and obstructiveness and to come to terms with the shift from didacticism of wartime propaganda to the advisory nature of public information. Animation's proven credentials in creating appealing and amusing message-led shorts, though, found its greatest purchase in the commercial field and the rise of television advertising in the mid-1950s. Bob Godfrey's Biographic studio, among others, was to find a ready role as companies sought out innovative ways to profile their brands and products in short commercials. This also served to propel Godfrey into the broader context of personal film-making and a series of shorts which came to define the themes of British animated comedy for the next 30 years. Godfrey's main preoccupation was

British attitudes to sex, exemplified in his 'exploitation' films, *Henry 9 'Til 5* (1970), *Karma Sutra Rides Again* (1971), *Dream Doll* (1979) and *Instant Sex* (1980), which all showed the typical 'little English man' dealing with the dull, pedestrian, repetitive nature of British life, indulging in sexual fantasies, which nevertheless are still characterised by the same passionless, mechanistic investment as sexual acts. Essentially, Godfrey points up the ineptitude and embarrassment of the British, even when apparently embracing the new freedoms of the permissive society. It is this tension between rhetoric and reality that is Godfrey's key subject, where innuendo takes the place of sensuality. The 'explicit' is rendered not as pornographic and erotic but as the taken-for-granted and predictable actions of an eccentric yet repressed masculinity that equates sex with formality and routine rather than liberation and excess.

This, of course, is the joke, one echoed in a slightly different way in Godfrey's documentary about Isambard Kingdom Brunel, *Great* (1975), in which the sadness of Brunel's death, and the sense of failure which permeated his final ambitious projects, is replaced by a musical finale charged with 'old school' Music Hall vulgarity, in which his ship, the *Great Eastern*, 'the Leviathan', is celebrated as a 'big one'. Somehow there

Figure 15.2 Bob Godfrey advertising his studio in the 1960s. Image author's own.

remains great security in the 'nob-gag' that reduces all things to the absurd and ridiculous; the actuality of the individual British 'penis' inevitably amusing in the light of the powerful promise, yet ultimate disappointment, of the national 'phallus'. It is a joke repeated on any number of occasions in British comedy, but in British animation most successfully much later in Joanna Quinn's *Girls Night Out* (1988), in which the buxom, middle-aged Beryl pulls off a male stripper's thong in an act of mischievous defiance and feminist reclamation of everyday power; and in Alison Snowden and David Fine's *Bob's Birthday* (1993), a classic exposé of British embarrassment. Margaret's surprise birthday party for her husband Bob goes hideously wrong as he plays out the angst of his mid-life crisis by criticising all those people hiding in his living room waiting to burst out and surprise him, and in his unwillingness to put on a pair of pants. 'The sight of 40-year-old genitalia too disgusting, is it?', Bob bemoans, as Margaret implores him to put on some trousers, finally evacuating the scene herself, to go up to her bedroom and hide behind a pillow.

But this is to anticipate the ways in which post-1980 British animation took on the observational comic tropes of Alan Bennett, Mike Leigh and Victoria Wood. Godfrey's sex films were part of a broader countercultural offensive, in which the surreal animation by Terry Gilliam in *Monty Python's Flying Circus* was testing the boundaries of taste, order and value. Gilliam argued: 'I have always tried to find the humour in a thing because it is a way of understanding it, and even admiring it ... I want things to be wonderful and wise, so I use humour as a way of testing them' (Sterritt and Rhodes 2004: 130). Crucially, Gilliam added: 'You get to be an impish god. You get to reform the world. You get to take the piss out of it. You turn it inside out, upside down. You bug-out eyes. You put moustaches on Mona Lisas. You change the world, and for a brief moment have control over it. You get to humiliate it for a while, and that's what all cartoonists get their kicks out of' (Sterritt and Rhodes 2004: 128) This desire to temporarily control and reform the world in a spirit of ridiculing the old order, shared by both Gilliam and Godfrey, has a strong anti-Establishment agenda, but it also becomes a witty take on Britain's post-war 'declinism' and the resigned yet defiant 'miserablism' that accompanied it. Arguably, this was actually bound up with an increasing realisation of Britain's loss of Empire and its decreasing influence in world affairs. Britain it seems is not as good as it was, and more to the point – and even more disappointingly – is not even as good as it imagined it was. Though both Godfrey and Gilliam reveal this with wit and irony, theirs is the satire of an emergent intelligentsia refusing the limitations of conservatism and the ideological status quo. This once more recalls Hill's version of English wit as a contradiction between critique and conformism, as their work operates in a spirit of playfulness rather than revelation or anger and, for all its social pertinence, distracts more than satirises and amuses more than it reveals.

This might be best summed up through a brief comment on Halas and Batchelor's *Tales of Hoffnung* (1964), seven short films using Gerard Hoffnung's amusing caricatures of classical music culture, and the well-known *Birds, Bees and Storks*, featuring the voice of Peter Sellers as an embarrassed father seeking to tell his son the facts of life. Influenced by Busch and Zille, Hoffnung became the master of the graphic pun, allying his own German tradition with English whimsy. To those intimidated by the seriousness of

Figure 15.3 Halas and Batchelor's *Tales of Hoffnung* (1964). Image author's own.

classical music, Hoffnung offered a point of access, innocently and affectionately sending up hopeless attempts to master an instrument physically and technically, and the pompous culture associated with classical music and performance. The Hoffnung cartoons were specifically directed at playfully engaging with the music itself, though, and were unambiguously about the orchestra, the conductor, the musician and their audiences. The credits to each cartoon note that the music is 'composed, re-composed, arranged, disarranged and conducted by Francis Chagrin', and includes the coda 'with acknowledgment and apologies to ... ' before listing the composers used in the film's music track. This alone foregrounds the sustained respect for the culture that is being parodied, but signals too that even if the graphic puns and exaggerated caricature that characterise the cartoons would appeal to children, there was nevertheless an intention on reaching and engaging with a classical music-literate viewer. This focus upon speaking to the specificity of the British middle- to upper-class audience, and its knowledge of classical music is a far cry from playful construction and populist recognition assumed of the fragmented scores in the Hollywood cartoon. In *The Hoffnung Maestro* (1964), both English literacy and classical knowledge is evoked by the parodic play of sending up musical terms: 'diabolico', 'pomposo', 'religioso', 'furioso', etc. Though Hoffnung's musical caricatures are used to extend the humorous effect, no one character is privileged as the presiding focus of the stories. While there is complete respect for the music, the visual jokes poke fun at the formality and austereness of the culture; once more valuing the socio-cultural milieu and its idioms, while using the animation itself to playfully undermine its anticipated rituals and solemnity. Such contradiction, ambiguity and irony were to change, however, in the contemporary era, with the rise of Aardman and the independent productions in the golden era of Channel Four.

'The stink of excellence in a world gone tits up': Subjectivity and subversion, 1980–present

Arguably, the ideological charge in English wit that plays out a dialectic between criticism and conformism in the post-1980 era might be best understood as a tension between Nick Park's unerringly nostalgic Wallace and Gromit adventures, set in an imagined mid-1950s northern England, and the rise of quasi-feminist comedy in the work of Candy Guard, Sarah Kennedy and Joanna Quinn, concentrating on the day-to-day seemingly self-defeating neuroses of contemporary women. Park's *Beano* and *Dandy* style gags, visual and verbal puns, and re-worked Hollywood genres through the filter of British culture, sat alongside Quinn's exposés of masculine ignorance and complacency in films like *Body Beautiful* (1991), Kennedy's embrace of the seedier normalities of British cultural life in *Crapston Villas* (1995–8), and Guard's closely observed revelations of women trapped in confines of the socially determined expectations about their bodies, outlooks and achievements, most notably achieved in *Pond Life* (1996–2000) (see Kitson 2008). Park's humour draws upon notions of eccentricity and faulty logic, while Quinn's, Kennedy's and Guard's insist upon recognition and empathy. Park can effectively re-enact the chariot race from *Ben-Hur* (1959) in a Wigan bedroom between a heroic dog and a villainous penguin in *The Wrong Trousers* (1993), while Quinn, Kennedy, and Guard point to the realities of domestic spaces and relationships, painfully drawing the humour from the everyday ineptitudes, pointless preoccupations, and mundane investments that characterise most lives.

Though Guard is perhaps best known for her character Dolly Pond, a contemporary descendant of comic strip characters Beryl the Peril and Minnie the Minx, it is her early films which best characterise her style. *Fatty Issues* (1988) is concerned with a young woman's good intentions to go on a diet, when finding every excuse to eat and avoid exercise; *Alternative Fringe* (1988) is focused on the significance of a young woman having her hair done, and the disaster it turns out to be; *A Little Something* (1988) is concerned with a young woman who is so paranoid about a mark on her nose, she wears a bag on her head (merely the start of a downward spiral in which her low self-esteem makes her believe that she is not competent to undertake the most menial and meaningless of occupational tasks, and which ultimately results in her being a homeless, eccentric bag-lady, dying barely acknowledged by anyone); *Wishful Thinking* (1988) is concerned with two friends, initially indifferent about going to a party, who then go through all sorts of anxieties about what they will wear, before arriving at the party thoroughly alienated from its yuppie milieu. The pair sit down, eat and drink, attract vague passing interest, and return home early in the morning wondering what they wanted from the party. It is this preoccupation with the minutiae of existence and the small things that fill lives that defines Guard's work as absurdist comedy; often bleak and black, it nevertheless comforts and amuses through the recognition of the commonality an audience recognises in the value it places on small talk, HobNob biscuits, haircuts and wistful aspirations for love and good times. There are no 'gags' here, as such, just the things that people say to amuse each other, and the things which strike an audience as amusing because they recognise the truth in the contradictions, flaws and obsessions that underpin everyday existence. There is no critique here; rather the delineation of the real conformism of psychological and emotional socialisation, instead of the more obvious conformism to social rules and regulations. Guard makes her characters' preoccupations and inadequacies the codes and conventions of existence, not institutional infrastructures or generic norms. The simple design and animation only draw attention to the issues of representation accordingly, painting a funny but challenging picture of what it is to know that fitting in to established, yet unfulfilling, modes of social experience is the only option available.

It is this absurdist comedy of embarrassment, restriction and acceptance that post-millennial British animation has reacted violently against. Chris Shepherd and David Shrigley's *Who I Am and What I Want* (2005) depicts a seemingly troubled outsider with mental health problems, who amongst other things brutalises babies and rabbits, and wants to be fried in a pan with some butter and garlic, be water soluble, an executioner, and talk to God. Though he is understood as outside social norms, he is ultimately vindicated by the film's view that it is equally mad to sign up and conform to the 'herd of twats' society is defined by (see Wells 2007: 74–7). Like Guard, Shrigley's designs are deliberately naïve and simple, drawing attention to the psychological and emotional conditions that actually inform personal representation in daily life. This corresponds to what Van Norris has suggested about Jon Link and Mick Bunnage's adult animation series *Modern Toss* (2006–8):

> On one level the concept could be seen to be implying a rather glib superiority in its register of a perceived cultural apathy that is rendered in the texts themselves and in the consistent abnegations of personal and social responsibility ascribed to their class-bound characters. Although, perhaps conversely the show can *also* [sic] be read as a painfully accurate actualisation of British attitudes and idioms and as an indicator of an isolationist mentality that pervades contemporary social experience.
>
> (Norris 2008: 234)

In whatever sense, there is a deep rooted, usually masculine subjectivity raging against the limits of existence, from the ball of anger that is Alan, to the signatory offence of Mr. Tourette, to the blasé, near-friendly insults of the Drive-by-Abuser, to the red Hulk-like figure, Barney, who merely destroys things around him through the release of the pent-up frustration provoked by something as petty as the mention of gardener and TV presenter Alan Titchmarsh. What is interesting here is once more the animation itself, mostly occurring as a hybrid with live action contexts, and of a fairly basic non-classical nature, privileging what the character means rather than what it looks like or how it performs/moves. The comedy here is both empathetic and cathartic as there is either recognition of the everyday irrationalities and frustrations that are repressed for the good of civilised conduct and communication, or release based on the desires to say and do anti-social and ultimately subversive things. Either way, as the *Toss* voiceover suggests, such animated comedy represents the more contradictory notion that there is a 'stink of excellence in a world gone tit's [sic] up'.[3]

Conclusion: An ontologically anxious organism?

In the comic art and animation project, Let Me Feel Your Finger First's *Ontologically Anxious Organism* (2010), an organism of uncertain status, resisting the notion of 'character', disguises itself as a boulder. Thereafter, it realises that it remains forever 'in-between', without closure or reference, unbounded by normal conventions of time and the security of clear identity or representation. This witty distanciation from the normal codes and conventions of the cartoon is also a ready commentary upon the ways British animators have used them, opening up these codes and conventions for revisionist play with, and the comic interrogation of, British socio-cultural idioms. Bob Godfrey put it another way: 'One of the things I want to do is *Hamlet*. With Robots. Get rid of the poetry and keep all the violence and the paranoia' (personal interview with the author, February 2001). There are bound to be some good jokes, too.

Notes

1 In six radio essays that I wrote and directed entitled *Laughing Matters* (1992, 1995, 2000), considerable attention was paid to the 'national characteristics' of humour. In a sample of 120 interviewees from six countries, 86 people noted this desire to make jokes in every circumstance as an aspect of the British outlook to humour.

2 Extract from *The Royal Magazine*, 1924. Re-published at www.studdying-with-bonzo.co.uk/interview.htm.

3 In a piece of this length, it is impossible to do justice to the myriad of exemplary animated comedy throughout its history. Apologies then to Phil Mulloy, Tim Searle, Peter Lord, Matthew Walker, and many others.

Bibliography

Babb, P. and Owen, G. (1988) *Bonzo: The Life and Work of George Studdy*, Shepton Beauchamp, Somerset: Richard Dennis.

Hill, C. (1993) *The Soul Of Wit: Joke Theory From Grimm to Freud*, Lincoln and London: University of Nebraska Press.

Kitson, C. (2008) *British Animation: The Channel Four Factor.* London: Parliament Hill Publishing and Bloomington: Indiana University Press.

Medhurst, A. (2007) *A National Joke: Popular Comedy and English Cultural Identities.* London and New York: Routledge.

Norris, V. (2008) 'Yeah, looks like it n'all': The "live action" universe and abridged figurative design and computer animation within *Modern Toss*', *Animation: An Interdisciplinary Journal*, 3.3 (November): 231–50.

Robinson, D. (1991) 'Masterpieces of animation 1833–1908', *Griffithiana*, 14.43. Pordenone: Le Giornate Del Cinema Muto.

Sterritt, D. and Rhodes, L. (eds) (2004) *Terry Gilliam Interviews.* Jackson: University of Mississippi.

Wells, P. (1998) *Understanding Animation*, London and New York: Routledge.

——(2007) *Scriptwriting*, Lausanne: AVA Academia.

——(2009) *The Animated Bestiary: Animals, Cartoons, Culture*, New York: Rutgers University Press.

Index